TRAVELS THROUGH THE SPANISH CIVIL WAR

NICK LLOYD

Travels Through the Spanish Civil War

HURST & COMPANY, LONDON

First published in the United Kingdom in 2025 by
C. Hurst & Co. (Publishers) Ltd.,
New Wing, Somerset House, Strand, London WC2R 1LA

Distributed in the United States, Canada and Latin America by Oxford
University Press, 198 Madison Avenue, New York, NY 10016, United
States of America.

A Cataloguing-in-Publication data record for this book
is available from the British Library.

ISBN: 9781805264149

EU GPSR Authorised Representative
Easy Access System Europe Oü, 16879218
Address: Mustamäe tee 50, 10621, Tallinn, Estonia
Contact Details: gpsr.requests@easproject.com, +358 40 500 3575

www.hurstpublishers.com

Printed and bound in Great Britain by Bell & Bain Ltd, Glasgow

To Mònica, Albert and Iona, with love

CONTENTS

ACKNOWLEDGEMENTS

I would like to thank the following people: Charlie Nurse for his selfless help in reading the text and contributing numerous suggestions and huge improvements. At Hurst, I would like to thank Alice Clarke, my editor, for her great help in improving the text in many ways, as well as Michael Dwyer, Tim Page and Daisy Leitch. Mònica Navarro, without whom I would never have written this book. Catherine Howley, who worked with me for many years in Barcelona and from whom I have learned much. Alan Warren, for always being there with an expert's eye. Víctor Pardo in Aragon, Andreu Caralt in the Ebro, and David González on the exile routes, from whom I learned a great deal on the road. Richard Blair, Quentin Kopp, Liz Kopp, and Pere Fortuny for sharing with me stories about their fathers; Dorian "Dusty" Nicol about his mother; and Antonio Cánovas and Alex Gabriles for their own tales. David Convery for help with Irish volunteers. Valerie, Tony and Frances Lloyd, and Andy, Ella and Lucy Godson for all their suggestions and encouragement. Josep Garcia for his help at Barcelona Zoo. Kathleen Hammond, Ricard Marco, August Andreu, and everyone from the Associació Francesc Boix. Brendon von Briesen, Isa Cacho, Armand Duch, Dr Andrew Flinn, Ricard Martínez, Alma Mašić, Alan Nance, Andrew Miller, Eli Pastó, Joan Sambró, and Archana Ramure for all their support and ideas. Paul Preston for the generous support.

And the following people for their kind help in numerous ways: Katharine Ainger, Marta Aladren Ribas, and Adrià Terol at Cementiris de Barcelona; Vicente Aupí, Francis Barrett, Richard Baxell, Roc Blackblock, Stephen Burgen, Alex Chip, Ricard Conesa, Sean and Jack Costelloe, Almudena Cros, Joan Delgado, Andy Durgan, Izabela Dziekan, and all the people at the Biblioteca de Poble-sec. Michael Eaude, Plàcid Garcia-Planas, Santiago Gorostiza, Gemma Grau, Judith Keene, John Kennedy, Rob MacDonald, Enric Masip, Marshall Mateer, Irene Mirando, Iratxe Momoitio (Gernika Peace Museum), Juan Carlos Salavera, Yvonne Scholten, Sean Scullion, James Stout (Olimpíada Popular), Paloma Teixidó, Elena Torralba, Andrea Vázquez, Steve Warren, Ali Zahid, Joaquín Ruiz Gaspar, Alberto Lasheras, Andrew Porter, Luis Gutiérrez, and Emma Lythgoe.

And finally to all those people who have been on my tours, often sharing extraordinary stories of your ancestors' experiences, and many of whom I should mention here. All your knowledge, questions and challenges have forced me to tell a better story.

Any remaining errors are my own.

N

★ 1. *Battle of Jarama*
  2. *Battle of Guadalajara*
  3. *Battle of Brunete*
  4. *Battle of the Ebro*

Bilbao — Gernika

Pamplona

Burgos

Huesca

Zaragoza

Lleida

Belchite

Barcelona

② ★
③ ★ ■
      ★ ①

Toledo

Teruel

④ ★

Madrid

Badajoz

Alicante

Seville

Granada

Cádiz

Málaga

Canary Islands

© S.Ballard (2025)

Francoist advances

| July 1936 | September 1936 | October 1937 | April 1938 | February 1939 | Last Republican zone until 1 April 1939 |

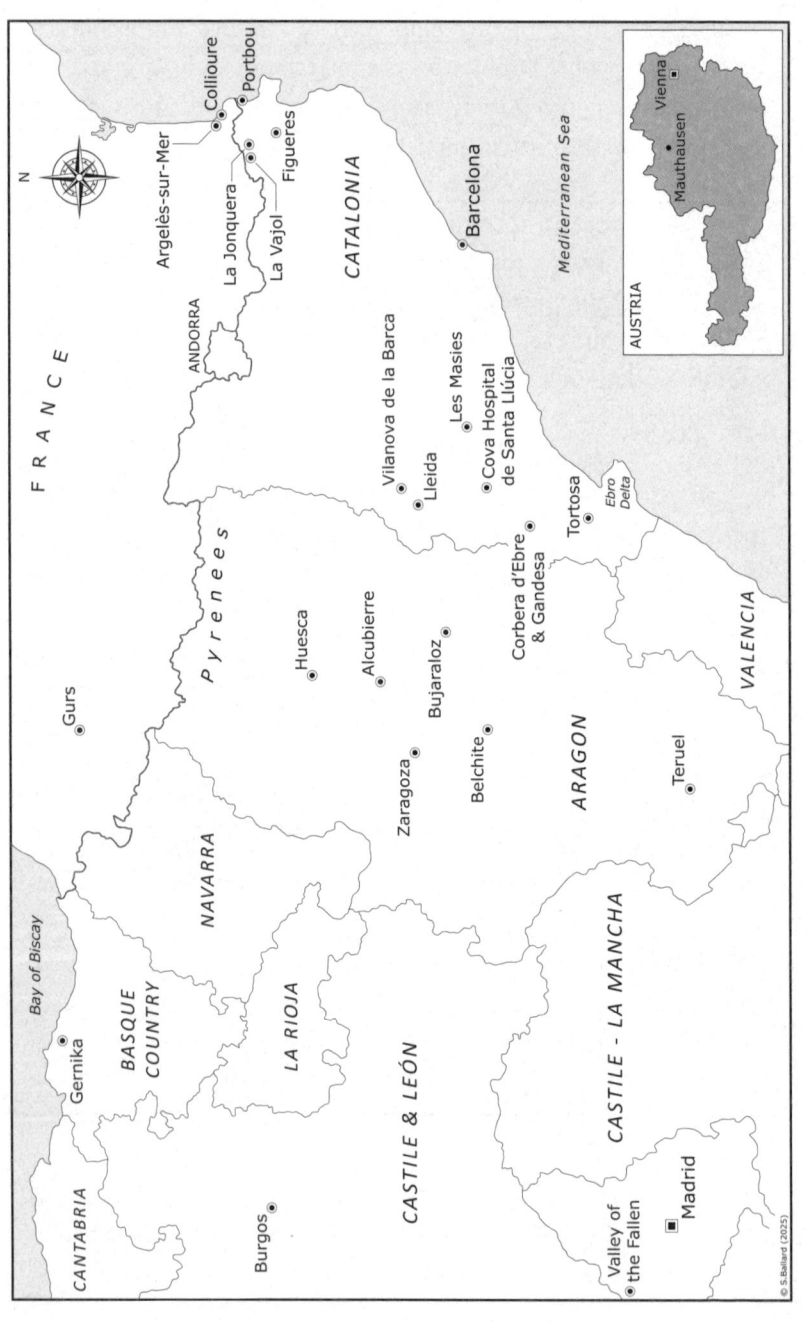

© S.Ballard (2025)

INTRODUCTION

I don't know when the Spanish Civil War first came into my mind, but I must have been very young. Perhaps it was my Uncle Tom tutting as I stuck the ugly, bald, 10-cent head of Francisco Franco, the Spanish dictator, into my stamp album. He certainly didn't look very nice, I agreed. Or maybe it was falling asleep, listening to my parents' friends singing the old Republican song "¡Ay, Carmela!", the lyrics, then just melodious syllables, I'd only later understand. In my teens came Laurie Lee's 1935 trek across Spain, *As I Walked Out One Midsummer's Morning*, one of the great walks of English literature, and The Clash's rousing "Spanish Bombs", an entry point for many British people of my time, followed by Granada TV's ground-breaking 1983 documentary series on the war,[1] which I watched aged seventeen, not that I could have understood much. Aside from knowing that the Republicans were good and Franco bad, I think all I took away was a terribly romantic idea of the conflict.

One day, probably in 1985, with Andy, a friend at university, I came across a wooden plaque in Manchester town hall. It was to the men and women from the city who had "fought against fascism in Spain" and was decorated with the names of places I'd never heard of: Jarama, Ebro, Belchite and Teruel, planting one-word poems of tragic resistance in my head. Andy, who was studying

1

history, filled me in with more, and the name of 'La Pasionaria' (real name Dolores Ibárruri), the famed Spanish communist politician whose dedication, bidding farewell to the International Brigades in 1938, was written on the memorial.[2] Later, on a rainy Manchester night heading for a long-since forgotten party, I found a blue plaque on a council house dedicated to Sam Wild, the last commander of the British volunteers, a serendipitous moment to which I only gave meaning years later. Andy also passed me a copy of George Orwell's *Homage to Catalonia* (1938). While I know his writing gripped me, all those ideological complexities on the left went straight over my head.

So, at some innocent level, along with my rucksack, the war was there in my cultural and political baggage when I arrived in Zaragoza in 1988 to work as an English teacher. I asked questions, probably rather naive ones, and read a few books, but I didn't really understand the war and its consequences in any meaningful way. A few years later, I moved to Barcelona. My interest in the war was always there, but only in the background.

Then, in 2001, a few weeks after settling in the neighbourhood of Poble-sec, I ran into a group of people a few doors from our flat, standing in our narrow street around a new plaque. It was dedicated to a photographer called Francesc Boix who was born there on 14 August 1920. The council had just named our new library after him. I became fascinated with this young man's story and what he did. It drew me in and led me to join a local history society.

I now realise I was going through a midlife crisis. A positive one. I was becoming bored stiff with my work—teaching English and translating—and felt pulled to experience more things outside of a relationship that wasn't working and a weekend social life of bars and parties. I had stopped caring about the fortunes of Barça. Meanwhile, new documentaries and novels were reflecting a growing interest in the war. Items started appearing on the news about local campaigns to open up the mass graves, and friends were becoming more open about their grandparents' experiences. Looking back, the war was in the zeitgeist. In 2010, I started doing tours on the war around the streets of Barcelona. I was manifestly unprepared when I began, but there is no better way to learn something than to teach it, and they quickly became my day job. This led, several years later, to my first book, *Forgotten Places: Barcelona and the Spanish Civil War* (2015).

At some point before COVID hit us all, I felt I had a reasonable grasp of the events in the city, but I knew I was ignorant of the wider conflict. So I set off on a series of trips, visiting several of the key battle sites and other places affected by the war and its shadow. I learned an awful lot through reading and from the people I met along the way, and as I travelled I tried to conjure up that past in today's landscapes. Visiting the sites helped me appreciate the scale of the war as well as providing me with a better understanding of its effect on Barcelona. It also gave me a sense of its sheer horror at a very local level. Many of the places I visited are surrounded by beautiful scenery, but they have seen too much history. Nature returned, but the traces of violence were still often evident. A peaceful land was turned into a bloody battlefield and then, after a while, became quiet farmland or a wild place again, from which bodies and bombs still emerge. A street in a provincial town that saw despicable events now plays host to a civic scene where children and couples stroll by. Stories of Franco's brutal assault and dictatorship appeared as I travelled, sometimes hiding in plain sight.

These explorations are the backbone of this book. The narrative follows the progress of the war and its aftermath in a more or less chronological order, starting in Barcelona. That said, there are disjunctures, parts where places and timelines don't coincide, and rabbit holes I wanted to explore. Woven into the narrative are tales of the people I met, although almost all of those who remember the war and its aftermath directly are no longer with us. I've also interlaced my own memories of living in the country for thirty-seven years insofar as it touches on this history.

Travels through the Spanish Civil War was born partly out of personal frustration. I love taking folk around Barcelona and showing them the story from the perspective of the city and its residents. The tours are easy enough to organise. People get in touch by email, and we agree on a date. I take the Metro for three stops, and five minutes later I'm in Plaça de Catalunya to meet them. It's an intense four hours or so, usually with lots of questions and discussion, but that's all. Then, I'm back home. I'd love to be able to take people farther afield, for example to sites on what was the Aragon Front or along the route the defeated took, fleeing Franco's army into exile in 1939. But you need several days away to cover these places, with all the logistical headaches that goes with running such a tour. Over the years, I've developed an understanding of these places and the stories associated with them—I slip in a bit about them here and there on tour in Barcelona. The trips were also sometimes simply an opportunity to get out of Barcelona's narrow streets to wider skies, although I made some of these travels in the city itself.

I've also included stories behind some of the objects I've collected and that now form part of my tour—what I like to call the walking museum of the Spanish Civil War. In 2010, I helped form an association to try to build a museum in Barcelona dedicated to the war. I won't bore the reader with the details, but we weren't successful. I continued to do my tours, still without objects. One day, an American woman signed up. She explained that her father was a Cypriot who had fought in the International Brigades. When we sat down for a coffee halfway through, she brought out Aris Hagis's old brigader identity card from Spain, unmediated by plastic, and passed it round the group.[3] I suddenly understood the power of an original object to take you back to a time and place. I had already gathered a few things, and so I started to introduce them into the tour. I slowly acquired more. Now I take people around with my rucksack packed with items: union cards, badges, postcards, newspapers, footwear, war material found in trenches. For many participants, holding something from the war provides a tangible connection to the past I'm trying to convey. I've bought some of the items; others I've been given. Some have made it into this text.

It is a mystery how many of these things have managed to survive. Was a trade union membership card hidden away at the back of the drawer by a brave old anarchist who couldn't bear to burn it? Was another item collected as a trophy by a victor of the war? Or was it taken into exile by defeated Republicans and returned after Franco's death in 1975? I haven't found much myself. Looking for buried artifacts isn't my thing and is now seriously frowned upon by archaeologists. I have, however, come across the odd piece on walks, including a bullet casing in a pinewood somewhere on the site of the Ebro battle, waged in the summer of 1938: it's Soviet, identifying it as being from the Republican army. It is one of the billions of munitions used by both armies to kill people. We weren't there in 1936, but through these objects, photos, stories and oral histories, we can follow in the steps of those who were. They invoke a remembrance of this time. That is the main goal of this book.

The book is more limited geographically than I originally planned. I had thought about driving down to Andalusia to the site where Robert Capa is contentiously alleged to have taken his famous photograph, *The Falling Soldier*, to try to unpick that story. I've been to Madrid a few times as a tourist or to visit friends, but I had wanted to go back and walk the Casa de Campo, where the battle for the city raged in the autumn of 1936. From here, I had planned to go to the battlefield of

Jarama, to cover the experiences of the British and American battalions in February 1937. Nor did I make it to the battlefields of Guadalajara, Brunete or Teruel, where Franco ground down the Republican army in a war of attrition. The war in Northern Spain is only discussed from the vantage point of a visit to Gernika, and I only make brief forays in this story to Castile, the only major area of Spain—Navarra, aside—where there was genuine, but not universal, support for the military coup against the Republic. The truth is, COVID scuppered one major trip I'd planned, and the practicalities of family life impeded other longer journeys, so most of the book is centred in Catalonia and Aragon, within three hours' drive of Barcelona. That said, Catalonia was a bastion of the fight against Franco and much of the war was waged in Aragon, while the biggest battle of all, the Ebro, was fought in southern Catalonia. Both regions give a good picture of the wider war and the revolution and violence experienced by its peoples.

After briefly explaining the war's origins, I start the story in Barcelona, where readers will find a basic introduction to the defeat of the July 1936 coup and the ensuing revolution as well as some of the main characters involved in this book. We then drive to Aragon, a region still relatively unknown to foreign visitors, where much of this book takes place. There is a short visit to the Basque Country, but most of the rest of the story is set in Catalonia, my home for more than thirty years, particularly centring on the terrible Battle of the Ebro in the summer of 1938. I then follow the route taken by the Republican army and refugees into France, and as far as Paris. There is a good deal to say about what happened to those who fled into exile and those who stayed behind.

It would be artificial to conclude this book in Spain in 1939, as it wasn't the end of the war for those who lost. This takes me reluctantly to the Valley of the Fallen, which I visited shortly before the dictator's remains were removed from this memorial to Spanish fascism. The story ends in Austria.

In addition to Boix, a number of characters come in and out of the text, including a six-year-old Barcelonan boy, a Catalan interpreter, a German International Brigader and, more obviously, Orwell. I hope I have reflected both the essential Spanish character of the war but also its world reach and how the foreign volunteers who fought Franco were more a phenomenon of much of Continental Europe than of English-speaking countries. The book also looks at examples of the war's national and international cultural impact and how the conflict echoes in today's Spain.

People frequently come on the tour because they have a personal connection to the war. Several times a month, there is someone whose family members fought in the International Brigades or whose ancestors had been forced into exile from Franco's Spain. They often bring moving stories that enrich the experience. I've included a few of them in this book. I was usually accompanied on a trip by one friend or another, a few of whom have also made it into the text. My partner Mònica was there with me on my first trip to Aragon and is in the background for a lot more besides.

I chose the photo for the front cover as it expresses the idea of travelling into the past. It was taken by the great Catalan photographer Agustí Centelles in Aragon in the summer of 1937. I think it perfectly expresses the contrast between the past and the modernity that had reached part of the country. Centelles travelled from Spain's only industrial metropolis of Barcelona to the front by car, perhaps a Ford, equipped with his state-of-the-art Leica III camera. Outside, there is an older Spain—a column of Republican mounted troops filing past along a dusty road. The Spanish Civil War often saw ultra-modern armaments pitted against weapons and equipment from a bygone age.

Franco's murderous war cost 600,000 lives as well as hundreds of thousands after the conflict—whether through violence, disease or hunger; it ruined many millions more, most of them innocent victims left with a lifetime of loss, racked by mental and physical pain. Spain is still paying the consequences. It's 2025 now. A general war in Europe now feels more of a threat than it has since 1945. We don't learn, do we?

While I hope I've provided enough structure to give the uninitiated reader a general background, this book is not intended as an all-encompassing history of the conflict. However, to aid comprehension I have included short sections to explain the war's progress. I have also suggested a few titles in the "Further Reading" section in the Appendix.

I plod my own eccentric path. I may have been studying the war for some twenty years, but I am not a professional historian in an academic sense. Nor do I have any personal attachment in the form of relatives who fought or were caught up in the war. But I can't say I am unbiased. I don't know how you can be unbiased about seismic political events: just as I have an opinion on the horror in Ukraine and Gaza today, I have sympathy for those who lost in 1939. Although the Spanish Republic was not perfect, which democracy was in the 1930s—or which indeed is today? Conversely, I also have sympathy for the anarchists' dreams for humanity, even though the world they sought to build in 1936 may seem very distant today. But I hope I have been fair and even handed: murder and inhumanity were not exclusive to Franco's side.

Another seed was the COVID epidemic. I couldn't work and found myself waking up every morning feeling trapped, a feeling probably familiar to many readers. I was saved when a friend suggested I try giving my own tour virtually. Talking about places on Zoom doesn't come close to actually being there, but the people who signed up often told me they felt a temporary escape from lockdown, as if they were really travelling. The format also allowed me to organise these make-believe trips to places that would be impractical in real life: to Aragon, the Basque Country, the site of the Battle of the Ebro, to Austria. I often pretended we were driving in a battered old bus, which helped build up the atmosphere. Each tour involved a lot of research, some of which has made it into this book. Imagine, if you will, then, that you're coming with me on a sort of road trip in that bus across the Spanish Civil War.

1

ORIGINS OF THE SPANISH CIVIL WAR

What follows is a necessarily brief summary of the lead-up to the Spanish Civil War, which hopefully goes some way towards explaining how Spain could have descended into such devastatingly bloody internal conflict. If you feel you already have a good grasp of this pre-war period of Spanish history, please feel free to skip the next few pages.

The immediate cause of the war lay in the July 1936 uprising carried out by a group of generals and their supporters who refused to accept the liberal democratic reforms put into motion by the centre-left government that had won the general election in February 1936. The coup itself half failed. After the first few days, 60 per cent of Spanish territory still lay under the nominal control of the Spanish Republic, with 40 per cent in the hands of the military rebels. Both sides had arms and the intent to win. This territorial division is what we call in English 'the Spanish Civil War'. However, the origins of the war go deeper.

A fractured society

Spain was a terribly fractured society in the 1930s, racked by extreme class divisions between the urban and rural poor and the elites who felt threatened by the spectre of the 1917 Russian Revolution, by the need for economic and social reforms, and by the mass political democracy that had spread across Europe after the First World War. Regional differences were huge. Spain was an economically complex country in the 1930s. Particularly in southwest Andalusia and Extremadura, land ownership was dominated by large semi-feudal estates. They were not "feudal" in any legal sense, but the landowners had so much power that they were able to treat the peasants and landless labourers as if they were serfs. In contrast, across most of Northern Spain, including Galicia, Asturias, the Basque Country, Aragon, Catalonia and most of Old Castile, small and medium-sized farms predominated. While there was a sizable industrial base around Bilbao based on engineering and steel production with smaller productive centres elsewhere, the only genuine industrial metropolis was Barcelona and its surroundings.

Castile is the heartland of Spanish nationalism, the supposed embodiment of the real Spain. In 1936, it was very poor, rural, conservative, Catholic, but crucially made up of small landowners. Many in Castile did not feel represented by the Republic's liberal reforms and felt threatened by its anticlericalism and cultural modernism. Rightly or wrongly, the new Republic had failed to gain their support.

Adding to this complexity were great ideological differences. The powerful right-wing forces were supported by an ultra-reactionary Catholic Church, big landowners and much of the army hierarchy, which found the idea of reforms abhorrent. On the other side was a highly divided centre-left and left: liberal republicans, Basque, Catalan and Galician republicans, a large and internally divided socialist party, a relatively small communist party and, uniquely in Europe, a huge anarchist movement. All of these organisations had very different ideas, but they were united at a certain social level by a desire to break the power of the old elites and the Catholic Church. By the time of the war, the right was also divided politically between conservative monarchists; Carlists (see Appendix); a new mass Catholic party, CEDA (Confederación Española de Derechas Autónomas); and the genuinely fascist Falange. While these groups had different visions, they were all united by their belief in the primacy of authority, social and gender hierarchy, private property, the military and the Catholic Church.

Economic and class tensions were heightened by the Great Depression, which led to a collapse in agricultural prices and steep reductions in industrial and rural wages, the latter already at near-subsistence level. The new Republic's land reforms— mostly from 1931 to 1933 and after the elections of February 1936—were met with fierce opposition from the landowning elites, while on the other side frustration was simmering among the landless peasants at the slow pace of the reforms.

The Spanish military

The most important single origin of the war was the attitude and culture instilled in a large part of the military officer class. The Spanish–American War of 1898 saw Spain lose almost all its remaining colonies: Puerto Rico, the Philippines and, most importantly, Cuba—the last treasure of its empire. This produced a belief in the Spanish military that it was their destiny to rule the country: despite their own manifest failings in contributing to the loss of Spain's colonies, they blamed what they saw as a national disaster on the political class. Senior officers now felt justified to step in to govern *La Patria* whenever necessary.

For their part, the Spanish peasantry and working class had become increasingly radical, often anarchist and deeply anti-militarist. This anti-militarism was due in part to how the common soldiers had been treated by their officers in Cuba, who, for instance, routinely syphoned off the rations of their recruits to engorge their salaries. Weakened by low rations, the biggest cause of death among Spanish soldiers in Cuba was disease: 22 per cent died of malaria and other afflictions between 1895 and 1898. After the defeat, many were returned to Spain and dumped on harbour quays, often sickly, hungry and missing limbs. Memories of this were very strong among the working classes in 1936.

Having only Spanish colonial Guinea and a few smaller dependencies, many in the military dreamed of a new empire, especially in North Africa. They looked to Morocco, where Spain had had a presence since the late fifteenth century, with murderous consequences on both sides of the Strait. Events took a turn in 1906, when the European imperial powers accepted the establishment of a French protectorate over most of Morocco while awarding Spain control of the north of the country. Driven by business lobbies and a monarchy greedy for mining profits, the imperialist dreams of politicians and an army and navy thirsty for glory after the defeat in Cuba, Spain was dragged into a series of colonial wars in Morocco, which were to continue intermittently until it finally subdued resistance in the Rif Mountains in 1926. The experience did more than anything to dehumanise and brutalise the section of the Spanish army that fought in Morocco and contribute to its messianic belief in its role as the Fatherland's saviour. This would have an effect in 1936, since the so-called *Africanista* officers, Franco among them, would play the central role in the coup. As Franco put it: "Without Africa, I can scarcely explain myself." Chilling words given the terror and killings involving his forces in Morocco, where he commanded troops who routinely committed atrocities against Moorish villages, involving chemical warfare, rape, torture, the decapitation of prisoners and the display of their heads.[1]

European context

The 1930s were a dark time in Europe. The Great Depression had ravaged economies and livelihoods, while the Soviet Union was being swept by the waves of Stalin's repression. But above all, the rise of right-wing authoritarianism and fascism was casting its shadow across the Continent, and not just in Germany and Italy. All over Central and Eastern Europe, the fragile new democracies formally proclaimed in the new states that emerged from the collapse of the Russian, Austrian and German Empires were being overthrown by right-wing dictatorships—of the rash of new democracies declared after the First World War, only the Irish Free State still existed on the eve of the new European war. Many had already turned to authoritarianism in the 1920s.

These new regimes relentlessly pursued political opponents and critics as well as identifiable minorities, pushing hundreds of thousands into an often-precarious exile in Western Europe and North America. By 1936, there were, for example, some 200,000 Jewish refugees in France alone.[2] They were accompanied by a similar number of political exiles, with plenty of overlap between the two categories, fleeing the rise of authoritarianism. They were a European diaspora. However, in Spain, unlike almost everywhere else in Europe, the attempt to overthrow a new democracy was resisted—violently—not only by the urban working class and landless peasants in the countryside but also by sections of the Spanish police and armed forces who remained loyal to the liberal democratic regime established in 1931.

As Julián Casanova, among the most readable and insightful historians of the war, points out in his *Short History of the Spanish*

Civil War (2013), Spain was not on an inevitable slide towards collective violence in the 1930s. However, hardly any country in Europe managed to resolve its tensions without the use of political violence in the 1930s and '40s, and one of its most "civilised" states took the terror to the most extreme form ever at the gates of Auschwitz and elsewhere. Individual idiosyncrasies aside, Spain's history was not independent economically, culturally or socially from the major currents affecting Europe.

The Second Spanish Republic

Before 1931, Spain was governed by a relatively light dictatorship, which dated from a coup in 1923 that overthrew the previous corrupt parliamentary regime. Headed by General Miguel Primo de Rivera, the regime was plagued with corruption. Primo's regime was never fully supported by the army, and the end of the 1920s economic boom and rising inflation led to his resignation in January 1930. King Alfonso XIII was blamed for having supported Primo and faced increasing opposition. To defuse tensions, municipal elections were allowed on 12 April 1931. While monarchist parties won the most votes, the left won by a landslide in the cities. The king was informed that the army would no longer lend its support. Alfonso fled first to Paris, before establishing an exiled court of sorts in a hotel in fascist Rome, where he died in 1941.

The declaration of the Republic on 14 April 1931 was greeted with euphoria by progressive Spain. Elections came in June, the first free and fair elections in Spanish history, which brought to power a centre-left coalition of socialists and liberal republicans, who rapidly engaged in a series of social, educational and land reforms. This led to a new constitution (see Fig. 1.1), which was passed in December 1931. The constitution had a number of ground-breaking features. Article 2 declared that all Spanish men and women were equal before the law, although in rural areas the elites did everything they could to obstruct this legal protection. Female suffrage was established. Women would vote for the first time in 1933, and civil marriage and divorce were legalised in 1932. Article 3 declared that the Spanish state had no official religion, while, further on in the document the clergy were prohibited from teaching, even in private schools; the Jesuit order was expelled; and religious processions made subject to government approval. These anticlerical measures were seen as an attack by the Catholic Church and many devout Catholics—some of whom could perhaps have been won over to other reforms. Article 6 renounced war as an instrument of national policy.

Until the arrival of the Republic and its reforming constitution, most of Spain's population simply had no rights, and this continued to be the case in many rural areas afterwards, whatever the law said. To many urban workers and peasants before 1931, the state was a distant, corrupt entity whose main effect on their lives was violence and repression. This helps explain why the anti-state ideology of anarchism took hold so strongly in Spain. Elsewhere in Europe, many people in working-class communities and their supporters believed the state could be reformed through parliamentary socialism, while others were attracted towards communism in order to reformulate the state. Many in Spain simply could not conceive of the state as a force for good. It seemed to offer them nothing—at least until 1931. The clearest example of this distant state was the absence of primary schools across huge areas of the country. The crowning achievement of the Republic was to create 16,000 schools between 1931 and 1939.

Internal tensions fractured the centre-left government just two years later, resulting in new elections in November 1933. However, the right was now better organised and engaged in vote-rigging in the countryside, while the anarchist CNT (Confederación

Nacional del Trabajo), which believed the Republic represented scant improvement on the previous dictatorship, called for an electoral boycott. These factors led to the victory of a right-wing coalition that rolled back most of the previous government's reforms, particularly after CEDA joined the cabinet in September 1934. CEDA was openly imitating the political style of the Nazis, and its leader, José María Gil Robles, regularly expressed praise for Hitler. Acutely aware of the Nazi takeover and the crushing of the left in Germany, in 1934 a general strike was organised across Spain in protest, which quickly developed into a revolutionary uprising in Asturias, led by the region's miners. Yet with the left weakened by factional divisions, the uprising would be brutally crushed after only two weeks by an army led by none other than General Franco, at an estimated cost of 2,000 lives. The right could now accuse the left of refusing to play by electoral rules, whatever the former's true intentions. For the left, it was a warning of what was to come.

The right-wing government, also an unstable coalition, collapsed in December 1935 due to corruption scandals, leading, after a failed right-wing attempt to form a substitute government, to a new general election in February 1936 fought between two now extremely antagonistic groupings. On the one side stood a right-wing alliance moving in the direction of something more modern—fascism—and on the other side, a centre-left alliance: the so-called Popular Front (Frente Popular). Although the latter included the small Spanish communist party (PCE—Partido Comunista de España), the largest element comprised the socialist party (PSOE—Partido Socialista Obrero Español) and centre-left parties such as Izquierda Republicana, Catalan and Galician social democratic parties and other smaller groups such as the POUM (Partido Obrero de Unificación Marxista), the anti-Stalinist Marxist party whose militia Orwell would later join. The Popular Front's manifesto, mainly reflecting the ideas of Izquierda Republicana, was less economically radical than, for example, Roosevelt's New Deal, but it did have a remarkable reformist agenda, which included resuming the 1931–3 land reform and the reforms to education and the armed forces. On 16 February 1936, it defeated the right, narrowly in terms of votes but by a comfortable majority in terms of seats: 263 out of 473. Even though the PSOE won the largest number of seats in the coalition (ninety-nine), the party's internal divisions led them not to join the government, preferring to support it from the outside. The resulting minority Republican government was made up exclusively of moderate centre-left reformers. Meanwhile, within three days of the victory, a group of generals and their supporters started to organise a coup d'état to stop the reforms and protect the old Spain. This planned coup was an open secret. Everybody knew it was coming.

The military rise in Morocco

The July 1936 coup began in colonial Morocco, where the army rose and swiftly crushed the weak Republican resistance. The executions of loyal soldiers and police, electoral officials and leftists began straight away—that night, 17 July, 225 people faced the firing squads in North Africa. It is often forgotten that in garrisons across Spain, the first victims of Francoism were soldiers and officers who remained loyal to their oath to democracy. The next day, the coup spread chaotically to Andalusia, with rebel officers rising in Seville, Córdoba and, unsuccessfully, in Málaga.

Within a week, Hitler and Mussolini had agreed to help with what became the world's first great airlift. Drawing inspiration from Wagner's opera *Siegfried*, it was named "Operation Magic Fire". Some 1,100 flights over two months aided by sea transport carried General Franco's 30,000-strong Army of Africa from Morocco to Andalusia. The force was made up of the Spanish

Legion as well as many young Moroccans, particularly from Ceuta and Melilla, who had fought under Spanish officers against their fellow countrymen and who, by 1936, formed a dedicated fighting force known as the Fuerzas Regulares Indígenas or, simply, Regulares. When this rebel army landed in Cádiz and Seville, its officers unleashed a wave of extreme violence against anyone they saw as opposing them, supported by proxy militias made up of local landowners, Falangists and other rightists. This would set a pattern as Franco's troops advanced north on their slow conquest of Spain.

2

BARCELONA
JULY 1936

I usually meet people for my tour in front of the Café Zurich in Plaça de Catalunya at the top of La Rambla. The old café was demolished in the late 1990s as part of a real estate operation, but they've recreated the structure, and the waiters are as grumpy as ever. After the failure of the coup in July 1936, it would be collectivised by the staff themselves, while the rooms above were taken over by Mujeres Libres—"Free Women"—the anarchist women's organisation.

In 1936, Barcelona was the only industrial metropolis in Spain. It was a port city with a complex industrial base that had developed from the textile industry in the mid-nineteenth century. These older factories now coexisted with advanced engineering operations producing, for example, one of the best cars in Europe: the Hispano Suiza. The fabric was completed by older craft-type businesses operating out of cramped workshops. Women, often non-unionised, formed an important part of the workforce.

The city had a rich literary and artistic tradition and a different language, Catalan, which was spoken on a daily basis by most of its population. It was one of the few places in Spain with a vibrant middle class. But Barcelona was also a city racked by terrible class divisions between rich and poor. This was reflected in the city's complex politics. The main pro-Republican party was the social democratic and Catalanist ERC (Esquerra Republicana de Catalunya), which had won the national elections in the region by a landslide in 1931 and 1936. While primarily representing the urban middle class and rural Catalonia, ERC pursued a wide-reaching modernisation programme that sought to build schools and improve the lives of the working class. Opposing ERC stood another Catalanist party, also strong, the Lliga Catalana, which represented right-wing Catalonia and its class interests, and which, while prepared to support the Republic, was wary of the changes threatened by the left.

Although the arrival of the Republic was welcomed by many members of Barcelona's militant, highly unionised and often anarchist working class, experience had taught them not to trust the state to deliver their needs. Often working and living in the most awful conditions, these men and women were quickly frustrated by the slow pace of change the Republic offered for themselves and their children, most of whom had no primary schooling in 1931, an atypical situation in the broader context of Western Europe at the time. The contrasts within the progressive but divided city, whose working classes often wanted radical change now rather than the reforms offered by the Republic, is key to understanding the magnitude of the events that would take place in the aftermath of the coup in Barcelona.

Francesc Macià and Lluís Companys

After dealing with the origins of the war and the context of Barcelona in front of the café, we head across the road to a large stone monument to the ERC leader Francesc Macià (1859–1933). A few hours before the Second Spanish Republic was declared in Madrid on 14 April 1931, Macià had unilaterally proclaimed a "Free Catalan Republic" within a non-existent "Iberian Federation" to an ecstatic crowd in Plaça Sant Jaume. However, several days later he was persuaded to back down and settle for what eventually became a statute of autonomy within the new Republic.

ERC had also won a landslide in the 1932 elections to the new Catalan parliament, known as the Generalitat, taking sixty-seven of its eighty-four seats, but Macià died a year later. He was replaced by Lluís Companys, who had a more strongly social-democrat profile and was prepared to give the Spanish Republic a chance, especially if it would lead to a federal Spain.

CEDA's entry to the government in Madrid in October 1934 had provoked armed resistance in Asturias, but elsewhere this received little support, save for Catalonia. On 6 October 1934, Companys declared a "Catalan State within the Spanish Federal Republic", an act for which he was arrested and sentenced to thirty years in prison, only to be released in February 1936, after the victory of the Popular Front in the national election. Companys was president of Catalonia during the war. A Catholic social democrat, he did much to prevent the revolutionary violence in Barcelona in 1936, saving large numbers of lives by giving exit visas to right wingers. In January 1939, he crossed the Pyrenees into exile in France—I will be following the route he took and his fate later in the book.

An alphabet soup

I like to use the shade of Macià's monument to outline the main ideological divisions within the left in Barcelona at the start of the war. Those new to the Spanish Civil War often stumble when confronted with the myriad political parties and organisations in Spain at the time. I certainly did when I first came to the subject. Orwell famously said that it looked as if Spain was suffering from a "plague of initials". A simplified outline of some of these divisions is given in the Appendix, which I hope will help aid understanding.

Defeat of the coup

Plaça de Catalunya is the place where the Old City's higgledy-piggledy chaos of streets meets the pure geometry of the Eixample (Extension), with its regular, planned blocks replicated 700-odd times for kilometres and kilometres across the Plain of Barcelona. As we start early, the square is usually fairly quiet: a couple of drunks on a bench enjoying the first cans of double malt Voll-Damm of the day, people sitting in the shade with their mobiles, a few young thieves still too drowsy to cause any bother, the kiosks selling overpriced snacks to the tourists, folk photographing themselves in front of hundreds of the estimated 85,000 pigeons in Barcelona. I like to allow birds to engage a part of my mind while I'm talking, chiffchaffs flicking among the bushes, the noise of monk parakeets above our heads in the holm oak trees, wagtails bobbing around, picking off the last of the *pipas* (sunflower seeds) left by young lovers around a bench the night before.

We stand in the shade of the holm oak trees. It was 18 July 1936, a Saturday morning and the hottest day so far that year. Word had reached Barcelona of the military rising in Morocco. A majority of the officers of the local garrison were preparing, not so secretly, to overthrow the local civilian authorities, as they were throughout the country. They could count on about 5,000 troops in the city, supported by several hundred civilians from far-right groups—mainly Carlists but also Falangists and others. Meanwhile, the Catalan government-controlled Guardias de Asalto, the Guardia Civil and other police units, numbering about 2,000, would almost certainly be loyal to the Republic. With them stood workers: a few communists and socialists, Catalan republicans, members of the POUM, and the anarchist CNT, the largest group of all (see Fig. 2.1). Some had already hidden a few pistols underneath their beds—it was the 1930s, a world away, and Barcelona was awash with guns bought cheaply and illegally from France after the First World War. As the morning wore on, workers tried to get hold of more weapons, raiding the arms shops. Others went to the Catalan government and demanded arms to save the city. From its perspective, the Generalitat, controlled by the moderate ERC, was in a rather difficult position. It was afraid of the military coup it knew was coming, but through experience it was also concerned about what Barcelona's angry militant working class might do with the weapons and so refused.

Few slept much on that torrid Saturday night. A febrile atmosphere swept the working-class districts as men and women prepared to defend their streets, ripping up the cobblestones to fashion makeshift barricades. At 4.30 on Sunday morning—temperatures having dropped—the coup leaders woke the conscripts, gave them a double ration of rum and told them they were to head to the centre of Barcelona to crush a supposed workers' revolt. A lie. But as soon as they left the barracks, spies positioned nearby got word to the city centre. At 5 a.m., the unions set off factory sirens across the city, a prearranged signal for people to rush into the streets to stop the rebellion. A general strike was also declared. Separately, the Catalan government went on Barcelona radio, denounced the coup and sent out its police. The rebel military, who had hoped they could take the city while it was still asleep, were immediately attacked by groups of workers, and by groups of police, often fighting together.

At 2 p.m., rather late in the day, the local detachment of the paramilitary Guardia Civil, seen as a traditional enemy of the working class and landless peasantry across Spain, also came out on the Republic's side. This is reflected in one of the watercolours by the artist José Rey (also known as Sim) in the first days of the war, which the anarchist CNT turned into postcards, as can be seen in the one depicted in Fig. 2.2 of two workers and a Guardia Civil fighting on the same side. Sim painted these with quick, urgent brush strokes to convey the heat, energy, anger and noise of that morning.

Chaotic, fast-moving situations developed in the morning, where there might be dozens of soldiers, all armed, on one side, and dozens of workers on the other, of whom perhaps only half initially had weapons. But the rebel army units were moving down what were effectively canyons formed by streets into hostile territory. Workers picked them off from the rooftops and built large barricades across the streets. The defenders felt they were fighting for their lives—many if not all must have remembered the crushing of the workers' uprising in Asturias and other recent episodes of extreme violence meted out by the state—and they knew what had happened in Berlin and Vienna. Crucially, the police were fighting on their side and putting up fierce resistance. Meanwhile, as the morning progressed, many of the army conscripts were slipping away or swapping sides, bringing more weapons with them. By no means all their officers supported the coup, and some didn't even leave the barracks.[1]

As a result of this complex situation, the coup was in massive trouble straight away in Barcelona. Yet, at about 6 on the Sunday morning, one military unit did arrive in Plaça de Catalunya. A terrible battle took place. Dozens of people were killed. It's perhaps a bit difficult to imagine all of this in the square today. One aid is the bullet marks—a recent study, with the help of a police ballistics expert, has identified eighty-eight in the *plaça*.[2] See if you can spot a few next time you're in Barcelona. I personally think the series of tragic photos taken by the great Catalan photographer Agustí Centelles help more. We see horses and men lying dead in the square. We can imagine the smell of burning buildings in the July heat. These images were shown around the world, including on the front page of the French magazine *L'Illustration* on 1 August 1936 (see Fig. 2.3).

The military were defeated within a day and a half in Barcelona by a combination of worker and police resistance or, to put it another way, by revolutionary and liberal democratic forces fighting together. Around 450 people were killed. There is no agreement on whether workers or the Catalan police were most responsible for the victory, and there probably never will be. It's probable that neither could have won without the other. The coup failed for similar reasons, different equations, across around 60 per cent of the country. Most importantly, it was unsuccessful in six of Spain's eight largest cities: Madrid, Barcelona, Valencia, Bilbao, Málaga, Murcia. But it did succeed in Seville, Cádiz and Zaragoza and in a huge swathe of Northern Spain, most of whose land, as we've seen, was divided into small farms. Here in the north, especially in Old Castile (approximately today's Castile and León), was the only place where a significant proportion, though not all, of the population enthusiastically supported the coup.

Historians have argued that the rebel success in Northern Spain would not have been enough. The Republic would have either mopped up rebel resistance in a few weeks or the war would have ground down into stalemate. What tipped the balance was the success of the coup in colonial Morocco, followed by Hitler's and Mussolini's prompt support in providing the aircraft to transport Franco's troops across the Straits. This turned a failing rebellion into a full-blown war.

A coup normally succeeds or it fails. In the case of Spain, neither side managed to defeat the other; both were armed, and were prepared to fight. The consequence was civil war. The territorial division shown in Map 1 shows the two sides within a few days. Like many conflicts, the war in Spain was several wars in one. It was a civil conflict that divided villages, towns, institutions and families. It also had a strong element of a class war waged by the rich and powerful against the poor—and by the poor against the rich and powerful. The airlift meant that the Spanish Civil War also immediately became an international conflict, one that is often seen as a prelude to the Second World War. At the time, many people also saw it as the precursor to an impending general European conflict. This was clear to the thousands and thousands of volunteers who came to fight fascism in Spain. It is also reflected in the 1937 postcard produced to help the Basque Front I picked up at an auction (see Fig. 2.4). Over Spain, we can see the child victims of Nazi bomb raids, while over France there is a still smiling child. It reads "Hoy España, Mañana el Mundo"—"Today Spain, tomorrow the world."

Two buildings

We head for the centre of the square, in 1936 strewn with bullets, acrid smoke in the air, horses lying dead. In one corner stands the Telefónica—the old telephone exchange and now a Movistar office. Orwell readers often ask me where it is as it plays a role in *Homage to Catalonia*. It was an important building in 1936 as it controlled communications with the rest of the planet. On Sunday 19 July, there was a heck of a firefight here, floor by floor, waged between workers, loyal police and soldiers on the one side and the rebel military on the other.

The battle for the Telefónica is reflected in the children's trading card, possibly anarchist in origin, depicting men in blue overalls attacking the building (see Fig. 2.5). A Pokémon à la 1936, as it were. In the fighting's aftermath, the building was taken over (the term is collectivised) by the trade union committee who worked there (jointly CNT and the Unión General de Trabajadores or UGT) and became a symbol of worker power in Barcelona. Keep this building in mind, because the spark that started the so-called "May Days" and the defeat of the workers' revolution just nine months later—not by Franco but rather by the left-wing Republican government—began here at the Telefónica.

A large building dominates the other side of the square. This is the site of the old Hotel Colón, which was demolished in the 1950s. The current building is now partially an Apple Store, but numerous photos taken during the war show the old building draped with large portraits of Lenin and Stalin. It was taken over by the PSUC (Partit Socialista Unificat de Catalunya), the pro-Soviet communist party. The ideological divisions of the Catalan left were there to see in the square: on the one side, the anarchist-run Telefónica, and on the other, the communist headquarters, glaring at each other with their very different ideas of society. These differences were shelved in the first heady days after the military's defeat, which saw all the groups on the left united against the rebel generals. And throughout the war, despite their heated and sometimes violent divisions, they remained on the same side. There was also a mass desire for change, particularly among Barcelona's working class, which made up the majority of the city's population in 1936, in favour of some form of social revolution—whoever they'd voted for in February.

Marina Ginestà and photography during the war

One photograph more than any other manages to evoke the spirit of revolutionary Barcelona and its pure optimism at the start of the war. It depicts a young woman, a Mauser rifle over her shoulder, on the rooftop of the Hotel Colón overlooking Plaça de Catalunya. It was taken by Cologne-born Hans Gutmann, who changed his name to Juan Guzmán when he came to Spain. The subject is a seventeen-year-old communist militant named Marina Ginestà. She is posing proudly and defiantly with a rifle slung across her back, oozing rebellion and youth. Behind her stands the square and the old city now engulfed by revolution. In reality, Ginestà was never a militia fighter, and the rifle belonged to a young militiaman who had lent it her for the photo shoot. He quickly grabbed it back off her no sooner had Guzmán finished.

The photo has often been taken as a universal image of the spontaneous rising of youth against fascism, but in truth her rebellion had more to do with her family background than with her age. Ginestà was born in Toulouse on 29 January 1919 into a staunchly left-wing working-class family. Her father Bruno Ginestà was a socialist militant and tailor. He had escaped to France in 1915 after being called up to fight in Morocco, encouraged by his own father, who'd fought in Cuba and knew how the Spanish military treated recruits.

In 1928, the family returned to Barcelona. Both parents were PCE militants. Marina herself joined the party's youth section in the early 1930s. Together with her brother Albert, she participated on the barricades in one way or another to defeat the military coup, although she later admitted she never fired a rifle at anybody. Guzmán came across Marina in the Hotel Colón and persuaded her to pose for the now famous photo. "It was pure propaganda," Ginestà later recalled. Guzmán quickly volunteered for a militia unit to fight in Aragon and later fought in the German-speaking Thälmann Battalion of the International Brigades, and so, while he took some of the best images of the war, most were never seen during the conflict, and many have yet to be properly published.

As Marina spoke native French, she quickly became an interpreter for the PSUC. Two weeks after the photoshoot, when the famous Soviet journalist Mikhail Koltsov arrived in Barcelona to cover the war for *Pravda*, she was assigned to help him (he was also fluent in French) and accompanied him to the Aragon Front. Although she was just seventeen, she seems to have been unflappable, as Koltsov remembered in his diaries: "We were awoken by explosions and gunfire. We got up quickly and took the guns. I went into the next room and lit a match. Marina was still asleep, dressed, long legs outstretched, with a childlike smile. She got up without asking anything."[3]

The Spanish Civil War was fought on many different terrains. But it was also an ideological war of words and images, often through the medium of photography explained with captions. This was the first war to be extensively photographed for a mass market, and its images were a powerful weapon in the battle for public opinion, in which the Republic proved more successful than Franco as the war went on. Photography reflected the world's fascination with the Civil War and how important its events were viewed as, but it was technological change that made this possible. First, the arrival of portable cameras now allowed the photographer to move around and get close to the action. The first and most famous was the Leica, which revolutionised photography with its superb lens, visor and fast shutter allowing images to be taken of moving objects. The war in Spain was the first conflict that really allowed these attributes to be tested.

The delivery of images was now made possible through wire transmission, which could be used to send a low-resolution image across the Atlantic in just a few minutes (Associated Press launched its Wirephoto service in 1935). The small negatives could be printed as large photos that could be distributed. By 1936, scheduled flights were connecting the major cities of the world, allowing a negative or high-quality print to arrive in a few hours in London and Paris and the next day in New York. And cheap, high-quality paper was available for the first time, which permitted affordable photo magazines (*L'Illustration*, *Life*, *Berliner Illustrirte Zeitung*, *Picture Post*, *Regards*, etc). The public lapped up this new, exciting, immediate artform as a way of understanding the conflict. The stark, powerful images from Spain were an anticipation of the television and internet eras, with photos that were often disturbing and that, theoretically at least, were unmediated by censorship. They showed not only images taken in the midst of battle and of exhausted troops but subjects that had hardly been documented before in war photography: civilian victims of bomb raids, distraught women, crying children, dead animals, the haunted face of an elderly man, as well as mothers breastfeeding babies, peasants bringing in the hay and children playing.

Many of the gifted photographers who documented the war were locals, such as Centelles. Others came to Spain. Their names are legendary: Robert Capa, Gerda Taro, David "Chim" Seymour and Kati Horna: all Central or Eastern European, anti-fascist and Jewish. The first three died violent deaths in foreign wars: Taro in Spain in 1937—the first photographer killed in any conflict; Capa in Vietnam in 1954; and Chim during the Suez Crisis in 1956. Horna, like Guzmán, ended up in a form of exile in Mexico, where her work continued to be highly influential until her death in 2000. Since 1939, the work of these women and men, and that of others, has continued to be widely published. Their images form part of the international memory of the war and help to explain why the conflict has continued to be remembered outside of Spain.

The People's Olympiad

One more story before we move on. That hot Saturday night of 18 July 1936, the eve of the coup, several hundred French men and women were sleeping in the square. They had come to Barcelona for a remarkable sporting event but were instead brusquely awoken at 5 a.m. to the sound of factory sirens and gunfire.

In 1931, there were two candidates for the 1936 Olympic Games, a pre-Nazi Berlin and Barcelona. The German capital won, but two years later Hitler came to power. After the February 1936 elections, in protest at the impending Nazi Olympics, Catalonia, with the support of the Spanish and French republics, organised an alternative games, the so-called Olimpíada Popular (People's Olympiad), which, as you can see from the poster in Fig. 2.6, was explicitly anti-racist in its message, well ahead of its time. The poster was done by a German Jewish graphic designer called Fritz Lewy, who had left Berlin with his wife shortly after the Nazi takeover and was now working in Barcelona: an example of the European diaspora that had spread to Spain. You can see his art with its characteristic single one-world circle plastered on the walls of the city in several photos of barricades from July 1936.

The Olimpíada Popular was a remarkable project. Some 6,000 athletes from thirty teams signed up to take part, especially from Spain and France. It also attracted a similar number of Spanish and foreign tourists. Most of the latter came from France. Léon Blum's Popular Front government had the month before brought in the first ever paid holidays for workers in Western Europe. They came down on the trains especially provided from towns such as Montpellier and Perpignan. In a way, this was the birth of Barcelona as a city of mass tourism, the day before the Spanish Civil War. But there was a massive problem with accommodation.

Athletes were sleeping in hotels, in private lodgings and at the Olympic Stadium. Many of the tourists slept wherever they could. There weren't enough hotels, and they just did not have the money we have today. Surely there had never been so many young foreigners in the streets of Barcelona, falling in love with each other and the locals and enjoying the fraternal atmosphere in broken Spanish. Perhaps most did not know much about the tensions rising across Spain. Among the small number of British tourists was the artist Felicia Browne, who was on a driving and sketching holiday in France with a fellow communist friend. We'll return to her story later. Journalists had also arrived in the city to cover the games and so were able to report on the fighting, among them the photographer Juan Guzmán.

The Catalan government cancelled the Olympiad on the Saturday night when it was clear the coup was going to happen. With the aid of foreign ships and trains to the border, it managed to get most of the athletes and tourists out, but about 250 chose to stay and became some of the first foreign volunteers to fight against fascism. One such case is that of an Austrian javelin thrower called Jaccod Menchter, who died in the attack on the Drassanes barracks on the morning of 20 July that brought an end to the coup in Barcelona. He was very possibly the first of the more than 9,000 foreign volunteers to die fighting on the side of the Republic. Nothing else is known about his identity, one of so many named and nameless lost in those terrible European years. Many of those who did return to their own countries played an important role in explaining the plight of the Republic and, in the case of some athletes, helped organise recruitment to the International Brigades before later returning to Spain. Among them was Alfred "Chick" Chakin, who had come as coach for the small American team. Back in New York, Chakin helped organise the American aid for Spain before returning in June 1937 as a volunteer with the International Brigades. The US team also included biracial boxer Charley Burley from Pittsburgh, considered pound for pound one the best fighters in the world.

Antonio Cánovas

In 2015, I was fortunate to meet a veteran from the Olympiad, aged ninety-five, in L'Hospitalet de Llobregat, Barcelona's poorer neighbour. As we sat down in his flat to talk, he quipped that his life had been like "un Far West"—a Western. Antonio Cánovas recalled the events in July in a fluent, lucid narrative:

> I was a member of Barceloneta Swimming Club. The day before the games were supposed to begin, we all dressed up in our green costumes and did exercises at the club. I was so excited. We all were. Just sixteen and the chance to represent my country. We weren't really interested in politics, but we also felt this was a chance for us workers to be champions and counter the Berlin Games. There was a fraternal atmosphere in the city the days before, but also fear—we all knew the coup was coming. But, hey, I was young, full of teenage enthusiasm and about to take part in a great sporting event. They [Franco and his generals] destroyed my life as it was then. It was such a disappointment not to be able to compete.

The next day, Sunday morning, as the military left the garrisons around the city, his parents told Antonio and his eighteen-year-old brother Alfonso not to go out: "We left anyway, and neither of us slept another night in the family home again." The two brothers fought on the barricades and then volunteered straightaway for the front with a communist militia, being involved in the failed attempt to take Mallorca a few weeks later in August 1936. He remembered how "[o]ne friend, just sixteen too, was hit by a bullet on the island. He died in my arms. His last words were 'mummy, mummy'."

Aftermath

As evening approached on 19 July 1936, workers felt they needed more weapons to finish the job as rebel army units were still entrenched in buildings around the city. Groups stormed the major barracks and seized about 30,000 weapons—old rifles in the main but weapons nonetheless: insufficient in quality to fight a war but certainly good enough to control a city. They then drove around the working-class districts and handed them out, more or less to anybody who insisted. Suddenly, the poor and the working class, those whose children often didn't have shoes on their feet, were armed and completely outnumbered the police. The city was now engulfed in what was described at the time as a revolutionary fiesta.

After five days, the CNT and UGT unions called off the general strike and told their members to return to work. Almost everyone did so, but many workers seemingly had a different idea and spontaneously began taking over their workplaces. Over the next few weeks, most of Barcelona's business and industry was taken over by workers' committees and collectivised. This is usually described as the greatest attempt at workers' self-rule in history, and, unlike what happened in the USSR, workers' control was not swiftly suppressed by the state but remained in the hands of local unions and community groups. At the same time, they were incensed by the coup that they saw as a threat to their lives, their communities and their ideals. While anarchist militants were hostile to the Republican project, it probably enjoyed the tacit support of much of the city's working class. But the rules of the game had changed. Now, workers, anarchist or otherwise, felt that if progress under the Republic was blocked, they would take advantage of the situation and do it themselves. Many workers probably had a foot in both camps—reform and revolution. The wind was now blowing forcibly towards revolution and was greeted with jubilation by the city's working classes.

Revolution in Barcelona

Some 3,000 companies were taken over by workers' committees and collectivised. Often, this was because their owners had stayed at home through fear or had fled. Faced with the need to keep the workplaces going—and, therefore, their wages—workers took power. Within three or four days, buses, trams, water and electricity, which had all been in private hands, were all under the control of self-managed workers committees and were all up and running perfectly well. An item in my walking museum that illustrates this is the 1937 annual report of Barcelona's metro system (see Fig. 2.7) run by the CNT. Aside from the attractive graphics on the front page, it is, like any decent annual report, a boring document crammed with details of investments, salaries and other technicalities, but it also gives an idea of the depth of organisation required to run an economy from below.

Huge swathes of Catalan industry were also taken over. Sometimes successfully, sometimes not. It was a mixed record. Some of the big industries were collectivised efficiently, such as the woodworking industry, which controlled the entire production chain from the forests of Girona to furniture shops in Barcelona. Others, such as the distribution sector, were a disaster. In 70 per cent of cases, owners were allowed to come back to work, especially if they had a good reputation, and would be employed as a technical manager or an accountant but within a self-managed cooperative structure, where at the beginning, at least, everyone had the same pay. I'm sure most were not delighted by this situation. Areas now controlled by workers' committees included public transport and taxis, power, gas and water companies; large-scale engineering and car plants;

and almost all other factories. Only the banks and most foreign-owned companies escaped the wave; the former were quickly nationalised by the Catalan government.

Another item illustrating the takeover of the economy is the milk bottle label shown in Fig. 2.8. Barcelona is a design city. That is true of the modern capitalist city, but it was also true of the revolutionary one. Catalans take design seriously. You can see this by walking around Barcelona and looking at the quality of the urban fixtures, the signposting in the Metro and in shops and bars. I always find Madrid, or, for that matter, Paris, London and Berlin, a bit messy in comparison. Design seems to be in the local DNA. Catalonia was an advanced industrial society, but, compared to similar societies at the time, it had relatively high levels of illiteracy and semi-literacy. Perhaps this encouraged the search for ways to get complex messages across to the part of the population who could not adequately read.

One interesting area of collectivisation was the entertainment industry, which included 250 cinemas, theatres and the film studios in Montjuïc, which was the centre of Spanish moviemaking. In 1930s Barcelona, the working class really had nothing. There was virtually no consumerism. Apart from a glass of wine, one of the very few "luxuries" workers could afford was a cinema ticket. Along with local productions, Hollywood and its escapist message was highly popular and in some ways fed into the aesthetic of working-class dress, with young men sometimes adopting the look of the gangster. In Fig. 2.9, you can see a cinema ticket for the Capitol Cinema on La Rambla dated 5 October 1937, where *Hija de Drácula* (Dracula's daughter, 1936) starring Gloria Holden was showing. A bit of mock American horror to escape from the real horror of the war by then.

In the weeks following the defeat of the coup, capitalism virtually disappeared from Barcelona as the means of production and effective political power passed into the hands of worker committees. Many anarchist writers have undoubtedly exaggerated the purity and success of what the German philosopher Hans Magnus Enzensberger called "The Short Summer of Anarchy." But a revolution did take place, and it was profound in almost all aspects of life. It was a revolution not only against fascism but also, while highly democratic at a local level, against liberal democracy and capitalism. The British correspondent John Langdon-Davies summed up these contradictions when he arrived in early August 1936: "I went on to Barcelona past barricade after barricade, giving the countersign every few miles to members of the Army in Overalls. I was approaching the strangest city in the world today, the city of anarcho-syndicalism supporting democracy, of anarchists keeping order, and anti-political philosophers wielding political power."[4]

Rents, a terrible millstone for most workers in the 1930s, were now municipalised and slashed by half. The acute overcrowding of working-class districts was abated, to an extent, by families moving up the hill into the houses of the wealthy, some of whom, but far from all, had left. The area where the revolutionaries and the authorities worked best together was probably education. Within a week, the Generalitat established the CENU (Consell de l'Escola Nova Unificada, or Council for the New Unified School), an authority that gave the right of free, secular education to all. It was influenced and led above all by anarchist pedagogues, but it was also characterised by its non-sectarian nature inspired by general principles of humanism.

Between July 1936 and June 1937, the number of children receiving free school education in the city rose from 34,431 to 116,846, and free nurseries were opened for the first time. Some of the schools were newly built by the CNT Construction Union, but most were set up in confiscated buildings, such as churches—although the church in front of our flat was used as a garage by the local CNT woodworkers' union.

At a talk at our allotment on the slopes of Montjuïc, I learned about another aspect of the takeover of the economy, until recently hardly mentioned, even among anarchist historians. As we sat in the shade of a fig tree, Marta Camps, a researcher on environmental history, told us about the CNT's urban farming collective in Barcelona. Before the war, Catalonia imported 45 per cent of its wheat consumption. The Francoist conquest of the wheatlands of Extremadura, western Aragon and, above all, Castile led to a huge drop in cereal imports and a massive rise in the price of bread in Barcelona, so people took to eating far more vegetables. Although the city had expanded massively in previous decades—almost doubling in population to just over a million between 1900 and 1936—there were still considerable areas of farmland within the urban limits, along with monastery possessions and private estates. All of this was seized by the CNT and formed into a single collective, which had the largest membership of any collective in Catalonia, employing 3,500 men and women. Despite the CNT's declared egalitarianism, older men were paid 180 pesetas a week, while all women, and men under twenty-five, were paid just 115. In 1937, the collective produced 35,000 tons of vegetables, which went a huge way in alleviating food shortages. Members could grow food for personal consumption—some of which inevitably ended up on the black market as shortages grew during the war. Meanwhile, workers informally created some 10,000 vegetable plots on bits of land around the city. As Marta pointed out, while the Second World War "Dig for Victory" campaign in the UK forms part of the British memory of that conflict, the huge efforts in Republican cities during the Civil War have been almost completely forgotten—a small example of the massive erasure of memory of the war arising from Franco's victory.

The working classes had been living dark, tunnel lives, working sixty-hour weeks with seemingly no hope of advancement for themselves or their children. They remembered in their memoirs the sense of liberation. Enriqueta Rovira, a twenty-year-old member of the anarchist Mujeres Libres, wrote:

> The feelings we had then were very special. It was very beautiful. There was a feeling of—how shall I say it?—of power, not in the sense of domination, but in the sense of things being under control. Of possibility. A feeling that we could together really do something.[5]

But there was also another part of the population, perhaps 5–10 per cent, who remembered living in a state of fear, for the revolution was accompanied by violent reprisals not only against supporters of the coup, such as right-wing militants, gangsters and the clergy, but also often against right-wingers, the wealthy and Catholics in general. Both of these contrasting memories and experiences were true, as we shall see later.

The militias leave for Aragon

While workers' committees were taking over Barcelona's industry and commerce, the rebel army was establishing control of around 40 per cent of mainland Spain. The military situation was critical. The Republican government in Madrid had disbanded all disloyal army units, which effectively meant that it now had no army. Into this vacuum stepped hastily organised worker militias that either attempted to defend Republican areas or drove out to confront the army rebels. As far as Barcelona was concerned, the principal threat was from Zaragoza, 300 kilometres to the west, which had fallen on the 19th. For the CNT, there was the added motive that the Aragonese capital had been a stronghold of anarchism. They wanted to take back the city to save their militants from being massacred.

Whatever the social and economic events in Barcelona, the threat from the rebel military meant there was a clear need for government authorities and revolutionary workers to come together against a common foe. On 21 July, the CCMA (Comité Central de Milícies Antifeixistes, or Central Committee of Antifascist Militias) was established in Barcelona by the Catalan government and the CNT with the prime aim of organising militia columns to send to Aragon. The first column to leave was led by the anarchist militant Buenaventura Durruti. On the morning of 24 July, the first 2,000 or so volunteers— older anarchist militants, young volunteers and a smattering of soldiers—congregated on Passeig de Gràcia. Film footage from the time attests to the unbounded enthusiasm of the volunteers and those cheering them on.[6] Many thought, as is often the case at the start of a war, that they would be back home in a few days or weeks once the job was done. There were similar illusions on the other side. The strange caravan of requisitioned trucks, buses, taxis and private cars drove out of the city at midday—in the words of anarchist militant Abel Paz, "to the delirious cheers, raised fists, and refrains from revolutionary songs". Durruti himself rode in a classy Barcelona-built Hispano Suiza that the CNT had seized.

The war was so much bigger than that fought in Barcelona's streets. It was time I also drove to Aragon to learn more.

3

HOMAGE TO ARAGON

It always gives me a bit of a frisson when I leave Catalonia, my home, and enter Aragon. Both are part of Spain, but even cocooned in your car you feel as though you are entering a different country. Not only are the road signs now in Castilian; it feels wilder, dryer and the sky is bigger.

A journey down from the French frontier through Aragon takes you through some striking changes. You begin in the Pyrenees, here the highest and most dramatic in the range, home to its last melting glaciers and dozens of peaks over 3,000 metres, rising to Aneto (3,404 metres). Descending, you pass through the wild limestone massif and deep gorges of the Pre-Pyrenees, and then, barely 100 kilometres from the border, in stark contrast, appears the vast semi-arid steppes of the Ebro Depression. Farther south, you again ascend into the rugged mountains of the Sistema Ibérico, which reaches its highest point in Moncayo (2,313 metres). On such a journey, you'd pass through Aragon's three provinces—Huesca, Zaragoza and Teruel—and if you avoided the capital of Zaragoza (most Spanish provinces are named after their capital) and its environs (home to 57 per cent of the region's population), you'd likely see very few people on your trip.

Aragon in the 1930s was, like most of Spain, a land of huge social differences. Although patterns varied, in broad terms there was a landowning class, particularly in the province of Zaragoza, which controlled big estates, but unlike in the south of the country, there was also a large number of smallholders, in many cases possessing barely enough land to make a living. At the bottom were desperately poor farm labourers who worked on the estates and small farms. Old social structures still dominated. The great surrealist film director Luis Buñuel wrote in his autobiography of his birthplace in Calanda in the south of Aragon that "the Middle Ages lasted until World War One".[1] Although migration to the big cities, capitalism and liberal republican and revolutionary ideas were beginning to erode the past, little had changed for many. In a similar fashion to the rural south, frustration at the timid land reforms after the Popular Front's electoral victory of February 1936 led to peasants and labourers invading estates in Aragon, demanding work. They would often be violently driven off by the Guardia Civil or hired gunmen.

The cosmopolitan maelstrom of Barcelona must have seemed a long way away. The role of women was particularly antiquated. A friend of mine's grandmother came from the town of Teruel. Mari told me that Pilar had come to Barcelona to serve with a wealthy family in an apartment on Passeig de Gràcia in 1935. They'd treated her well enough, but also for the first time in her adult life on free days she could walk the streets at night without being chaperoned by a family member. Across Spain, the old provincial elites hated this new role for women.

Los Monegros

At Sariñena, we turn south to Bujaraloz into the arid heart of Los Monegros. Geographers call this semi-desert of low hills and plains a pseudo-steppe. It was formed by low rainfall, poor soils, ancient deforestation and overgrazing. Temperatures rise to 40°C in the summer and regularly drop to -5°C in the long winter. As the old Castilian saying goes: "Nine months of winter, three months of hell" ("Nueve meses de invierno y tres de infierno"); an exaggeration of course, but spring and autumn are short and getting shorter in the Iberian hinterland. Much of the war was fought under such extremes, with many succumbing to the cold, frostbite, heat exhaustion and thirst.

Los Monegros probably take their name—The Black Hills—from the Spanish juniper (*Juniperus thurifera*) and pine trees that once covered part of the area. They were felled, you'll often hear people say in Aragon, for the ships of Philip II's Armada, built to invade England in 1588. It's an appealing story that conjures up the image of Aragonese trees entombed in the North Sea after storms wrecked his fleet, but juniper is not used extensively in shipbuilding, and, more importantly, areas of the Ebro Depression have never been heavily wooded, at least not since before the last Ice Age. Much of the soil is saline, and there's just not enough rain. The tale forms part of a traditional belief that Iberia was once a sylvan idyll, forested uninterruptedly from the Pyrenees to Cádiz, and that a hypothetical red squirrel could make such a journey hopping from tree to tree: an Eden from which a harsher Spain had apparently descended. Whatever the case, the unirrigated part of the Monegros today is a place of vast vistas, very occasionally broken by crumbling farm buildings scattered here and there. Dry, stony cereal fields lie between rougher ground. The people who worked them in the past must have suffered to gain just enough to eat. The land can't yield much today. The natural vegetation is made up of tough little plants and low shrubs, eking out a living in the arid soil. Apart from the occasional pine plantation and lone juniper, there's hardly a tree in sight. The light is blinding.

We come across an abandoned residential estate and turn off to drive along its roads, scrub invading each plot, some planted with a concrete frame, others unbuilt. Signs, zebra crossings and lampposts are all neatly laid out, one of numerous half-built schemes across Spain. They are a legacy of the boom years of the early 2000s and a potent symbol of the Spanish capital's love of easy money in construction and property over industry and innovation. The roadscape, I later learned, was part of Gran Scala, a mega water-guzzling project to build a European Las Vegas in the Monegros, a "destination city of leisure for all ages". The dream consisted of thirty-two casinos, seventy hotels and half a dozen major entertainment parks, which would, the promoters claimed, attract 25 million visitors a year by 2025. With the financial crisis, this greedy 27 billion-euro fantasy was definitively ditched in 2012.

Context: the war in Aragon

Aragon was cleaved in two by the July coup. The western half and all three provincial capitals fell to the rebel forces, unleashing a vicious repression against the left by the military and its allies. In contrast, the rebellion was defeated in eastern Aragon in large part due to the rapid intervention of militia columns from Catalonia. This zone experienced a remarkable social revolution through the collectivisation of agriculture, but it was also accompanied by violent reprisals against the supporters of right-wing parties and the Church. There were now two Aragons, divided by a front strung 350 kilometres from the French border. After a few weeks, as neither side appeared capable of breaking through, both dug in and fortified their positions. Individuals found themselves in radically different situations, with their experiences and fates dependent on which half they happened to find themselves in, their political ideas and their economic class. As the conflict dragged on, the region experienced some of the war's most brutal battles, particularly at Teruel, Belchite and around Huesca, besieged for twenty months by Republican troops. But killing went on all along the line in long-forgotten minor assaults and from sniping, shelling and aerial bombing. And when Franco's army broke through in March 1938, a new wave of brutal rearguard violence came in its wake.

Bujaraloz: the militias arrive

After leaving Barcelona, the Durruti Column advanced triumphantly into Aragon, taking the small town of Caspe in a bloody skirmish with the Guardia Civil and mopping up other pockets of resistance. On the way, they picked up thousands of Catalan and Aragonese volunteers. The column finally became entrenched some 30 kilometres southeast of Zaragoza on around 27 July, halting at the village of Pina de Ebro. Durruti meanwhile set up his temporary headquarters 30 kilometres behind the lines at Bujaraloz.

We park in front of the church. It's noon, and the July sun is fierce. Like most of the villages in the Monegros, Bujaraloz is made up of narrow streets lined with low houses, few trees and not many old buildings: most people were living in fragile adobe homes well into the twentieth century. About 1,000 people still reside here, its population slowly falling, although less so than elsewhere in the Spanish hinterland. While lyrical on the tongue, Bujaraloz is not somewhere most urbanites would consider moving. When I suggest we do so, Mònica shudders and tells me I am on my own. Aside from the out-of-the-wayness and the smell drifting in that day from the pig farms, the climate is not easy. Months of freezing winter, sharpened by the cierzo winds, precede a short, sweet spring and then a hellishly hot summer in a treeless, steppe-like landscape, although absolutely not one without its beauty. I pull out a few black and white photos showing the Durruti Column in the village and imagine the caravan of vehicles passing through in July 1936. Mònica, who is better at such things, manages to find several of the locations. She holds up our copies, squaring them with today's scenes. We come to a fine eighteenth-century brick manor house, one of the handful of attractive buildings in the village, decorated with a noble family crest. This was Durruti's HQ. The push quickly wore down into a stalemate as both sides lacked arms to mount a serious attack against well-defended lines.

The anarchist leader met the Soviet journalist Koltsov in Bujaraloz on 14 August accompanied by Ginestà, famed subject of the Hotel Colón photo in Barcelona. They found the village covered in red and black flags and plastered with decrees issued by the column. Another image, again by Guzmán, shows the three of them hunched around a campaign map, together with other fighters. Durruti is wearing a black and red militia cap; Kolstov, a beret. They argued about how to wage the war. Kolstov claimed the Spaniard was excessively emotional, a fanatic even. Durruti hardly trusted the Russian.

Ginestà was convinced that the conversation in Bujaraloz cost both men their lives, claiming in an interview with El Público in 2008 that they were killed "because Stalin was spying on them and didn't like what they said". Although we can never be sure, she was probably mistaken. The anarchist was killed during the defence of Madrid on 20 November 1936, probably either from a sniper's bullet fired from Franco's lines or more likely because the pistol he was wearing went off. Kolstov himself, a superb writer, had become just too popular for Stalin. He was called back to Moscow in November 1937 and showered with honours. One month later, bathed in the glory of Stalin's praise, he was inevitably arrested, one of the many victims of the Great Purge, and eventually shot in February 1940.

Standing in front of Durruti's old HQ, I wonder if anybody else comes to Bujaraloz as a tourist. I guess the odd anarchist following Durruti's path must pass through. Mònica pushes me from the heat to the only restaurant open. For the first course, we have *Borraja con patatas* drizzled with olive oil and vinegar. It's delicious. Borage is not something you see often in Barcelona, although we eat Swiss chard (*acelgas* in Spanish, *bledes* in Catalan) once a week in a similar fashion. It's Mònica's comfort food. There's a big plate of lamb, always good in Aragon, for the second course. I pull out my tablet so we can watch a video I've downloaded from YouTube, an anarchist propaganda film made in 1936. *Los Aguiluchos de la FAI por tierras de Aragón* begins in Bujaraloz. Buses, painted with the letters of the CNT, are parked in front of the church, and militiamen rest in the shade of the village's streets. Others stand around laughing for the camera. Most are smiling, some are smoking. It's all optimism in early August 1936. Some are so young. "They look like boys," says Mònica. One group herd sheep to a slaughterhouse to feed this strange army. The film then accompanies the column as it drives, red and black flags flying from lorries packed with militia fighters, through arid fields bleached white by the sun, heading for the front a few kilometres farther west. Hardly a tree breaks the horizontal. It's an interesting document of the times, heavy with propaganda of the heroic proletarian struggle.

Back in Barcelona, the CCMA continued to organise new columns: anarchist, Catalan Republican, communist. On 25 July, the first POUM column made up of 2,000 volunteers departed for Aragon. This would become the so-called Lenin Division that Orwell later joined. The next day, the first PSUC column left with another 2,000. Its members included a group of German anti-fascist exiles led by former communist Reichstag deputy Hans Beimler, who would be killed on the Madrid Front in November. These foreign fighters would later form the nucleus of the German-speaking Thälmann Battalion of the International Brigades. More columns soon headed out, taking different routes from Barcelona and Valencia towards the front line. Their swift action and the opposing push from the insurgents established the Aragon Front, saving a huge swathe of land nominally in the hands of the Republic. This kept Barcelona relatively safe and far from the fighting—unlike Madrid, which was soon besieged by Franco's forces.

The militias were a potent symbol of anarchist power representing the idea of the "People in Arms" and were depicted in numerous propaganda posters and magazines. Composed mainly of urban workers, they had certainly proved themselves effective in street fighting against the uprising in Barcelona and showed a great deal of initiative in the first weeks by establishing a stable front, but they also understood little of military campaigning in open countryside. *Los Aguiluchos de la FAI por tierras de Aragón* emphasises the technical means with which the column was endowed. A biplane gets plenty of coverage, as does the column's artillery and telescope. We see a truck being repaired by mechanics. In reality, however, the militias were very poorly armed and equipped. As POUM leader Jordi Aquer later remembered: "We didn't have maps, and I am not talking about proper military maps, but a simple Michelin road map."[2]

We continue to watch the documentary as our dessert arrives. A very young militia woman, a girl really, appears on the screen. Mònica rolls her eyes at the triumphant anarchist commentary: "Smiling, this attractive female militant from Barcelona who didn't have the patience to wait for news of the final victory and joined the column as the bravest and most beautiful soldier.

What else could a woman want!" Mònica interjects: "She's almost the only woman I've seen in the whole film and all they're talking about is her beauty. It mustn't have been easy for her. You want to know what happened to her. She's so young."

Women at the front

The Republican and revolutionary press printed hundreds of photos and drawings of women armed with rifles (see Figs 3.1 and 3.2). It is one of the enduring images of the Spanish Civil War. However, rather than seeking to inspire women to fight, they were aimed at men—as a way of encouraging or shaming them into joining the militias. Relatively few women fought on the Aragon Front and across Spain. We'll never know the true figure, but numbers vary between 500 and just over 1,000. Most were young and accompanied, or even in some cases chaperoned, by a husband, a boyfriend or a brother. Despite the revolutionary rhetoric in support of women's liberation, once at the front many were quickly relegated to traditional female roles such as cooking and nursing. By the autumn of 1936, all anti-fascist organisations, including the CNT and the anarchist women's organisation Mujeres Libres, were advocating for women to be reserved for ancillary tasks or sent back to the rear-guard.

The most famous use of the image of a woman to shame men into fighting can be seen in the 1936 recruiting poster by Cristóbal Arteche depicting an armed woman in tight-fitting overalls exclaiming in Catalan "Les milicies us necessiten!"—"The militias need you!" Three flags are flying—anarchist, communist and Catalan—at a time when anti-fascist unity still seemed possible. It is a clear take on the posters from the First World War: Lord Kitchener pointing at the viewer, "Your country needs you" and Uncle Sam's, "I want you for the US army." All the fighters pictured in the background are male. The woman was based on Marlene Dietrich.

At the same time, the social revolution that swept across Republican Spain in 1936 was accompanied by an incipient yet remarkable sexual revolution, particularly among young working-class women. This was reflected in the numerous powerful images of women such as Ginestà armed with rifles at the start of the war. Others show women having taken over their factory. These changes had deep roots. The Republic had certainly broken barriers with the vote and the right to divorce. Large numbers of women had also joined the labour market in the previous decades, slowly undermining the traditional dominance of men. However, as will come as no surprise to female readers, we should not kid ourselves that women had suddenly stepped into a feminist utopia. Spain, and with it Catalonia, was still a terribly sexist society in 1936 and not just in right-wing circles. As has almost always been the case with leftist revolutions around the world, women were fighting a double battle: first against reaction and, in the case of Spain, against the Catholic Church, but second against the attitudes and practices of their own male comrades. It was also not unusual for anarchist collectives to pay women lower wages than men.

At the forefront of this struggle was the anarchist women's organisation Mujeres Libres (see Fig. 3.3). Founded in 1936, the organisation had some 30,000 members across Spain and played an important role in promoting health and literacy and driving trams in Barcelona. They campaigned in favour of women joining the workforce and fought against brothels and prostitution. At times, the organisation had a rather problematic relationship with the CNT itself, many of whose men, and a few of the women, did not like the women organising separately.

Women initially played little part in managing the collectives, though their role increased as the war continued. Many women also worked in education and vocational training—both of which saw an unquestionable improvement in provision for both sexes. As the war went on, the propaganda line on women's roles also became more conservative. One poster produced by the Catalan PSUC in December 1936 gives you an idea of the flavour. It proclaims: "Dones! Treballeu per als germans del front"— "Women! Work for your brothers at the front." It depicts a soldier in a trench coat and a young woman knitting. However, like in the UK and the United States during the Second World War, as men were sent to the front, more and more women found work as tram drivers, in heavy engineering and in more managerial roles—something not in any way mirrored on Franco's side, where women, when allowed to work, were restricted to professions such as nursing and more menial factory work.

Revolution

After the anarchist documentary finished, I pulled a slim book out of my bag, a Spanish edition published in Madrid in 1930. Mònica stroked its old cover, leafing through the pages with the care we show for old things. Peter Kropotkin's *The Conquest of Bread* was probably the single most influential text on the Spanish anarchist revolution—and more recently on the Occupy movement around the world. Published in France in 1892, it first lays out the defects of feudalism and capitalism, which the Russian believed needed both poverty and scarcity to prosper. He then puts forward a decentralised economic system based on mutual aid and voluntary cooperation. Underlying his ideas is a belief that the "basis for such organisation already exists, both in evolution and in human society". In revolutionary Spain of 1936, while the village church would often be set on fire to be used later as a garage or a latrine, the school, either opened by the Republic or newly formed by the revolutionary committee, was a building to be revered, and an edition of Kropotkin's text such as mine would often be placed on the school desk as the Bible had been placed on the altar. I imagined extracts from my worn copy being passed around and read aloud by the militants in Bujaraloz—in the shade of a building, in a requisitioned hall, in trenches by candlelight at the front. In revolutionary Aragon and in other areas still under nominal Republican control, Kropotkin's ideas, which had for decades been discussed openly in worker classrooms or in secret meetings, whispered in bars and explained in public rallies, were now in the matter of a few short days being put into practice. One extract reads: "The most important economy, the only reasonable one, is to make life pleasant for all, because the man who is satisfied with his life produces infinitely more than the man who curses his surroundings."

As in much of rural Spain where the coup had failed, eastern Aragon had been wrenched out of government control and was undergoing a profound social revolution that sought to sweep away the old order. This was far more radical than that offered by any of the parties that supported the Republic. The militias and the peasants disbanded the old village councils, replacing them with revolutionary committees and made declarations in the village squares that libertarian communism, as anarchism is also known, had arrived. The committees collectivised fields, mills, factories, shops and entire villages. But others, some equally poor, looked upon the arrival of these militant workers from Catalonia's factories with concern or fear as they saw their old world crumble. In October 1936, the revolutionary collectives were brought together under a single administration: the short-lived Consejo Regional de Defensa de Aragon (Regional Defence Council of Aragon). Sometimes described as the only anarchist "government" in history, it was based in the small town of Caspe under the presidency of CNT leader Joaquín Ascaso, functioning as a quasi-state within the Spanish Republic.

The process of collectivisation was depicted in Ken Loach's moving film *Land and Freedom* (1995). In a newly liberated village, we see POUM militia fighters, local peasants and smallholders gathered together and debating in an open assembly whether to collectivise the land. Lawrence, the only American volunteer, argues that the war effort should come before taking the revolution further, pointing out that the Republic desperately needed the support of capitalist governments such as the United States and Britain to buy weapons and that the collectivisations were scaring them off. In contrast, a German militiaman argues that war and revolution need to be waged at the same time, exclaiming "in Germany revolution was postponed and now Hitler is in power". Loach's film is essentially a retelling of Orwell's *Homage to Catalonia*. The director had been unable to acquire the rights and instead retold the story through a fictitious lens, putting forward the POUM's, and Orwell's, position that the only way those on the Republican side could have defeated Franco would have been by fighting a revolutionary war. Most historians would today disagree, putting the prime responsibility for Republican defeat on the huge amount of military equipment Franco received from Hitler and Mussolini, while the Republic was fatally encumbered by the refusal of the Western democracies to sell arms to a fellow democracy, forcing them to turn to Stalin's half-hearted, overpriced and politically poisoned aid. Divisions on the left did not help the anti-Francoist cause either, nor did the Republic's need to re-create an army from scratch.

The attempt by the anarchist workers and peasants to build a new society was one of the most remarkable revolutionary experiments in world history, comparable in depth to the Paris Commune of 1871 or Petrograd in 1917. (A more recent example is the ideas of direct democracy and decentralised economy developed in Rojava, northeastern Syria.) All revolutions involve a dual process of destruction and creation. One reason for the revolution's ultimate failure in Barcelona and rural Spain was that this process of creation was immediately curtailed by the need to fight Franco: so much energy and resources went into fighting what quickly became a full-scale war. But the CNT/FAI (Federación Anarquista Ibérica) leadership in the summer of 1936 was also clearly unprepared for the swiftness of the events and often had difficulties in knowing how to put its ideas into practice.

Anticlericalism

We left the restaurant and headed for the church. The heat still fierce, I brought out another black and white photo showing church bells lying on the ground among the rubble here in 1936. While for part of the population of Bujaraloz and villages like it, the collectivisations were greeted with joy, for others they were met by fear. The parish priest Eusebio Antolín Moliner was among the latter. We got back in the car, now a furnace, and drove through scrappy outskirts past warehouses offering agricultural supplies and a gaudy sign advertising a "club"—a brothel—as you get in so many small Spanish places on the road to somewhere. As is commonplace in Spain, the cemetery was outside the village. Antolín, along with fourteen other men marked out as rightists, were shot against its low, whitewashed walls shortly after the arrival of the Durruti Column. Inside the quiet space lined by walls of niches, they are remembered by a stone cross erected by the Franco regime between cypresses.

Across Spain, the clergy were victims of some of the worst violence. On the eve of the war, the Spanish clergy comprised some 115,000 people—45,000 nuns and 15,000 monks, with most of the rest being made up of priests—representing around 1 per cent of Spain's working population. They would soon bear the brunt of the anger unleashed by the failed coup as the country saw their slaughter on an unprecedented scale. In all, some 6,800 members of the clergy were murdered in Republican Spain during the war, one of the worst levels of anticlerical violence in history.[3] And unlike the assault on the church in revolutionary France or the anticlericalism in communist states, it was not directed by the state. In Spain, the violence was generally committed at a local level by local actors, which the Republican state, shocked by the events, was incapable of stopping.

The causes of anticlericalism in Spain lie in the Catholic Church's central position at the helm of reactionary Spain, offering the ruling class almost total support in their policies of repression and justification for their wealth. The Church vociferously campaigned against the right to organise trade unions, and while the clerical hierarchy preached the poverty of the cloth, they themselves lived in opulence. Although it had lost much of its agricultural land to liberal reforms in the nineteenth century, the Church still held considerable possessions. This was particularly the case in the cities, where it was a powerful landlord; it also held important financial interests, further wedding it to the elite. It can thus be difficult to decipher whether the violence was merely anticlerical or part of a wider class war. In contrast, in much of Spain, the working class and the landless peasants were offered little but the promise of salvation. The Church also imposed a suffocating rule over social life, particularly in villages. It is therefore unsurprising that Spain, as much as being a Catholic country, was a deeply anticlerical one. According to Anthony Beevor in *The Battle for Spain* (2006), the pre-war rate of churchgoing for the whole of the state was around 20 per cent—the lowest in Christendom at the time. If one considers that churchgoing on the right, and among the smallholding peasantry of Castile, Navarra and Galicia, was relatively high, the figure must have been very low indeed among most workers and landless peasants in other regions. A further cause of opposition was the Church's association with militarism. This is crudely portrayed in a famous poster issued by the socialist UGT trade union in 1936 entitled "Como ha sembrado la Iglesia su religión en España"—"How the Church Has Sowed Its Religion in Spain". We see a priest, a swastika swinging around his neck, a sword at his waist, sowing little crosses of death, associating the Catholic Church with militarism and fascism.

Until the 1930s, most of Spain's schools were run by the Church, which made up for the so-called "absent state" by running its own institutions, although as we have seen these were woefully inadequate to cover demand. Although the liberal-left Republican governments of 1931–3 and 1936 were hardly revolutionary, they were unstintingly radical in their anticlericalism—expelling the Jesuits, long seen as the Church's elite 'shock troops', in 1932, for example. So it is unsurprising that sections of the Church saw the February 1936 election as a crusade, their sermons threatening excommunication of those who voted for the left. Officially, the defence of religion did not form part of the initial justification for the rising, but the anticlerical violence played into the hands of the military rebels, allowing them to claim they were engaging in a holy war in defence of Christianity.

The violence was reported in the world's press, often in lurid detail, particularly in Catholic newspapers, which greatly exaggerated the events when not telling outright lies. On 14 August 1936, London's *Catholic Herald* reported that "[t]he innumerable ex-convicts who had taken refuge in Barcelona have become the masters of the situation". It went on to justify the military rising, claiming: "Republicanism in Spain has always brought revolution in its wake. A tremendous work against public order and against religion has been accomplished in the course of the last years." While many of the revolutionaries condemned the violence in general terms, they were sometimes less than critical when it was directed at the Church. The

CNT's *Solidaridad Obrera* was explicit, stating on 15 August that "[t]he religious orders should be dissolved, the bishops and cardinals should be shot; and church property should be expropriated".

When Franco won in 1939, he handed all the schools in Spain, including the 16,000 created by the Republic, to the Catholic Church, which used them as centres of indoctrination. The parents of those who lost the war couldn't, of course, complain. This produced a generation gap between an older, more anticlerical generation—with huge regional and class differences—and a younger one, which tended to be more Catholic. That said, being anticlerical is not the same thing as being antireligious. As Alfredo González-Ruibal points out in his superb *Archaeology of the Spanish Civil War* (2020), crucifixes are a frequent find in digs of Republican trenches and in excavations of mass graves of Republicans executed by the Franco regime. Organised religion is one thing; spirituality another. And many on the Republican side were in fact Catholics and abhorred the burning of the churches, whether or not they had regularly attended them before the war. In some villages, the local priest was murdered after being forced to watch religious parodies, while the bodies of murdered clergy were frequently doused in petrol and set alight.

The Aragonese town of Barbastro, 80 kilometres to the north of Bujaraloz, saw the worst bout of clergy killing anywhere in Spain. In this small town of 8,000 inhabitants, some 105 members of the clergy were murdered, representing 54 per cent of those living in the town. Yet very few nuns were killed across Republican Spain. This was in part due to a taboo in Spanish society against the murder of women, as opposed to widespread domestic violence, but nuns were also often viewed by the left and in particular by the anarchists as victims to be liberated—whether they wanted to be or not—arising from a widespread belief that many young working-class women who entered convents had been forced or tricked into doing so. Moreover, the little charity the Church did give tended to be provided by nuns. In *The Spanish Holocaust* (2011), Paul Preston cites a study that estimates that 296 nuns were murdered during the war, representing around 1.3 per cent of the nuns who found themselves in Republican Spain, a percentage that contrasts dramatically with the 18 per cent of monks and 30 per cent of priests who were killed—a total of 2,365 and 4,184, respectively. Despite Francoist propaganda, and however shocking the individual cases were, rape as an act to sow wider terror in Republican Spain was uncommon, unlike on Franco's side, where it was used as a very deliberate tactic of terror.

In village after village, militias and jubilant locals threw religious artefacts from churches and homes on to the streets along with "municipal and ecclesiastical documents and property registers, religion and order inextricably united".[4] The whole lot would then be piled on to bonfires in village squares and set alight when darkness came. Many people were enthusiastic; others looked on in horror. Academics are divided as to what lay behind the need to systematically destroy the physical objects of the Church. Perhaps it was an attempt to demonstrate that these sacred objects really had no power. Or perhaps it was a way of hurting those who believed in their power and materially demonstrating to all that a new order had arrived.

Revolutionary violence

The clergy were not the only victims. In all, fifteen right-wing men were shot in Bujaraloz by the militias or locals at the end of July 1936. The counterpoint to the revolutionary euphoria that swept Catalonia and eastern Aragon was the wave of general violence that engulfed both regions during the summer of 1936. As the columns moved forward, militia members and locals took advantage of the breakdown in social order to murder large numbers of so-called fascists: far-right militants but also right wingers in general, conservative peasants, Guardia Civil and the clergy. This was part of the wider violence across Spain in areas where the coup failed, as the Republican state collapsed and scores were settled. The violence arose both from the anger unleashed by the coup itself and as a response to grievances that had been simmering for decades, in what was a class-ridden and sometimes violent society. Some of the worst cases happened in places where violence meted out by the elites had been endemic, particularly in the semi-feudal estates of the south of Spain. A study by Joan Villarroya and Josep Maria Solé i Sabaté estimates that, in Catalonia, 8,360 people were killed behind Republican lines during the war. This figure includes legal executions and murders committed for non-political ends. Of these, 2,328 died in Barcelona city. In Aragon, the figure has been estimated as 3,901.[5] Throughout Republican-held Spain, much of this violence took place in the summer of 1936. It continued at a much lower level in the autumn and had almost ended by the spring of 1937.

Among the worst cases was the Catalan town of Lleída, where 250 people had been killed by the time order was restored in October 1936. In areas where locals took over the villages themselves, it was usually smooth and relatively non-violent. But in places where the militias arrived and were confronted with local opposition, often from very poor peasant landholders who resisted the collectivist ideas of these industrial workers, it was accompanied by violence.

Ending the violence in Republican Spain

Much, though by no means all, of the violence in Catalonia and Aragon was committed by people who were members of or associated with the CNT. Leaders of all leftist groups tried to save people. The mass extrajudicial killings of July, August and early September fell dramatically by early October with the entry of the revolutionaries—CNT–FAI and POUM—into the Catalan and Spanish governments and the formation of the anarchist-dominated Regional Council of Aragon. This was coupled with the re-establishment of control by more experienced, older anarchist militants, who sent some of the worst culprits to the front.

Although Franco's regime grossly exaggerated the numbers, some 55,000 people were murdered behind Republican lines across Spain as a whole—victims of revolutionary and other forms of violence. This figure is known with relative precision, not just because the Francoist state invested huge sums in investigating it as part of what was termed "La causa general" (The general cause) but also because the Republic itself also recorded and investigated the crimes. This is a key bullet point for understanding the Spanish Civil War. Atrocities were certainly committed on both sides. On the Republican side, the violence was largely committed due to the breakdown of social order because of the coup and was eventually stopped and condemned. On Franco's side, in addition to the greater numbers murdered, it was the state itself together with its proxies—the Falange, the Carlists, landowners—that was behind the terror.[6]

Before leaving Bujaraloz, I needed a coffee, so we headed to another bar. I was surprised to find framed photos of the war, including the militias we had seen arriving in Bujaraloz. Fernando, the owner, now retired, explained to me: "Look, we managed to leave behind the tragedy of the war. We live together in peace today in Bujaraloz, whatever our politics. For most people it's forgotten but I like to remember the war with these pictures because it is the most important thing that's happened to my village."

Zaragoza

Zaragoza was founded on the banks of the Ebro by the Romans as Caesaraugusta—in honour of the first emperor in 14 BCE—as a colony to settle army veterans from the bloody Cantabrian wars, the final episode in Rome's protracted 200-year conquest of Hispania. Barcelona (Barcino) was built for the same purpose. Today, almost 700,000 people live in Zaragoza. Many came in the 1960s and '70s, while often maintaining strong connections with their village—part of the Spain-wide abandonment of rural areas. It was the first place I lived in Spain when I arrived, aged twenty-two, to work as an English teacher back in September 1988. I quickly made friends. I'd ask them what must have been naive or even crass questions about the war and their family's involvement. In one bar, an older student asked me to keep my voice down when discussing Franco with him. In other bars, it wasn't a problem.

One friend, Luis, took me to the huge Plaza del Pilar, one of the largest squares in Western Europe. At one end was a massive bronze statue of Franco astride a horse. I knew little of Spain's history, and it shocked me that here was Hitler's ally in full public view. Luis, a firm PSOE supporter, didn't like the dictator's presence, but that was the past. Spain was exciting, and modernising now, he explained, although he was always happy to share his family memories of the war. The statue presided over the entrance to the Military Academy that Franco had directed between 1927 and 1931. It was closed by the first centre-left Republican government in 1931. He never forgave them. The statue itself wasn't removed until 2006. In fact, the last public statue of the dictator in Spain didn't come down until 2021. It was located in the North African Spanish enclave of Melilla, where the local government, seemingly in the permanent hands of the right, refused to accept that it was illegal under the 2007

Spanish National Historical Memory Law, which mandates the removal of all Francoist symbols from public spaces across the state. They argued it celebrated his role in defending Melilla from Moroccan forces as commander of the Spanish Foreign Legion during the Rif War of 1921, not as Caudillo of Spain, as he became known as the dictator of the country. This seems an odd defence given Franco's brutal role in the Moroccan wars, where he came to learn that terror, killing, rape and torture were efficient tools to keep the local population in check. This is crucial to understanding the role he played in the later war in Spain.

Presiding over the Plaza del Pilar is the huge Cathedral-Basilica of Our Lady of the Pillar, today the iconic image of Zaragoza (see Fig. 3.4). Its fortress-like walls and sheer size are perhaps best appreciated approaching from its back, crossing the Ebro along the Puente de Piedra, itself built on Roman foundations. From here, you can get a sense of how the building and its contents represent the Church's power. The Virgin del Pilar is Spain's patron saint. By royal decree, she has been a field marshal (*capitán general*) of the Spanish army since 1908. Here we see Catholicism wedded with the military writ in stone. Luis insisted we stood in the queue to pay her a visit in a dark, intimate alcove. She's rather small, just 38 centimetres high. So much power has been emitted from this little statue.

Luis also wanted to show me, somewhat amused, the bombs on permanent display on one of the central columns of the cathedral. On 3 August 1936, two weeks after the military coup, a plane probably from the then Llobregat airfield, now Barcelona's international El Prat airport, flew low over Zaragoza and dropped three 150-kilogram bombs on the cathedral. One missed and fell in the square—a cross marks the spot. The other two hit their target, piercing the dome. The first ripped through a fresco by Goya; the second fell barely 10 metres from the holy figure. Miraculously, or due to a technical issue, none of the bombs exploded.

I asked Luis in 2025 if his attitudes towards the war and the Franco regime have changed. "I was interested back then and had my family's direct memories," he explained,

> but now there is just so much more in the public sphere: movies, documentaries, novels, the internet and everything else. But I don't think my son Antonio—he's twenty-six—and his friends have the same level of interest. It's so long ago. He didn't know people with direct memories of the war.

Violence in rebel Aragon

While eastern Aragon, nominally under Republican control, underwent a social revolution, the western half of the region had fallen to the rebel forces. Its experience was starkly different. Here, a vicious military-sanctioned repression was unreleased against the left, killing at least 10,000 men and women, many of whom were shot in ditches or against cemetery walls, others pushed, still living, into sinkholes.

Some of the worst violence was seen in Zaragoza itself, a stronghold of the anarchist CNT, where at least 3,543 people were shot, mainly against the wall of the Cementerio de Torrero, and buried in ditches, most of them in the first months of the war. Following the return of democracy, the remains of around 2,500 were moved to a mass grave. In 2024, I visited with Luis and his wife Emma. At the entrance stands an understated memorial in the shade of pine trees, where 3,543 steel posts are laid out in a spiral route, each topped with a plaque, detailing the name of a murdered man or woman and their age when they fell (see Fig. 3.5). We walked in silence past name after name. Emma found one naming a boy aged thirteen; another was seventy. People had added little family homages, anarchist stickers or bunches of flowers in the colours of the Republic. Around 600 have never been identified. Their plaques read "man" or "woman". A cemetery map took us to the wall where some 2,000 were shot. It looked like most of the bricks had been replaced, although some still bore the scars of bullets. An ugly railing protected the site with a sloppily designed, officious sign telling people not to leave homages on the wall. It seemed a purposeful insult by the city council, in the hands of the Partido Popular (PP), the Spanish conservative party, to the families of the victims. With a darkening sky, we turned away from the wall and stood imagining their last view in a cold dawn light all those years ago.

General Emilio Mola, one of the key Africanist generals and the "director" of the coup, declared on 19 July: "We must sow terror—we have to create a sensation of domination, eliminating without remorse all those who do not think like us." We will never know how many died behind the lines in Francoist Spain, though the figure perhaps lies between 150,000 and 200,000. Local and national estimates go up each year. Rebel units entered village after village, executing trade unionists, electoral officials, leftists and teachers from the new Republican schools. This was accompanied by mass rape and torture to spread the terror. Interviewed by the American journalist Jay Allen on 29 July, just twelve days into the war, Franco exposed the intentions of the rebels for the whole world to read: "'We are fighting for Spain. They are fighting against Spain. We will go on at whatever cost.' You will have to shoot half of Spain, I said. He shook his head, smiled and then looking at me steadily: 'I said whatever the cost.'"

4

ORWELL IN ARAGON

Eric Blair

As I greeted the group outside the restaurant, Richard showed me his wrist. It was red and sore. Ten minutes earlier, they had been walking across El Raval, Barcelona's vibrant, cosmopolitan and sometimes edgy working-class district adjoining La Rambla. Suddenly, a robber lunged out, grabbed his wrist and ripped off his Omega watch. It's a speciality, I soon learned. Thieves snatching expensive watches. Although clearly hurt, Richard, seventy-eight years old, was remarkably unperturbed and stoical. "It kept good time," he concluded, "but perhaps I shouldn't have been wearing it. Lesson learnt."

Richard Blair was leading a group from the Orwell Society, following in his father's footsteps around Catalonia and Aragon. Accompanying, as always, was group organiser Quentin Kopp, son of Georges Kopp, Orwell's commander in Spain, and his wife Liz, whose father was a Slovak International Brigader. This unfortunate start to the trip was forgotten for the time being as the group consumed huge plates of rabbit and onions and too much rough wine. The next day, after guiding them around

Barcelona, we headed for the police station to report the theft. While we waited, Richard joked that perhaps he should keep quiet about who he was just in case the June 1937 arrest warrant was still out on his father, but that's getting ahead of the story.

At the outbreak of the war in Spain in July 1936, Eric Blair, better known to the world as his pen name, George Orwell, was at home in the small Hertfordshire village of Wallington. Together with Eileen, his wife, he was running the little village shop, tending a vegetable plot and chickens and writing *The Road to Wigan Pier* (1937), which would become the writer's first successful work. Near the end of the book, Orwell notes: "As I write this the Spanish Fascist forces are bombarding Madrid, and it is quite likely that before the book is printed we shall have another Fascist country to add to the list."

At some point in the autumn, Orwell decided to come to Spain. He claimed in the first pages of *Homage to Catalonia* that he was attracted by the idea of doing some journalism and once in Barcelona had been enthused by the atmosphere to take up arms, although there is some indication he had already made up his mind to fight before leaving London. Orwell initially sought papers through British Communist Party General Secretary Harry Pollitt in London, but Pollitt claimed to have been repelled by Orwell's old Etonian accent, a strange reason given that he had happily accepted other public-school boys for the International Brigades. As Orwell realised, the more likely reason was his socialist, and at times quirky, politics, laid out in *The Road to Wigan Pier*. Pollitt had already seen the manuscript before its publication, and he would later savage it in a review for *The Daily Worker* as the work of "a disillusioned, little middle-class boy",[1] claiming that Orwell said that the working classes smell. This assertion became a very common stick with which to beat Orwell. I myself believed for some time that he had written these words, and I am ashamed to say I occasionally repeated them in the past on tours in Barcelona. The problem is he never wrote such a thing, instead declaring that "we were taught [by middle-class people, such as his parents] that the lower classes smell". Some on the left still use this slur today. Stalinism continues to cast its shadow.

As a second option, Orwell approached the Independent Labour Party (ILP), a left socialist breakaway from the Labour Party and in a sense the British sister organisation of the POUM. The ILP were organising their own small unit of volunteers to send to Spain and invited Orwell to join. They were set to leave in early January, but Orwell, now armed with a letter of introduction to the ILP representative in Barcelona, elected to leave straight away, departing around 23 December. He stopped off in Paris, a city he knew well from his time as a dishwasher but also from the French side of his family. While in Paris, he picked up safe-conduit papers and then took the midnight express from Gare d'Austerlitz to the Spanish frontier. It was virtually a troop carrier packed with tired Czech and French volunteers. His own third-class carriage was full of "very young, fair-haired, underfed Germans in suits of incredible shoddiness".[2]

Arrival

Orwell's train arrived at Barcelona's Estació de França on the bright winter's morning of 26 December. The memories of his future comrade Stafford Cottman were typical of the greeting the volunteers received, recalling a brass band accompanying them to their lodgings playing "L'Internationale" as well as "La Marseillaise", in 1936 still seen as an anti-fascist anthem— think of the stirring scene in the classic 1942 movie *Casablanca*. New to many of those arriving to Spain would have been the anarchist anthems "Hijos del Pueblo" and "A Las Barricadas". The latter, in all surety the song most associated with revolutionary Barcelona, is, as its Slavic melody hints at, Polish in origin. The tune is based on the late nineteenth-century Polish socialist song "Warszawianka", which may have been brought to Barcelona in the early 1930s by German anarchists, with the Spanish lyrics written in 1936. Orwell was travelling separately from the ILP contingent and so perhaps missed this typically rousing welcome. He probably walked from the station along the seafront, then flanked not by a pleasure marina but by docks and a large fishing port, before reaching the foot of La Rambla at the Columbus monument. As he made his way up the city's most famous street to the Hotel Continental, he was stunned by what he saw, later narrating one of the most famous descriptions of a revolution anywhere, inspiring young radicals from Paris to Kurdistan.

"It was the first time that I had ever been in a town where the working class was in the saddle," he wrote:

> Buildings were draped with red flags or with the anarchist's red and black flags; walls were scrawled with the initials of the revolutionary parties; most churches had been gutted; most shops and cafes had been collectivised, as had the bootblacks with their boxes painted red and black. Waiters and shop-assistants now looked their clients straight in the face. "Tú" had replaced "Usted". Trams and taxis had been painted red and black. Loudspeakers in the Rambla were blasting out revolutionary songs.

Despite his initial impressions, Orwell had arrived at the tail-end of the revolutionary period. And, as he soon recognised, there were many in the city against the anarchist experiment. Some of the wealthy had fled, others were dressing down, even wearing their servants' clothing, or in hiding, while most of the large Catalan middle class, reactionary or progressive, were also disturbed by the events. He promptly decided to volunteer to fight for the POUM and was taken to the Lenin Barracks for training. The first person he describes meeting in *Homage to Catalonia* was a young, nameless Italian militiaman. He returns to him in his 1943 essay *Looking Back on the Spanish Civil War*:

> When I remember—oh, how vividly!—his shabby uniform and fierce, pathetic, innocent face, the complex side-issues of the war seem to fade away and I see clearly that there was at any rate no doubt as to who was in the right. In spite of power politics and journalistic lying, the central issue of the war was the attempt of people like this to win the decent life which they knew to be their birthright. It is difficult to think of this particular man's probable end without several kinds of bitterness. ... This man's face, which I saw only for a minute or two, remains with me as a sort of visual reminder of what the war was really about. He symbolizes for me the flower of the European working class, harried by the police of all countries, the people who fill the mass graves of the Spanish battlefields and are now, to the tune of several millions, rotting in forced-labour camps.

The complex, known as Cuartel de Lepanto before and after the war, was demolished in 1996. Nothing remains of the buildings today, save for a few sections of the cobblestones. The site is now occupied by Catalonia's main law courts, composed of a half-dozen brutalist towers, looking very much like a Ministry of Truth, whatever their real function.

Barcelona to the Aragon frontier

Around 2 January 1937, Orwell's unit of young Catalan volunteers were marched, crowds cheering all the way, from the Lenin Barracks to the Estació del Nord, where they boarded a packed troop train headed for Aragon and the front. No trains leave from here anymore—it's now the city's main bus terminus. Back then, it would have been decorated with revolutionary posters. These days, along with the Romanian and Polish, the adverts are in Ukrainian for coach services to visit relatives in another war: Barcelona to Kyiv forty-eight hours, 2,943 kilometres, leaving at 6 a.m. most mornings.

For our part, we were travelling in two comfortable hired minivans, Richard and Quentin at the wheel, which took us along the A2 *autovía*, bend after bend, through the rugged, empty heart of central Catalonia and then across the scrappy, prosperous fertile plain of Lleida. Meanwhile, Orwell and his trainload of still-eager volunteers "crawled out of Catalonia and onto the plateau of Aragon at the normal wartime speed of something under twenty kilometres an hour". We stopped for lunch at a roadside bar Quentin knew. The waitress with her gentle Lleida Catalan accent served us spinach omelette, lamb, *butifarra* sausage and big plates of white beans drizzled in garlic and olive oil. Foreign volunteers, Orwell included, often complained about the white beans and lentils in Spain, but they hadn't tried these deliciously mellow ones. Then again, we didn't have to eat them day after day. The bill came. For the same quality, we'd have paid double in Barcelona. Back in the vans, it was a short drive along a minor road over a low sierra and then into Aragon.

The road took us over the Cinca, flowing fast in May, carrying the Pyrenean melt on its way to the Ebro. The river helps to irrigate the miles after miles of fruit trees along our route: apples, pears, peaches. We pass the turnoff for Mònica's mother's village. Saidí (Zaidín in Spanish) was founded during the Islamic period. A possible translation of its name from Arabic is "land between waters"; another connects it to an important Shi'ite family, the Zyadi. Etymology is a hazy business. During the Civil War, the village was collectivised by the CNT. Mònica's older relatives, gone now, were very young children and had no direct memories. Juan, her great-uncle, told me he had voted for the PSOE since the return of democracy. "The anarchists did bad things. Franco did worse things. Now things are better." He was named after his Uncle Juan, who had been taken to the *barranco* and murdered when Franco's army took the village in April 1938.[3] His body has never been found.

María, Mònica's mother, shared few memories of the village during the war with her daughter. One was of working in the fields, aged about six, with her mother. Planes came over. Her mother grabbed her, and, in the panic, María lost a shoe. She never found it again. It was her only pair. The loss stayed with her for the rest of her life. In the 1950s, she was sent to serve in a wealthy home in Barcelona, and old ties slowly fell away. We've visited Saidí a few times, and relations with the family there are cordial enough, but nothing more. Mònica's cousin Mari Carmen took us around her farm one day. Hundreds of hectares of peaches and nectarines flourish in the hot summer, aided by irrigation. The physical work these days is done by Bulgarians. Several Bulgarian villages moved en masse to Saidí in the 2000s. Bulgarian is the second language spoken on the streets today. But although we're in Aragon and people identify themselves here as Aragonese, the first language isn't Spanish, it's Catalan. Aragon is home to around 30,000 Catalan speakers living in La Franja, the eastern fringe of the region bordering Catalonia. As elsewhere in Europe, linguistic frontiers often have a messy correspondence to national ones.

We drive on. Quentin points out that the barley is "ready for a brewery in Barcelona". He informs me it's hairy, unlike wheat. "They need a lot of bloody barley in Barcelona," he says. The fields, barley to the left, and wheat to the right, are skirted by poppies growing in deep bright-red strips in their millions. I find myself gasping at their sheer beauty. Somebody in the back asks me if the flower has any significance in Spain. As in the rest of Europe, poppies have some relationship with eternal sleep. There's none of the symbolism of sacrifice and slaughter they have uniquely acquired in Britain since the First World War, where they form part of the national story of what that war represented. In Spain, there is no national narrative to its terrible war but rather ideologically conflicting understandings of the conflict. This may well be an issue in Spain, but an overarching state-controlled national story can also be problematic. I recently learned—I like to collect these things in my mind—Iberian words for poppy: *amapola* (Spanish), *rosella* (Catalan), *mitxoleta* (Basque), *papoula* (Galician), *papoila* (Portuguese). There are probably a hundred more local ones, slowly disappearing. They're all lovely, but the Catalan wins it for me. We pass old, crumbling villages, superseded after a thousand years by neat, identical new houses with gardens built on their outskirts. White storks are nesting everywhere they can: on church towers, electricity pylons and the stark grain silos found across much of Spain, incredibly ugly yet oddly resonant with the Spanish landscape. These days, you'll see storks all year round. Winters are warmer of course, but they can also feed month after month in the huge, irrigated fields. They're after the insects, the lizards, the frogs, the mice. We drive by one field watered with 10,000 spray poles. Flat-topped hills rise here and there.

After a petrol stop, I sit next to Judith Keene, an engaging historian and academic from the University of Sydney. She's published two books on the war in Spain. Her first, *Fighting for Franco* (2007), tells the story of the Irish, White Russians, Romanians and French, together with a motley crew of other adventurers, right wingers and fascists, who fought against the Republic. Judith wrote to me later:

> Many groups on the inter-war right, fascists, conservative Catholics and those antagonistic to liberal democracy were attracted to Franco's cause. They believed that Franco was holding the line against secularism, modernism, women's suffrage and free thought in general.

Some 250 plus individuals, men and some women, moved by ideology and adventurism, came as volunteers where they anticipated a warm reception. For almost all of them it was neither warm nor welcoming.

I'd learn more about the 700 Irish, a case apart, who fought for Franco later on in my journey. She's also edited *The Last Mile to Huesca* (republished in 2023), which brings together the diaries of Agnes Hodgson, an Australian nurse who travelled to Spain and to the Aragon Front, one of more than 1,000 medical staff, ambulance drivers and humanitarian staff who came to aid the Republic. Hodgson describes the often-appalling conditions in frontline Republican hospitals, wrought by factional differences, and the tribulations in acquiring medical equipment. Judith also explained to me:

> The Australian nurses on their homecoming were physically exhausted and overwhelmed with despair, what Albert Camus described as an evil wound that stayed in the heart, left by the memories of their own sacrifice and that of their Republican comrades left to face the savagery of Franco's victory. On arrival in Sydney, Agnes Hodgson stated that she had "never seen such dreadful wounds and suffering as those that result from warfare" and that "what I have seen in Spain made me a militant pacifist forever".

We pass Lanaja. To the right, there's a *torrellón*, one of the weird sandstone formations that stand out here and there in the landscape, looking every bit like something from the American Southwest, although here there are no cacti or tumbleweeds. This one is called "La Cabeza de Perro" (Dog's Head). Jock, Judith's down-to-earth geologist husband, explains they were formed by the surrounding softer clay soils eroding, leaving harder sandstone standing. The wind, a bit of rain and several million years took care of the rest. A black kite, recently arrived from its African winter, drifts above.

Alcubierre

By a crumbling adobe wall on the outskirts of the village, Richard related Orwell's arrival on around 3 January 1937. We then walked into Alcubierre, sturdier now than the "mass of mean little houses of mud and stone huddling round the church" described in *Homage to Catalonia*. Only our steps echoed in the mid-afternoon. It always seems quiet in such places. So many people have left for the cities. Richard paced alone past the old barracks, imagining, it seemed, his father's presence. In the main square, Víctor Pardo and Elena Torralba were waiting for us. Víctor, dogged journalist, historian and expert on the war in this part of Aragon, would be our guide for the weekend. Jovial most of the time but deadly serious when talking about the past and its echo today, he laid out to the group the context of the war in Aragon and Orwell's journey to Alcubierre. Elena, a local schoolteacher, acted as translator. Richard wondered where the bullet marks on the facade of the *ayuntamiento* (village hall) had gone. Víctor says they had been plastered over since his last visit. A shame, he thinks. "It's a bit of history they could have protected." Erase the traces, it is easier to deny the past. Orwell believed the marks had been caused by rifle-volleys where various fascists had been executed, but Víctor told us what really happened. On 19 July 1936, after overthrowing the civilian authorities in Zaragoza, Falangist units started driving out to the surrounding villages to sow terror. When they arrived at neighbouring Lanaja, they forced all the local men into the square. Ten were picked out and pushed on to a lorry. The Falangists brought them to Alcubierre to be machine-gunned against the village hall before driving back to the capital. Two of the men, although wounded, managed to crawl away to tell the tale.

Somebody in the group asks Víctor how the war is remembered in Alcubierre. He sighs, saying that the reigning spirit in the village and across Aragon today is a lack of interest. It comes, he explained, from the long duration of the dictatorship and the lack of teaching about the war in schools. Elena disagrees. She teaches the war in her classes, as do many of her colleagues. Young people are more interested today, she points out. And, she says, Víctor's own work on historical memory has enjoyed some success. Víctor shrugs his shoulders, through modesty but also perhaps hardened by innumerable battles with politicians, the media and wider society over bringing to light the story of those who lost the war. He is obviously the expert here, but Elena is younger and perhaps sees changes in the younger generation. We left the plastered wall covering the past and headed for a quick coffee in the bar.

Later, as we drove through the sierra, I reflected this ignorance of the past is perfectly normal in any modern society. We can berate young people today for their general lack of interest in learning about the Second World War or the Holocaust, but if I'm honest, the vast majority of people I went to school with in the 1970s probably had absolutely no interest in these matters either, aside from the widespread nationalistic pride in the British armed forces' role in defeating the Nazis and the enjoyment of all those war films on the TV.

What we did have were the memories of our grandparents during the Second World War. My grandfather Edward Hind was perhaps not untypical in that he just didn't want to talk about it, despite my badgering, interested as I was aged eight in guns, planes and tanks. Edward once, and only once, opened up to his two sons-in-law over a few pints in the pub. He had got lost with his mates in the French countryside somewhere near Dunkirk. They had a map, but nobody knew how to read it. They were terrified of the Germans, and they were terrified of the dark. He'd never been outside his industrial streets of Stockport. It was an alien territory for him. Somehow, they managed to reach Allied lines and cross back to Britain in one of the boats. We know he was later at Normandy but not much else. He also told my father and uncle that night that he could never fire at the Germans, instead aiming over their heads. This was common. It takes a lot for a human being to kill another human being, which is why the American army and others invested heavily in the psychology of teaching soldiers how to kill after the Second World War. Maybe it's easier in civil war. Florence, my grandmother, was much more open. For her, the war meant the bombing raids over her streets and the rationing but also a great sense of solidarity and purpose. Nothing extraordinary about these memories, or lack of them, for any family back then in Britain, except of course for the individuals who experienced them. But Florence's right to remember, and Edward's right to forget, not because he was forced to but because he wanted to, was not possible in Spain for those who lost.

The front

On the third morning, the rifles arrived. To his dismay, Orwell was issued with an 1896 German Mauser—"one glance down the muzzle showed that it was corroded and past praying for," he grumbled. Then, his column of about 80 men "wound raggedly up the road ... between yellow infertile fields, untouched since last year's harvest," and into the Sierra de Alcubierre, a line of steep hills that fringe the Monegros to the far west. They were led by Georges Kopp, Quentin's father, astride a black horse, the stout and apparently Belgian commander (in fact he was born in Saint Petersburg to Jewish parents) with whom Orwell would soon become close friends. Orwell was secretly afraid. He was old enough to remember the Great War, although he had been too young to fight. "War, to me, meant roaring projectiles and skipping shards of steel; above all it meant mud, lice, hunger, and cold. It is curious, but I dreaded the cold much more than I dreaded the enemy." For our part, Richard and Quentin drove us bumping and jolting in the minibuses.

We arrived a few minutes later at the position dug into the hilltop that Víctor had restored and recreated with mocked-up sandbags and barbed wire as a representation of where Orwell was stationed, although the exact position is not known (see Fig. 4.1). In front of us lay a wide ravine, at the bottom of which runs the Zaragoza Road. On the other side stood the Francoist line, 500–700 metres away across no-man's land, controlling the main heights of the sierra. Orwell claimed he felt "profoundly disgusted" when he found that the enemy was so far away. Quentin shuddered: "My father must have felt terribly exposed on this hill in these trenches—they're primitive, barely scrapings." I asked Richard how he felt: "It's so surreal, walking here in my father's footsteps. I feel like I'm with him all those years ago. Mind you I'm not being sniped at, with the shit lying around and the terrible food and the cold. It's humbling," he ended, visibly moved.

We explored the trenches and recreated bunkers. Víctor had put up information panels explaining Orwell's time at the front. A copy of a 1936 campaign map inside one bunker showed the ideological complexities on the Republican side along the front line. Our hill was controlled by the POUM, the next by the PSUC, then the POUM again, then the CNT. Farther along, ERC. And so on.

After a few photos, I forced my phone away and found a quiet corner to contemplate the scene through a gap in the sandbags. It wasn't difficult to let your mind drift back to 1937. When I'm talking to groups in La Rambla about revolutionary Barcelona, it takes a degree of suspension of disbelief, lots of photographs, storytelling and a bit of theatrics to help people filter out the thousands of tourists flowing past, the branded shops, the commercial bustle of a twenty-first-century city. You have to will them away to form a sense of the time and place. But here, in these old hills, things haven't changed very much. So much easier to conjure up the red flags, filth, mud, lice, rusting guns and whistling bullets that Orwell so intimately described. I wondered what journey his German rifle had made before reaching him in these hills. Was it employed to kill Asturian miners in the 1934 uprising or Moroccans in the Rif wars? Had it arrived in Spain after the First World War from the German army and been used in the killing fields of Flanders by a Bavarian private? Was it employed in the Herero and Namaqua genocide of 1904–8 in German South West Africa? Or was it bought new, greased, Swedish steel still glinting, in 1897 and shipped to Cuba or the Philippines in Spain's failed attempt to hold its colonies in 1898?

I wandered away from the trenches. It had rained a great deal in recent weeks, and the hillsides, usually parched, were now a riot of wildflowers like I'd never seen them here before, softening the harsh landscape. A cuckoo, the first I'd heard that year, called from a small wood to the right, and to the left among the billowing clouds a vulture soared—there always seems to be a vulture somewhere above your head in Aragon. Today, the Sierra de Alcubierre is covered by low scrub and replanted pinewoods, but, as old photos and Orwell's writings attest, in 1936 it was mostly bare save for "stunted shrubs and heath" thanks to centuries of felling and overgrazing. Spain has undergone a remarkable reforestation since the 1950s, beginning soon after the war with large-scale replanting of pines, usually non-native species, for timber and pulp carried out by teams of Republican forced labourers and free workers directed by the Ministry of Agriculture and the Falange. This has continued over the decades, with a massive natural rewilding as the rural hinterland has emptied. One of the main reasons why there are so many fires in Spain today is because there is an awful lot of dense pinewood and scrubby woodland to burn.

Before heading back down, we gathered around Víctor as he explained the "static" nature of much of the fighting in this part of Aragon. By early 1937, Republican forces numbered around 42,000 soldiers on the Aragon Front. They faced a similar number of rebel troops across the line. The former's forces were divided, as we've seen, into several columns: anarchist, communist, Catalan Republican and the POUM's so-called Lenin Division, in which Orwell and his small number of ILP comrades fought. While almost all the POUM fighters were from Spain (in particular Catalans), they did include an estimated 600 foreign fighters, many of whom have never been identified, as the records no longer exist.[4]

Víctor also listed some of the stuff they had unearthed during the excavation: inkwells, glass bottles, belt buckles, rubber soles, shrapnel, cartridge cases, metal plates and pans, tins. All remains from Orwell's time. They'd also found grenades and several 7.5-millimetre howitzer shells the Guardia Civil bomb squad had to deactivate. Finding unexploded ordnance from the war is a common occurrence in many parts of Spain.

Francoist positions

After crowding for a photo around a great big POUM flag that Richard and Quentin always bring along for the occasion, we got back in the vans and followed Víctor for a few kilometres to a Francoist military camp he had also helped restore. The difference in quality of the facilities compared with the Republican militia positions was striking. Quentin, an engineer by trade, exclaimed: "What chance did they have—an untrained people's militia, fighting a battle-hardened professional army. This camp is relatively sophisticated. There are concrete floors. Orwell's lot had dirt." Víctor agreed: "You can tell who was going to win the war by comparing these positions and the concrete." Of course, the Republicans did use concrete extensively in their defences, but the Francoist army had more and were able to deploy it more quickly, more frequently and at more inaccessible sites. Organisation aside, the chief reason was because they had so many more trucks. The American companies Ford, Chrysler and General Motors sold more than 10,000 to Franco on advantageous long-term loans. Perhaps even more important was the provision of American oil, particularly from the Texas Oil Company, now known as Texaco. Its chairman Torkild Rieber broke several US laws and ripped off his own shareholders by selling at below-cost prices to Franco. In all, the American company shipped more than 3.5 million tons of oil to the rebel army. José María Doussinague, under-secretary at the Spanish foreign ministry, was perhaps not exaggerating when he remarked in 1945: "Without American petroleum and American trucks and American credit, we could never have won the Civil War."

We huffed from the camp up to a hilltop known as San Simón, on which stands an ugly little monument (see Fig. 4.2). Quentin stayed behind. "It's a bloody fascist shrine. Once was enough, no thanks," he explained. The stone tower bearing a metal cross remembers a group of Falangists who lost their lives here. On the night of 9 April 1937, a group of Catalan Republicans of the Macià-Companys division silently crept up on the position and killed fifty to eighty men. Many of the defenders had their throats slit in their sleep so as not to not raise the alarm. The Catalans only managed to defend the position for another night. The Franco regime anointed those who died as martyrs, and the site, as Víctor succinctly told me, became "Aragon's Valley of the Fallen", a place of annual pilgrimage remembering the slaughter for the regime and its local supporters. An information board shows the hill in 1974 with several thousand Franco supporters who had come to pay homage. These days, just a handful of old people turn up on the anniversary accompanied by a dozen or so neo-Nazis who daub their slogans on the concrete trig point. Anti-fascist locals daub their messages too.

As dusk approached, we headed to our hostel. Albergue Monegros is housed in a tall, austere sanctuary on the top of a steep hill. The building dates from the thirteenth century, although much was destroyed in the Peninsular War and the fighting in the summer of 1936. That evening, choughs danced around the roof, their yellow beaks golden in the evening light. After huge plates of griddled lamb, stories from the group and too many spirits, we slumped to our bunks.

After breakfast, I took a walk around the hill with Liz Kopp as she told me about her father. Unlike her husband Quentin's father, Jan Geza Pošner's story is hardly known outside the family. Her knowledge was often fragmentary, much lost to time and the ravages of the twentieth century, but how many of us know the details of our ancestors' lives of the 1930s and '40s? Jan was born in 1906 in what is now Slovakia, then part of the Austro-Hungarian Empire. Probably a communist in 1936, he fought with the International Brigades in the defence of Madrid and elsewhere at the front, one of the 2,200 Czechoslovak volunteers. I'll pick up his story later.

Orwell had a remarkable ability to evoke a place in his writing. In *Homage*, in sentence after sentence he manages to convey his time using the sights, sounds and often unpleasant smells of what it was like to be freezing and bored on a largely inactive front. Among the most unpleasant features he remembered was the presence of lice. Soldiers at the front on both sides often spent more time fighting these delightful insects than their human enemies. They didn't just have to contend with head lice (*Pediculus humanus capitis*) but an even more unpleasant creature: the body louse. *Pediculus humanus humanus* is thought to have diverged from its cousin some 100,000 years ago, coinciding with our adoption of clothing (animal hides, etc). Indeed, a better name would perhaps be the "clothing louse", for it is inside the hems and cracks in garments that they hide and breed, emerging at night to feast on the body. This is the louse associated with typhus and trench fever, penury, mass exodus, natural disasters and war. Typhus was widespread, particularly on the Republican side, due to a lack of soap.

Lice featured strongly in the memory of one young recruit, Joaquim Oller Viladrosa, who had been called up to fight in the Battle of the Ebro when he was just seventeen years old:

> The whistle of the machine guns, the low flight of the planes and the feast of the lice as big as grains of rice, and the scarcity of food and the terrible thirst which sometimes even overcame the constant fear ... You'd wake up with your fingernails impregnated with blood. It was from the lice. During the night they had a party in the trenches and swelled up like little purple balls. Soldiers would pop them as they scratched while sleeping.[5]

Everybody had them at the front. Carlist soldiers from Navarra, Barcelona anarchists, socialist miners from Asturias. I dare say there are letters from fascist Italians and Nazi Germans reporting these parasites. I suspect one week of mud and lice would cure almost anybody of the romanticism of war.

Orwell vividly complained about the lack of equipment in addition to the weapons. This list I've collected is not exhaustive:

- no tin hats, no bayonets;
- no maps or charts;
- no range-finders, no telescopes, no periscopes, no field-glasses except for a few privately owned pairs;
- no flares;
- no wire-cutters, no armourers' tools;

Fig. 1.1: The Spanish Republican Constitution. Approved on 9 December 1931, it established a democratic state based on the rule of law. It immediately faced opposition from conservative groups and the Catholic Church, as well as the revolutionary left who saw its reforming project as insufficient.

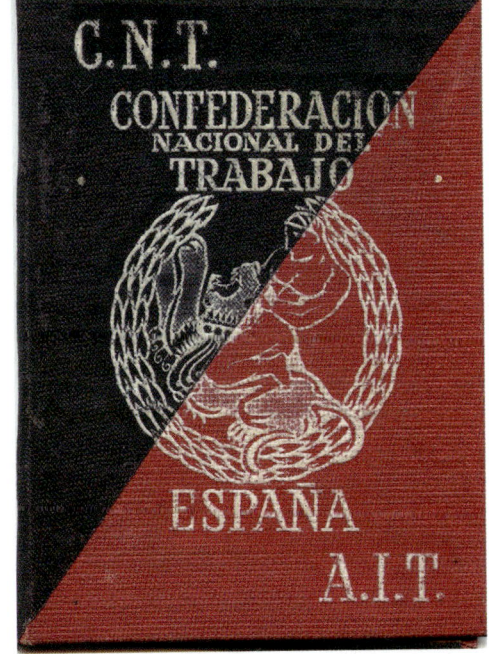

Fig. 2.1: Anarchist trade union card. It was issued on 19 July 1936 in Barcelona, the same day as the rebel military rose in the city.

Fig. 2.2: This watercolour, by José Rey AKA Sim, shows two workers and a Guardia Civil fighting on the same side. Rey's 1936 paintings quickly came to represent the revolutionary events in Barcelona. The CNT sold them to raise funds in Spain, Paris, London and New York as postcards and in the album *Estampas de la Revolución Español: 19 Julio de 1936*. Rey died in Paris in 1983, aged 82.

N° 4874 — 94ᵉ ANNÉE

1ᵉʳ AOUT 1936

L'ILLUSTRATION

LES HEURES SANGLANTES DE BARCELONE

APRÈS LA RENCONTRE PLAZA CATALUÑA : DES CORPS D'HOMMES ET DE CHEVAUX TUÉS ET BLESSÉS
SONT RESTÉS SUR PLACE... ET LES PIGEONS FAMILIERS SONT REVENUS PICORER

AVEC CE NUMÉRO L'ABONNEMENT N° 1 COMPREND "LA PETITE ILLUSTRATION" CONTENANT

UNE PIÈCE EN TROIS ACTES

TU NE M'ÉCHAPPERAS JAMAIS, par MARGARET KENNEDY
Adaptation française de PIERRE SABATIER

13, RUE SAINT-GEORGES, PARIS (9ᵉ)

Voir au verso les tarifs d'abonnement.

Fig. 2.3: The 1 August 1936 edition of French magazine *L'Illustration*, featuring a photo by Agustí Centelles of the aftermath of the fighting in Plaça Catalunya, Barcelona on 19 July 1936.

Fig. 2.4: A 1937 postcard with the words "Hoy España, Mañana el Mundo" (Today Spain, Tomorrow the World), re-purposing the original design made by German anarchists in Barcelona in 1936. The back reads, in Spanish, "Children destroyed yesterday in Madrid, today in the Basque Country, tomorrow... throughout the world, if working people do not wake up in time to crush fascism. Aid Committee to Euzkadi and the North – Barcelona".

Fig. 2.5: A children's trading card depicting workers attacking the Telefónica in Plaça Catalunya, Barcelona, on 19 July 1936. Part of the series "España en Armas", possibly created by Gráficas Marco, 1936–8.

Fig. 2.6: Poster for the 1936 Olimpíada Popular. It was designed by German Jewish artist Fritz Lewy who had arrived in Barcelona in 1933, fleeing from the Nazi regime. He managed to emigrate from Barcelona to the US in 1938, where he died in Cincinnati in 1950.

Fig. 2.7: Annual report for the Transversal line (known as L1 today) of the CNT-run metro system. It details investments and salaries, including substantial differences between ticket staff and engineers. It notes, for example, the successful incorporation of women due to men joining the People's Army, the opening of the platforms as bomb shelters, and financial help for families of metro workers in the army.

Fig. 2.8: Milk bottle label produced by the CNT-run dairy industry.

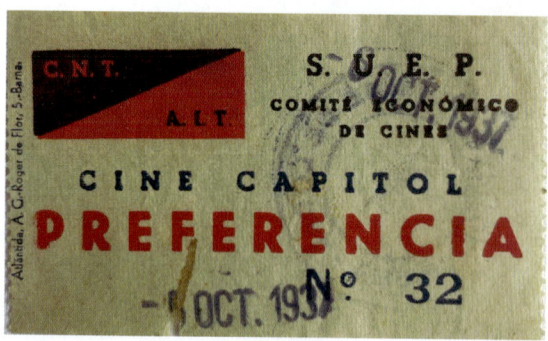

Fig. 2.9: A ticket for the Capitol Cinema on La Rambla, dated 5 October 1937, where the film *Hija de Drácula*, starring Gloria Holden, was showing.

Fig. 3.1: Front cover of the magazine *Crónica*, 11 October 1936. The photo was taken by Agustí Centelles in Loporzano, on the Aragon front.

Fig. 3.2: A watercolour of a militia woman by José Rey. See also
Fig. 2.2 for more about Rey.

Fig. 3.3: The October 1937 front cover of the magazine of the anarchist women's organisation Mujeres Libres (Free Women). This is a beautifully produced faithful facsimile by the Fundación Anselmo Lorenzo. It features articles on women in Goya's art; Emma Goldman; Picasso; women in China; maternity, including a photo of a woman breastfeeding (not seen in the UK until the 1970s); refugee children in Mexico; and housing. There is a single redacted article praising the taking of Belchite in September 1937, while criticising Republican army policy for inaction.

Fig. 3.4: Cathedral-Basilica of Our Lady of the Pillar in Zaragoza, by tradition the first church dedicated to the Virgin Mary. It was hit by bombs dropped by a Republican plane on 3 August 1936.

Fig. 3.5: Memorial to the victims of Francoism created in 2010 in the Cementerio de Torrero, the largest cemetery in Zaragoza.

Fig. 4.1: Recreated trenches in the Sierra de Alcubierre as a representation of where Orwell was stationed.

Fig. 4.2: San Simón. The stone tower bears a metal cross remembering a group of Falangists who lost their lives here on the night of 9 April 1937. A key site for the victorious side's memory of the war in Aragon.

Fig. 4.3: A box of matches produced by the Collectivised Chemical Industries of the CNT.

Fig. 4.4: Republican army–issue espadrilles. Inside, the faded letters read "suministro militar" (military supply) together with the mural crown depicted on the Republican Constitution in Fig 1.1.

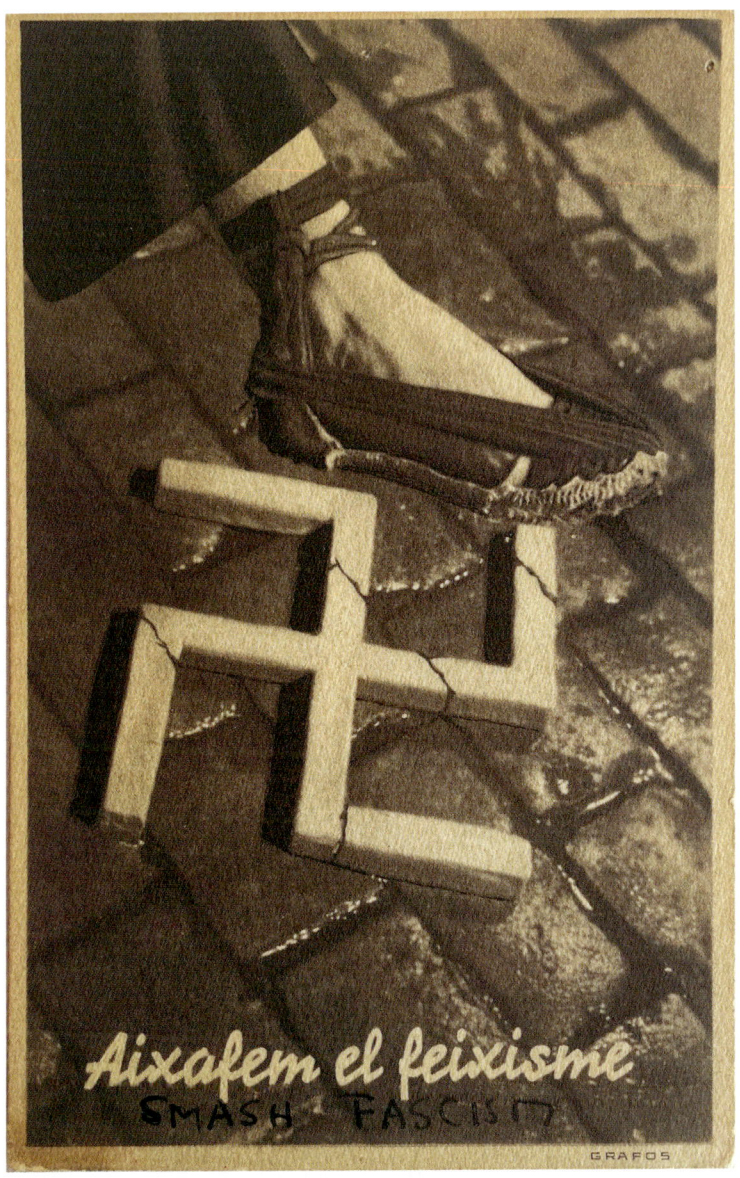

Fig. 4.5: Postcard reading "Aixafem el feixisme" (Let's crush fascism), created by Pere Català i Pic for the Catalan government in October 1936. I bought this on eBay from Australia. A former owner had written a translation on the postcard in English in fountain pen: "Smash fascism". I wondered if it belonged to one of the sixty Australians to fight in Spain, but the seller had no information.

Fig. 5.1: Orwell and his British comrades in the environs of Monflorite, March 1937. The author of the photo is believed to be Georges Kopp, but this has not been proven. Harry Milton, the American who later saved Orwell's life, is squatting to the left wearing a black cap and holding a rifle. Eileen Blair can be seen, also squatting, at Orwell's side.

Fig. 5.2: La Cartuja de Nuestra Señora de las Fuentes (near Huesca): Carthusian monastery, anarchist militia headquarters, Condor Legion base.

Fig. 5.3: The huge courtyard of La Cartuja de Nuestra Señora de las Fuentes. The Nazi Condor Legion used the site as a base to bomb Catalonia from April 1938. Restoration of the buildings, which contain an important assemblage of eighteenth-century murals, is ongoing.

Fig. 5.4: All that is left of the Republican Airforce runway at Sariñena. A few lonely information panels elsewhere on the site of the airfield remember the history.

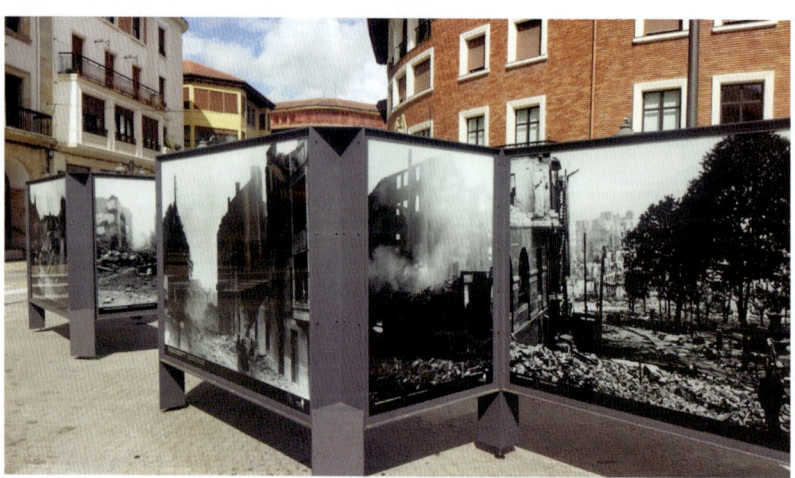

Fig. 6.1: A public display in Gernika of large photos documenting the destruction of the town. The town council has also opened up several bomb shelters for guided visits.

- hardly any cleaning materials;
- no lanterns or electric torches;
- tea—milkless, seldom sugar;
- cigarettes. Initially, his unit was issued a packet a day. This dwindled to five a day and then "ten deadly days when there was no issue of tobacco at all".

Although they started out with matches and candles, as the months wore on, the supply ran out, making "life a misery". He continued: "You do not realise the importance of these things until you lack them. In a night-alarm, for instance, when everyone in the dug-out is scrambling for his rifle and treading on everybody else's face, being able to strike a light may make the difference between life and death." A popular item in my walking museum is a box of matches produced by the Collectivised Chemical Industries of the CNT (see Fig. 4.3). Orwell would have jumped on them.

Alpargatas

While Orwell was lucky enough to own leather boots, some of his Spanish comrades must have dreamt of owning a pair. They often wore espadrilles—*alpargatas* in Spanish, *espardenyes* in Catalan—whose soles were woven from *esparto* grass. I have an old pair in my walking museum (see Fig. 4.4). They are stamped with the Republican anti-monarchical mural crown and bear the words "Suministro militar" (Military supply). How on earth could they have won wearing shoes with soles made of dried grass against the might of Hitler's military machine, Mussolini's Italy and Texaco's oil? *Alpargatas* were the standard footwear of the southern and eastern Iberian peasantry and working class, unable even to afford leather shoes until well into the twentieth century. I can hardly imagine wearing such things in a trench month after month in the freezing cold or in the torrential rains of the war. Nor can I imagine wearing them for any distance. They can't offer much protection against stony ground, which is most of Spain. Whenever available, the rubber from a blown tyre would be repurposed to fashion sturdier soles. Militia fighters and common soldiers wore them on both sides as decent footwear was lacking across the country, but this was much more pronounced on the Republican side.

The rope sandal also came to be seen as a symbol of the dogged resistance of Republican fighters to Franco. A famous and powerful example is the photomontage (*Aixafem el feixisme*— "Let's crush fascism") created by Pere Català i Pic for the Catalan government in October 1936, showing an espadrille-clad foot crushing a swastika on a wet, cobbled street of Barcelona. I have an original postcard (Fig. 4.5) of the work that I bought on eBay from Australia. Somebody has written the English translation of the title at the bottom using a fountain pen, which dates it. Perhaps, a kid in Adelaide did it on his grandmother's old card in 1968, hoping to help, vandalising it forever. Perhaps it was written with more meaning by one of the sixty-odd Australian men and women who came to Spain. The seller was unforthcoming. The work has two readings. It suggests that it is the poor who will crush the fascist threat, but it is also a symbol of Catalonia—the owner of the photographed foot was in fact a Catalan Mosso d'Esquadra police officer. Australian surrealist poet Mary Low mentions seeing the poster after an evening at the theatre in Barcelona in 1936 in her *Red Spanish Notebook* (1937): "We stood outside the columned portico, in front of us a poster flapped in the rain, a foot in a Catalan sandal crushing a swastika with negligent, unquestioned strength." After Franco won in 1939, the fight was continued against all odds by guerrillas known as the *maquis*, as is movingly remembered in the 2009 song "Suela de alpargata" (Sole of espadrille) by classic Pamplona hard rockers

Barricada. The song forms part of the concept album *La tierra está sorda* (The land is deaf, 2009) about the Civil War and the struggle to recover memory.

> Espadrille sole that will never succumb
> Neither to icy waters nor frozen nights
> Espadrille sole with damp, sodden clothes
> You must cross the river before it gets light
> Espadrille sole pushing on up the mountain
> Through thorny scrub and over scratched stone
> Espadrille sole hidden deep in the land
> Those who must whisper, who sleep with the stones.[6]

With higher wages and synthetic materials, the sun slowly set on the *alpargata* and *esparto* industries, and most makers had closed by the 1990s. Now the sandals are enjoying a revival as comfortable summer wear and even as high fashion, the latter commanding huge prices (250 euros for the poshest brands). Very, very few are made these days with *esparto*. Even those made in Spain are usually manufactured from jute, imported from Bangladesh. Jute is easier to weave but is less durable and, as I have found, quickly turns soggy in the wet. *Esparto* is an altogether darker, coarser weave, chosen since Neolithic times for its resistance to a stony, inclement land. Perhaps unsurprisingly, *alpargatas* are a common find in excavations today of mass graves of Franco's victims, for it was the poor (landless labourers and workers) who were murdered most often.

Robres

Before leaving the Monegros, we visited the great little museum Víctor helped to create in the village of Robres. In just a few rooms, it manages to cover the whole of the war on this front. I was most struck by a mural listing the names of 8,913 Aragonese men and women who were shot by the Francoists during the war and in the following years until 1944. Víctor pointed out that if he did the piece again, the number would be more than 10,000. He has done a great job in recovering the memory and history of the war in Aragon and in helping to attract tourists to this often-forgotten corner of the region. I've visited several times over the years. It's an example of how anti-Francoist culture is not at all restricted to Catalonia, as some Catalan nationalists would have you believe. I had considered donating a few items to their collection, which has an air of permanence about it, although with the threat of the far-right Vox party to historical memory in regions such as Aragon and in Spain in general, I am no longer sure. The museum seems safe for now, but it does not seem far-fetched that funding for such places could quickly dry up.

Bullfighting and bullrings

Orwell's train from Barcelona had taken the militia fighters 225 kilometres west to Barbastro, where the clergy had been massacred months before. Although it was a long way from the front line, the small town looked "bleak and chipped", while "swarms of militiamen in shabby uniforms wandered up and down the streets, trying to keep warm". On a "ruinous" wall in the town, Orwell came across a poster from the previous year:

> "[S]ix handsome bulls" would be killed in the arena on such and such a date. How forlorn its faded colours looked! Where were the handsome bulls and the handsome bullfighters now? It appeared that even in Barcelona there were hardly any bullfights nowadays; for some reason all the best matadors were Fascists.

As the original poster shows, the *corrida* was held on 8 September 1935. One of the bullfighters, Jaime Noain, found himself in Republican territory at the start of the war. He took part in several fights including one in Albacete, headquarters of the

International Brigades, in which he ended saluting the crowd with a raised fist, and a second held in Barcelona in honour of the Basque government on 12 May 1937, two weeks after the bombing of Gernika and as Franco's forces advanced on Bilbao. One month after this fight, taking advantage of an invitation to Bordeaux, Noain slipped across to Francoist Spain, as did most *toreros* when given half the chance. In truth, as Orwell noted, there was little work in Republican Spain for most bullfighters, and only a small number of bullfights took place in Republican cities—mostly during the first months of the war. There was certainly a tradition of anti-bullfighting on the left, particularly among anarchists, who argued it was an ancient cruelty, comparable to the Inquisition. They also maintained that to enjoy the suffering of another creature was a debasement of the human condition. For many more, bullfighting was a hated symbol of wealth and privilege.

While peasants faced severe underemployment and borderline starvation, swathes of the best land were often used for breeding fighting bulls. At the outbreak of the Civil War in Andalusia and Extremadura, many of the landless labourers invaded these hated estates, symbols of the ostentatious wealth of the landowners, and slaughtered their bulls; these were acts of social revenge, but they were also driven by sheer hunger. For many, it was the first time they had tasted red meat. Meanwhile, in areas where the military coup succeeded, these estates were protected. And their owners often played a key role in the terrible violence unleashed by the rebel army and its proxies against the left.

My own introduction to bulls was probably the classic children's picture book *The Story of Ferdinand* by American author Munro Leaf. It was published coincidentally in September 1936, barely a month after the start of the Spanish Civil War. Ferdinand is a bull who would rather smell flowers than fight in the ring, and as such came to be seen, whether the author meant it or not, as a

89

pacifist symbol, an anti-Francoist or even as a Red. It was banned by the Franco regime until after the dictator's death, and copies were burned by the Nazis under Hitler's orders as "degenerate democratic propaganda". It was also prohibited in the USSR. The book has since sold millions, been translated into sixty foreign languages and has never gone out of print. I guess now it was the first time the land of Spain came into my mind, aged five, three years before sticking that stamp in my album.

The enclosed nature of sports stadiums and entertainment venues have often proved useful locations for internment and mass murder. The Pinochet regime's use of the Estadio Nacional in Santiago de Chile in 1973 is a chilling example. Similarly, dozens of bullrings, stadiums and such were used to imprison, torture and kill by the military rebels during and immediately after the war in Spain. The most widely reported and appalling case is that of Badajoz. When the rebel army under General Juan Yagüe entered the town on 14 August 1936, hundreds of people including many women and children were simply slaughtered in the streets. Under Yagüe's orders, thousands more—mainly civilians, as most Republican fighters had escaped—were rounded up and herded into the Plaza de Toros. The organised executions began the same night, either in the bullring itself or against the walls of the Cementerio de San Juan. A number of foreign journalists were present in Badajoz and reported on the events. Mário Neves, the correspondent for the *Diário de Lisboa*, described bodies littering the town, while American journalist Jay Allen, who had interviewed Franco two weeks before, wrote in the *Chicago Tribune*:

> They were young, mostly peasants in blue blouses, mechanics in jumpers, "The Reds." They are still being rounded up. At 4 o'clock in the morning they were turned out into the ring through the gate by which the initial parade of the bullfight enters. Their machine guns

awaited them. After the first night the blood was supposed to be palm deep on the far side of the ring. I don't doubt it. Eighteen hundred men—there were women, too—were mowed down there in some 12 hours. There is more blood than you would think in 1,800 bodies.[7]

Foreign journalists were only allowed to work in the rebel zone under close supervision, and their dispatches were strictly censored. Allen's report was one of the first and few occasions when a reporter did manage to get through—he reached Badajoz from Portugal without official permission. This allowed international newspapers to print an authoritative account of one of the widespread massacres carried out in the aftermath of the army's advance and thus counter the dominant narrative in the foreign press that most violence against civilians was occurring in the "Red" zone. We will never know the number killed in Badajoz, but most historians put the executions carried out by Yagüe's men at between 2,000 and 4,000 in a few short days.

I must confess I have never been to Badajoz, but I have travelled there in one sense. One of the virtual tours I organised during the pandemic was a five-part road trip around Spain. We made a brief stopover in the town to talk about the massacres. I'd assumed I'd be able to take people via their Zoom screens to the bullring. While preparing the talk, I learned that the building had been demolished under the regional socialist PSOE government to build the new Palacio de Congresos, inaugurated in 2006. Protests by local memory groups who argued it was wanton destruction of a key site of historical memory were ignored. Although a memorial to the victims was later erected, a chance was lost to preserve a powerful witness in stone and iron to the violence at the heart of the Franco regime, which may have been the intention. Similarly, the bullet marks that dotted the cemetery wall were also destroyed in 2009 by the city council, in this case in the hands of the conservative PP, again despite protests from local groups and leading Spanish historians. As at Alcubierre but on a far bigger scale, a testimony to the past was erased.

There is a witness to the killings much closer to my home. The Museu Nacional d'Art de Catalunya (MNAC) in Barcelona has an excellent permanent section on the Spanish Civil War. One of the most dramatic exhibits is a large painting (221 x 327 centimetres) by Joaquim Martí-Bas called *Fusilamientos en la plaza de toros de Badajoz* (Executions in the Badajoz bullring). Painted in 1937, it depicts the horror of those days. On the left, a crush of people: working-class men—some in characteristic blue overalls—women and children are being cut down by bullets in the central open space. Some have raised fists, one a red star on his shirt, which identify the victims ideologically. On the right, watching the spectacle from the shaded, expensive seats of the amphitheatre are the supporters of the coup: priests, Carlists, the wealthy, Guardia Civil. On the front row, legionnaires mow their machine guns into the human mass.

5

THE SIEGE OF HUESCA

Context: the battle for Madrid

Franco's Army of Africa swept through western Andalusia and Extremadura in the face of poorly armed resistance, which, in many cases, can scarcely be called militias as they had so few guns between them and little or no military training. These two regions saw the worst violence of all both during and after the war. Throughout Spain, Francoist conquest of territory was followed by extreme violence against those parts of the civilian population that did not support the rebels, but Andalusia and Extremadura suffered the most. In Andalusia, at least 45,566 were murdered before being thrown into 708 mass graves.

By the start of November, the rebel army had reached the edges of Madrid. With the capital in danger of falling, the Spanish government decamped to Valencia on 6 November, leaving a defence council, the Junta de Defensa de Madrid, in charge of the city. Panic about the presence of a fifth column—the term was in fact coined at this time—led to some 5,000 rightist prisoners being transferred from the city. On the way, 2,000 to 3,000 were murdered at Paracuellos in the Jarama Valley.

This was the biggest single atrocity—by a long way—committed by the Republican side during the war and was probably ordered at a local level, mainly by communist officials and certainly not by the Republican government. The Franco regime portrayed the massacre as the definition of "Red barbarity", and it is still a major *cause célèbre* for the Spanish right.

Meanwhile, several factors averted what had seemed like the inevitable fall of the capital. The spirited resistance of local defenders, backed by the newly formed International Brigades, plus the arrival of Soviet tanks and planes, captured the world's attention. There was also the difficulty of capturing a heavily defended city, fighting street by street or even house by house. This was a challenge for which Franco's army had neither training nor experience.

By December 1936, both sides were exhausted, and the battle for Madrid ground to a halt. The remains are still there in pill boxes, trench lines and bullet-scarred walls. I often point out on my tours to people planning a trip to Madrid that there are far more tangible ruins to see around the capital than in Barcelona, as the front reached its edges. Sadly, Madrid's rightist city council has done nothing to memorialise these sites.

As the months wore on, the Republican government slowly formed the militias into a new, professional Republican army. This was a long process: it was achieved relatively quickly around Madrid, but it wasn't complete along the Aragon Front until 1937. Overall, the Republic's great task was to rebuild its army and state, which had collapsed because of the military coup. It was eventually successful in creating a regular army capable of fighting proper battles with complex troop movements and supply chains. But by the time it had done so, it was too late.

The militias showed a great deal of initiative in the first weeks of the war, at least in the drive into Aragon, by stopping the military rebels' advance and setting up a front 300 kilometres from Barcelona. By the end of October, after minor offensives by both sides, a stalemate was reached on the Aragon Front. While tens of thousands of enthusiastic young people volunteered in the first months, there were never enough, forcing the Republic to gradually introduce conscription.

Train to Huesca

After the sleek and high-speed AVE train from Barcelona to Zaragoza, I enjoyed the contrast of the two-wagoned diesel that took me at its own pace north towards Huesca. At some point, we crossed what would have been the front between 1936 and 1938 and shortly after stopped at Tardienta, 20 kilometres south of Huesca itself. It was only June, but it looked hot out there, red kites wheeling over yellowing wheat fields. Militia fighters and locals had managed to secure the village at the start of the war, which proved important as it allowed the Republic to bring up troops and supplies by rail from Catalonia. The front lay just a couple of kilometres west. Rebel planes bombed its streets on several occasions. A famous image taken by Agustí Centelles in September 1937 depicts a group of refugee women and children fleeing along the road after a bomb raid on Tardienta. It featured in numerous publications, including the front page of the Paris magazine *Regards* on 2 December 1937, which used it as a warning of the dangers posed by French fascism. A swastika is superimposed over the photograph. In the centre of the cross is a fleur-de-lis, the symbol of the far-right Action Française. "They'd like to make France a new Spain," the subtitle reads. It's worth remembering that many of the French brigaders who fought in Spain had already been involved in some violent street confrontations in Paris and elsewhere. After several attempts by Franco's forces, Tardienta fell in March 1938. Much lay in ruins. In villages and towns across Aragon and the rest of Spain, many fled their homes during the war never to return, others afterwards escaping grinding poverty and local repression for the anonymity of the cities or abroad. Many places never recovered from this mass exodus.

My interest in Tardienta that day lay in another story. On 25 August 1936, a group of ten communist militia fighters set out from the village. Their plan was to dynamite a rebel munitions train as it passed over a bridge. Among their number was a thirty-two-year-old bespectacled English woman. All seemed to have gone well as they pulled back to watch after rigging the explosives at the foot of a stone pillar, but on their way back, a Francoist patrol caught up with the group. Felicia Browne was killed trying to rescue a wounded Italian comrade, becoming the first Briton to die in the war—and the only known British woman to do so fighting.

Browne had studied fine art in England before moving to Germany in 1928 to study sculpture. After witnessing the Nazi takeover, she returned to London and joined the Communist Party. In 1936, she had been on a driving and sketching holiday with a fellow communist friend, the photographer Edith Bone, in France. They decided to go to Barcelona after hearing about the People's Olympiad, where Browne was soon captivated by the revolutionary atmosphere following the defeat of the coup. On 3 August, despite her male comrades' attempts to dissuade her, she joined a PSUC militia, declaring "I am a member of the London Communists and I can fight as well as any man." Although her body had to be left where she fell, her comrades managed to retrieve a few belongings, including her sketchbook, which she had filled with drawings of fellow fighters and Aragonese peasant women and children. These were sold in London in October 1936 by the Artists' International Association to raise money for Spanish relief and now form part of the Tate collection.

As for the operation in August, while the blast missed the train, the bridge was sufficiently damaged to stop other trains laden with troops, munitions and food for six weeks, which must have had an impact. Engaging in more guerrilla actions like this would have surely strengthened the Republic's weak hand at a lower cost in human lives than conventional warfare. The actions of a Republican guerrilla group are famously portrayed in Ernest Hemingway's *For Whom the Bell Tolls* (1940), which is set in the Guadarrama Mountains to the northwest of Madrid, but in truth such forms of warfare were not widely used by either side, despite the success of guerrilla groups against Napoleon during the Peninsular War. Indeed, the term *guerrilla* comes from the Spanish diminutive form of *guerra* (war), meaning "little war", which was coined during the fight against the French.

Huesca

Twenty minutes later, we pulled into Huesca. The town is one of the smallest provincial capitals in Spain, and it was only a short walk from the Renfe station on the outskirts to the old centre, its unhurried, cobbled streets making a welcome break from the tourist hotspot that Barcelona has become. In many ways, it's a typical provincial Spanish place with its tasty local specialities, customs and pride. And like every other one, Huesca hides a recent history of murderous violence.

The military rebels and their civilian supporters left the local garrison on 19 July 1936 and swiftly crushed the leftist resistance in the town, while Republican forces moving from the east soon captured most of the surrounding villages, almost encircling the town but failing to take it in an offensive in October 1936. To bolster the besieging forces, the small ILP contingent was transferred 45 kilometres north on around 15 February 1937. As Orwell recalled, the trucks took the men from Alcubierre across "the wintry plain, where the clipped vines were not yet budding and the blades of the winter barley were just poking through the lumpy soil". Their destination was the La Granja estate, whose "new trenches" formed part of the Republican lines almost encircling Huesca, just 4 kilometres away, which "glittered small and clear like a city of dolls' houses".

After militia forces had taken the nearby Siétamo in September 1936, an overly optimistic commander claimed: "Tomorrow we'll have coffee in Huesca." But despite months of bloody attacks, it still had not fallen. In the same fashion, Francoist general Mola proclaimed similar words in October during his failed onslaught on Madrid. Orwell quipped: "If I ever go back to Spain, I shall make a point of having a cup of coffee in Huesca."

I'd come to the town to meet Víctor again. In homage to the writer's time in Spain, he had created a superb exhibition: "Orwell toma un café en Huesca". It expertly charted Orwell's journey from his birth in India in 1903 to his arrival in revolutionary Barcelona and his time on the Aragon Front. Perhaps the local council missed a huge opportunity to turn it into a permanent exhibition on the writer, which would surely have attracted visitors, but maybe it's best it has avoided tourism's wrecking ball. The exhibition was held in the town museum located in a medieval palace. As we left, Víctor pointed to the arched rooms. "Hundreds and hundreds were imprisoned here. Hungry, beaten, scared, never knowing if each night would be their last." We went for lunch, where he explained what had happened in the town in 1936.

On 19 July, the summer heat pressing down, Huesca fell to the insurgents. What occurred in the coming days, months and years is illustrative of the fate of similar towns across Spain. That morning, unarmed civilians were gunned down in the street, and hundreds were rounded up and imprisoned in the medieval palace and other makeshift jails. Many were shot against the cemetery wall in the early mornings. The killings were carried out by the so-called *escuadrón de la muerte*—death squad—made up of local Falangists and landowners directed by General Gregorio Benito, one of the *Africanista* officers. Out of a population of some 17,000, 533 people were executed in the town in the coming years, although many had fled on the first day. Most were killed in the first year. Thirty-eight more died of abuse in prison. Even though the town's lodge had fewer than a dozen members, 100 of the victims were accused of being Freemasons. The worst single day was 23 August 1936, when ninety-five Republicans were shot, including a pregnant woman. If those orphaned were lucky, they were taken in by friends or relatives, although, in doing so, these adults also risked being denounced. Others spent traumatic childhoods in hospices run by the Catholic Church.

A two-volume book, *Todos los nombres: Víctimas y victimarios* (All the names: Victims and victimisers, 2017), Víctor co-wrote with fellow historian Raúl Mateo has helped shed light on what happened in the town. It comprises a massive 1,488 pages of detailed biographies of every single victim and, unusually for Spain, also includes biographies of their executioners in Huesca, compiled from archives and hundreds of often painful interviews with descendants. The book was, Víctor said, "a plea against forgetting". These four words sum up the principal aim of the history and memory movement in Spain, formed by thousands of tireless researchers—some professional historians, many poorly paid, as well as many unpaid amateurs—aimed at breaking the silence and remembering those who lost the war. In Víctor's case, he has no traumatic family story from either side, no dead relative lying in an unknown ditch. "But we have the right and the obligation as a society to remember what happened in the past as an act of justice. It's a debt to the families of the victims," he explained. "When we first gave a conference in Huesca on the violence a deathly silence descended on the packed hall, even though 95 per cent of those present wanted to hear it. It's easier to breathe now in Huesca."

Ramón Acín

After lunch, Víctor took me back up the old streets to a well-appointed house called Casa Ena (Calle de las Cortes, 3). It's an arts centre now, but in 1936 it was the home of Ramón Acín. As parents with chattering children passed by, Víctor explained: "He is perhaps the most famous victim of the Francoist repression in Huesca. On 6 August 1936, the Death Squad came for him." Acín was a multitalented artist, teacher trainer, local leader of the anarchist CNT and a man renowned for his pacifist views, greatly loved and respected in the town, even by some on the right. In 1932, El Gordo, the famed Spanish Christmas lottery, fell on Huesca, and Acín won a tidy sum, which he used, fulfilling a promise, to fund his friend Luis Bruñel's classic film *Las Hurdes: Tierra sin pan* (Land without bread, 1933). "He so hated the idea of personal freedom being restricted that he even painted a collar and lead on his dog rather than let it be led by a real one," Víctor added.

As news of the spreading coup reached Huesca on 18 July, a fractious meeting was held in the town square. Acín managed to persuade the participants not to take up arms, as he felt the situation was under control, and, if they feared for their lives, he recommended they leave for the countryside. The next day, the town was in the rebels' hands, and the killing spree began. Acín himself managed to hide in a secret space behind a wardrobe here in his house. Night after night, the Falange appeared and beat up his wife Concha Monrás in front of the couple's daughters, demanding she reveal his hiding place. On 6 August, unable to take it any more, Acín came out from his hiding place. Ramón and Concha were dragged from the house, their daughters screaming. Acín was brutally tortured and shot the next day. Concha was one of the ninety-four to be executed on 23 August.

Víctor points to the plaque he had erected in 2004 on the side of the house remembering Acín's murder. It recreates his famous twin bird sculpture, *Las Pajaritas*. Before I took the train home, I visited the original work, located since the 1930s in a corner of the town park. Acín folded white metal sheets as if they were origami paper to form two birds that face each other. They somehow managed to survive forty years of the Franco dictatorship. *Las Pajaritas* are today very much a proud symbol of progressive Huesca and its people, created by an anarcho-syndicalist artist who abhorred violence. The Huesca museum has a room dedicated to Acín with a dozen or so works, most notably *Fair at Ayerbe* and *The Fair*, vibrant paintings of people having a grand old time, full of fun and humanity. He is Aragon's Federico García Lorca. They were close friends. Acín was murdered thirteen days before the Granadian poet. Both were killed for their huge talent and their ideas.

Víctor later decided to create a memorial to Orwell in a park in Huesca. After the then socialist (PSOE) town council backed out from a promise to pay for it, a campaign organised locally by Víctor and internationally by the Orwell Society managed to raise the funds. With several hundred people in attendance on 19 May 2024, Richard Blair inaugurated the frieze. Víctor chose three pieces of music to be performed by the four-piece band. The first was Shostakovich's "8th String Quartet", officially dedicated to the victims of fascism and the Second World War, but also understood as remembering victims of all forms of totalitarianism. This was followed by "Anda Jaleo", a traditional Andalusian tune arranged with lyrics by Lorca, who was famously associated with the Republic and progressive ideas. As the song came to an end, Richard touchingly turned back to the memorial and blew a kiss to his father's face. The event was completed with Christy Moore's International Brigader classic "Viva la Quinta Brigada", with the lyrics changed to pay tribute to the ILP volunteers in the POUM. All in all, it was a moving morning, and the memorial now stands in the park as a permanent testament to Orwell as well as to Víctor's tenacity in keeping alive the memory of those who fought against Franco.

La Granja

Orwell and his British comrades arrived at La Granja in late February 1937 (see Fig. 5.1). The estate, a couple of kilometres behind the Republican lines, was used by the POUM as a cookhouse and store. Orwell disdained the way the militias had wrecked the buildings. Every room was smashed up or employed as a latrine. He admitted it gave him "a sneaking sympathy with the fascist ex-owners". Now, it's an altogether more pleasant place. We arrived hungry after the trip from Alcubierre at midday and were welcomed by today's owner, Pedro Mainer, who jovially treated us to a huge and delicious *rancho aragonés*—a rice-based dish packed with rabbit, pork, snails, asparagus, peppers and artichokes served in two huge earthenware *cazuelas* and washed down with plenty of the local Somontano wine.

Fuddled with the wine and several helpings of the *rancho*, I wandered around the courtyard, amused at the gaggle of irate geese defending their patch by honking at me, and wondered about the rats Orwell had described gorging on food left around the courtyard. They were "as big as cats, or nearly; great bloated brutes that waddled over the beds of muck, too impudent even to run away unless you shot at them". "They're still a problem," Pedro later informs me. Although Orwell had written about them before, it is in *Homage* that his fear and disgust of these rodents really come to the fore. In Aragon, he lived in close proximity to them in the trenches. Rats fed on their food and devoured their leather belts and cartridge pouches. Perhaps it was these intimate experiences in Spain that above all concentrated his mind and fears, leading to that awful room in the Ministry of Love.

Republican troops continued to besiege Huesca throughout 1937 and engaged in a major offensive to take the town between 11 and 19 June, by which time Orwell was away from the front. Although it was never completely surrounded, this was the longest siege of the Civil War, lasting for 611 days until Franco's advancing armies arrived in March 1938 to relieve the town. To weaken the resistance, Huesca was heavily shelled and bombed by Republican artillery and planes—900 tonnes of metal fell on the small town. Some 119 people were killed and 212 wounded, many of them children. These were among the heaviest bombing raids committed by the Republican side, the most severe being on the Asturian capital of Oviedo. Numerous photographs attest to the destruction. Meanwhile, Francoist planes systematically targeted villages on the Republican side in Aragon. For many locals, these were the first flying machines they had ever seen. People learned to recognise the engine sounds and the silhouettes of Soviet Polikarpovs, German Junkers and Italian Savoia-Marchettis. They soon knew whether to cheer them on or take cover in fear.

In early March, a minor cut on Orwell's hand had become badly infected, so he was sent a few kilometres behind the lines to a field hospital at Monflorite. As we arrived in the village, jackdaws, swallows, martins and swifts danced around the crumbling Romanesque church of the Plaza Mayor, which in 1937, Víctor explained, was used as a military store. Red kites patrolled just a few metres above our heads. Suddenly, a peregrine falcon flashed low across the square. I marvelled at the sheer proximity and fecundity of this birdlife, something that seems a memory in most places. We gathered in the shade in front of a plaque celebrating Orwell's stay. Richard did another reading from the book describing his time here, arm in sling, when "Monflorite was the usual huddle of mud and stone houses, with narrow tortuous alleys that had been churned by lorries till they looked like the craters of the moon."

Carthusian monastery

On the road from Huesca, Víctor informs me that "[t]his village has children ... This village doesn't ... This one has had none since 2010." Depopulation stalks the Spanish hinterland. Dozens of buzzards pose on telephone poles and hover above the fields. It must be a good year for voles. Poppies again are uncountable in the verges. It's *abadol* in Aragonese, Víctor proudly tells me. Another word for the collection. Half an hour later, we pull up outside the imposing stone gatehouse of an old monastery (see Fig. 5.2). La Cartuja de Nuestra Señora de las Fuentes, as the name states, was endowed with a spring and was run by monks of the Carthusian order. They owned a big chunk of the best land around, although they lost the estate in 1835 as part of the Spanish government's confiscation and sale of ecclesiastical lands. We were greeted by Alberto Lasheras, a friendly and very knowledgeable local historian, who explained this older history and how in 1936 the place was taken over by the Durruti Column. He points out the anarchist graffiti written across the walls by militiamen marking their arrival all those years ago. There's also a large, well-drawn bird—I think a sparrow—"a symbol of freedom," says Alberto.

We're then taken into a walled yard as big as a football pitch, such a huge space, we thought, for the twenty monks who lived here in silence and solitude (see Fig. 5.3). At the entrance to the monastery itself, Alberto pointed down to some curious marks that had been scratched into the tiles. He told us archaeologists have worked out they were made by a Soviet T-26 tank as it turned around here, perhaps after the site had been taken over by the Republican army. Simple, ugly scour marks vandalising the floor they might be, but for me, they were incredibly evocative of that time and place: a group of Republican soldiers shouting in Spanish at the crew to turn around (they rarely knew much Russian); the crew, who couldn't understand Spanish, shouting back in Russian. I'd learn more about these vehicles farther on in my journey. Alberto explains the marks might have been made after the war. La Cartuja was used as a grain store, and they often turned these captured old tanks into tractors.

The monastery itself turned out to be relatively new, dating from the mid-eighteenth century. Most of the walls had been decorated with bright and colourful frescoes by Goya's brother-in-law Friar Manuel Bayeu. He spent most of his life on this work, which covers a couple of thousand square metres of walls and ceilings. Some were half completed as if waiting for him to return. A few had been vandalised as a statement of anticlericalism or boredom. I wandered around the maze of rooms and corridors. The names of dozens of soldiers were written on walls, some on the frescoes, some in the spaces between, together with anarchist and communist graffiti. The hammer and sickle. The red star. CNT, FAI, PSUC. The alphabet soup. Alberto has discovered more graffiti since our visit—one written across Friar Manuel's work proclaims in Spanish: "Religion is the crutch of the stupid and ignorant." As we wander through the empty rooms, he says he's also taken descendants of the authors around. "Showing grandchildren their grandfather's writing," he says, "is incredibly emotional." One reads in careful loping letters—calligraphy being important back then—"Every drop of your blood is today a seed: tomorrow a flower of freedom." It suddenly felt like they'd only just abandoned the place. The dust of time lay everywhere. Back outside, Alberto explained that after Republican Aragon fell in March 1938, the Condor Legion, the military unit sent by Hitler to aid Franco, moved in. After the war, the monastery was left to fall into decay until it was bought in 2015 by the local government. I hope they continue to restore the monastery. But not too much. Friar Manuel's unfinished paintings, all the names on walls, the badly lit corridors, the dust; nothing to stop you from wandering, all adding to a sense of history you could almost touch, a portal to another place.

Before lunch, we drive to what is left of "Alas Rojas", the site of a major Republican airbase at Sariñena, where we are met by another local historian and dogged chronicler of the Monegros, Joaquín Ruiz Gaspar. In front of an information panel, he explains that this was the Republic's largest airbase in eastern Spain, more important during the war than Barcelona's El Prat airfield, due to its strategic position 50 kilometres behind the lines. More than 1,000 people worked here, aiding the Russian and Spanish pilots who used it to attack the front and to bomb the Francoist-held towns of Zaragoza and Huesca. They also built dummy airfields nearby, explained Joaquín, with fake planes to confuse enemy air raids, a tactic picked up from the First World War.

One of our group, Dorian "Dusty" Nicol, an American geologist, explains that his mother's uncle, Alfonso de los Reyes González, a renowned Republican pilot, was in charge of setting up and running the base, before going into exile in Mexico after the war. In March 1938, with the fall of Aragon to Franco's army, the Condor Legion used the base to bomb Catalonia. Joaquín then takes us to the site's main air raid bunker. The steps that lead down are filled in with rubble, so we can't visit, but it's an emotional moment for Dusty. His mother Isa Reyes, born to a well-off Madrid family with Republican leanings and fifteen years old at the start of the war, lived on the base for several weeks on her way out of Spain into exile. "She often told me," he explained, "how terrified she was of going down these dark steps when there was a bomb raid—she suffered from crippling claustrophobia all her life ... I can now understand why. Look at how narrow and cramped the space is."

While her father and uncle continued to fight for the Republic, Isa was sent by the family to France, where she made a living dancing flamenco and singing in nightclubs and even represented a neutral Spain at the 1938 Miss Europe contest organised by *Le Monde*. In 1939, circumstances led her to perform unwillingly at Hitler's fiftieth birthday in Berlin, an unusual fate for a Republican exile, as her son pointed out. Dusty later adapted his mother's remarkable memoirs in *"Miss Spain in Exile": Isa Reyes' Escape from the Spanish Civil War* (2020). It's a fun, moving and exciting tale that manages to capture the fading glamour of 1930s Europe on the edge of catastrophe from a very atypical viewpoint, that of a young woman who had managed to escape from the war in Spain. "I promised my mother that one day I'd tell her story," Dusty told us. "It means a lot to me to visit a site where she had stayed on her way out of Spain."

On the way back to the cars, we stop to look at what's left of the runway. Another of our group, Steve Warren, an air traffic controller and pilot who knows about air warfare, tells us this was one of the very few concrete runways in the world—even the RAF only used grass at the time. He points out the compass marked out on the ground, allowing pilots to orientate their planes on take-off. The runway is in a sorry state, as Víctor laments. Most of it has been destroyed, and what's left is largely occupied by a cow shed and large piles of dung (see Fig. 5.4). It seems a fine metaphor for the burial of historical memory in Spain. As a swarm of flies finds us, we head for the cars.

The International Brigades

On the early morning of 12 February 1937, while Orwell and his three dozen British volunteers were freezing in the hills of Aragon and hardly managing to kill anyone, the British Battalion of the International Brigades went into action to the east of Madrid.

After Franco had failed to take Madrid in the autumn of 1936, he decided to launch offensives near the Spanish capital—first Jarama in February 1937, followed by Guadalajara in March. At the Battle of Jarama, the British Battalion were effectively annihilated as a fighting force in a few short days. Three days later, they were followed by the Americans of the Abraham Lincoln Battalion, who suffered the same fate. Both units formed part of the International Brigades. As British brigader John Lepper chillingly wrote, remembering Jarama: "Death stalked the olive trees / Picking his men / His leaden fingers beckoned again and again." At Jarama, they had the same training, or worse, as Orwell's volunteers in the POUM, woefully limited equipment and the same wrong cartridges for rifles that wouldn't load. In truth, most Republican army units were very badly trained and poorly armed at the start. This did change, and the Republic managed to create a reasonable army, but as we'll see later, by the time they had done so, it was too late.

The International Brigades are unique in terms of numbers and importance in history, a phenomenon very much of their time and place. With thousands of young volunteers coming to Spain, the Comintern, the global organisation established to promote world communism, agreed to form an international column in late September 1936 with the support of the Spanish Republican government. More than half of the recruits were members of their national communist parties. Although their ranks certainly included many hard-line Stalinist cadres, and others were hardened during the fighting in Spain, most were young, working-class men who came to fight against fascism, not for the geopolitical interests of the Soviet Union. Women were not allowed to join as soldiers, although many did so as nurses. These volunteers came from all around the world. There were sixty Chinese, a handful of Indians and as many as 800 Arabs, mainly from Algeria, who fought in Spain together with their Jewish comrades. There were volunteers from Iceland and New Zealand. Around 2,500 were from Latin America. Most, however, came either directly from Central Southern and Eastern Europe or were first- or second-generation exiles from those countries who were living in Western Europe and North America.

The International Brigades can be seen as a symbol of the European diaspora I mentioned in the sections on the origins of the war. This concept is eloquently put forward by the British historian Helen Graham. To paraphrase her writings and talks, they came from the new states of the old Austro-Hungarian Empire, and by extension Germany, Poland, Greece and Italy, whose lives had been made a misery by local fascist bully boys in provincial towns. They were now living rather precarious lives in the Western democracies. Some 20 per cent of the volunteers were Jewish, which comes as no surprise. They wanted nothing better than to get even with those fellas back home. How could they do it? They could come to Spain. Additionally, many of those who travelled from Western European democracies had already been involved in some violent confrontations with local far-right groups, most famously in the UK's case at Cable Street in London. Others had fought at Liverpool, Hull and Glasgow. Many of those who managed to lay a punch on the face of a British fascist later came to Spain.

We can also see the International Brigades as a symbol of the Great Depression, which had destroyed the lives of millions across the world. By 1936, in macro terms at least, economies were recovering, but things certainly weren't getting better for many of the working class. They saw Spain as a hope, a beacon in a darkening Europe. While many saw the USSR as a model, some also saw in the Republic a third way—or third ways in the case of revolutionaries—between the disasters of capitalism and the Soviet Union.

If we include smaller numbers who fought with the CNT (about 3,000), and—as we've seen—with the POUM (about 600), some 35,000 foreign volunteers fought on the side of the Spanish Republic, although exact figures will never be known. Around 9,000 died; 70 per cent were wounded. These terrible casualty figures need explaining. First, they were ideologically committed and prepared to risk everything; second, they often had scant or no military experience before coming to Spain and particularly in the first year of the war received little or no training; and third, they were often used as shock troops, perhaps sometimes criminally so, in search of great propaganda victories. Some 80 per cent were working class. They came from more than fifty countries. The largest group of volunteers, around 9,000, were from France, although some of these were exiles, born farther east; 3,000 of them died. These were followed by 5,000 Poles, 4,000 Italians, 3,000 Germans and 2,800 Americans (the Abraham Lincoln Battalion), of whom around 700 were killed. All of these figures are estimates.

The Abraham Lincoln Battalion is famed as being the first desegregated American fighting unit, although of course it was not in any way supported by the American government. The Lincolns were also the first American fighting unit to be commanded by a black officer, Oliver Law, who was killed at the Battle of Brunete, west of Madrid, on 9 July 1937. Around eighty-five African Americans volunteered. In their letters home, they made an explicit link between the fight for the Spanish Republic and the fight against the semi-feudal system in the south of Spain and the struggle against Jim Crow, the legal system that enforced racial segregation and discrimination against African Americans back home. Fellow brigader Tom Page told James Yates, author of the memoir from *Mississippi to Madrid* (1988):

I remember how sometimes a whole town would turn out when they heard there was a Black man around. Spain was the first place that I ever felt like a free man. If someone didn't like you, they told you to your face. It had nothing to do with the color of your skin.

The experiences of these men are movingly told in the documentary *Invisible Heroes: African-Americans in the Spanish Civil War* (2015). The film also relates the experiences of Salaria Kea, who in 1936 was rejected for flood relief work in the American Midwest. In 1936, she travelled to the Spanish Republic, which was unconcerned by the colour of her skin. She worked as head nurse at the American Villa Paz hospital at Saelices, Cuenca, tending the wounded at the Battle of Jarama, where she was head nurse over five white American nurses.

Although their military value has, perhaps, been exaggerated, and although they constituted a small part of the Republican army, the International Brigades' arrival in the autumn of 1936 brought an injection of energy and had a great impact on the defenders of the Republic's morale, making them feel that they did not stand alone.

6

GERNIKA AND THE MAY DAYS

A market town destroyed

On the evening of 26 April 1937, a Basque town some 600 kilometres to the west stood ablaze. At 16.30 that afternoon, bombers and fighter planes of the German Condor Legion and the fascist Italian Aviazione Legionaria began their murderous assault on Gernika, dropping some 45,400 kilos of high-explosive and incendiary bombs. Fighter planes also strafed the surrounding roads, causing numerous civilian casualties. As they pulled back to their bases three hours later, the town lay in ruins. Gernika in Basque, Guernica in Spanish: another name to add to the world's gazette of place names of infamy. Nobody knows how many died, as it was a market day and so was packed with people from the surrounding villages, and above all there was an unknown but large number of refugees fleeing through the province of Vizcaya from the advancing Francoist army. As most of the men were at the front, a high proportion crowding the streets would have been women, children and the elderly— these demographics are reflected in the figures in Picasso's *Guernica*: four women, a child and a horse, in addition to a fallen male soldier and the much argued-over bull. The town fell three days later.

The Francoist authorities announced they had found precisely zero bodies, hardly surprising since they claimed to the international press that it was the Basques themselves who had blown up their own town. This extreme form of negationism was still prevalent in Franco's Spain until the 1970s, when the great lie became untenable in its pure form, leading the regime's historians to admit the town had in fact been bombed, inevitably laying all the blame on the Nazis and claiming the figure of a few dozen victims. A few days after the attack, the Basque government declared that 1,645 persons had been killed and 889 wounded. Studies by Basque historians in the 2000s brought this figure down to 300 or fewer. Basque historian Xabier Irujo's superb and comprehensive study, *Gernika: Genealogy of a Lie* (2019), estimates at least 2,000 were killed in the successive waves of the attack. Lieutenant Colonel Wolfram von Richthofen, who planned the attack, noted in his diary that Operation Rügen had been a "technical success". The raid was part of the offensive to take Northern Spain, which began on 31 March 1937 with General Mola's chilling but also mendacious words, "I have decided to rapidly terminate the war in the North: those not guilty of assassinations and who surrender their arms will have their lives and property spared. But, if submission is not immediate, I will raze all Vizcaya to the ground, beginning with the industries of war."

After a long August family drive across the scorched peninsula, the air-con having given up as soon as we left Barcelona, we reached the deep verdant valleys of the Basque Country, light drizzle giving way to sunshine as we entered Gernika. As we wandered around the pleasant, well-ordered streets with our ice creams, it was difficult to imagine the horror of that day. Since my previous visit twenty years before, the local council had installed a considerable number of information panels, and there were impressive new public displays of large photos documenting the destruction that certainly helped in understanding the atrocity (see Fig. 6.1). Not a single old building remains in the centre: it was all reduced to ruins in 1937. Everything we saw had been rebuilt—much of the work being done using Republican forced labour.

The new town was part of the regime's failed attempt to create a new past. As an architectural friend had directed me, this was most evident in the town hall's attractive façade, erected like other new public buildings across the state in a similar style to the monastery-palace complex of El Escorial, built on the orders of Philip II outside Madrid between 1563 and 1584. This aping of another age looked to connect the Franco regime with the "glories" of Philip's empire, at a time when the state reached the height of its influence and power. This period is sometimes called the Spanish Golden Age, when the crown ruled over the entire Iberian Peninsula, European territories such as Naples and the Low Countries, and had completed the conquests of the Inca and Aztec Empires and the Philippines. These municipal buildings would help signify a united Spain, epitomised in the forever repeated Francoist slogan "¡Una, Grande y Libre!"— "One, Great and Free!"—on thousands of public buildings. To cap it off, Franco was named an "adoptive son" of Gernika in thanks for his work recreating the town he was responsible for annihilating. These municipal buildings are on a modest scale. For a full-blown vision of a building imitating El Escorial, have a look at images of the Air Ministry building in Madrid.

Across the square from the town hall is the Gernika Peace Museum. Opened in 1998, this was one of the first institutional centres to remember the conflict. It expertly narrates the wider war in Spain and the key events in the Basque Country with original objects and images, before focusing on the destruction of the town itself. The central installation impressed us most. You are guided through into a recreated darkened 1930s room of a middle-class Basque family, where a woman's voice narrates from her Gernika home the effects of the war on those around her. Something happens as the old clock on the wall strikes 4.30 that brought home to me and my family the shock of that day, as far as this is possible in a museum space. I don't want to spoil the experience for anybody reading this who wants to visit, but to get an idea, see Fig. 6.2.

Although the central part of Gernika was destroyed, most of the outskirts were untouched, including the higher part of the town where several palaces, wealthy homes, convents and most notably the Casa de Juntas (Assembly House) are located. After the museum, we sat in the shade of the Casa de Juntas' garden and looked through the railings at the famous Tree of Gernika (*Gernikako Arbola*), a common oak, where male representatives from the region of Vizcaya would traditionally meet to hold quasi-democratic assemblies. Castilian and Spanish kings would also stand under its branches and promise to respect Basque liberties. The tree, the Casa de Juntas and the ceremony have all come to represent these freedoms. To this day, the Basque president, the *lehendakari*, is sworn in under the tree. The oak survived the bombing but died in 2004. We were looking at its "grandson", as the Basque call it. The famous Renteria bridge was also spared, which, had the intention of the bombing been military, might have been an expected target aimed at impeding the retreat of the Basque forces. Also untouched, surprisingly or not, was the town's industrial zone, including the major weapons manufacturer Astra-Unceta y Cía. Its output and other Basque industries would prove very useful in supplying Franco's army as the war continued. Today, the building is an arts centre, producing culture instead of guns. The centre also houses the old works siren that sounded the warning on 26 April 1937. It is set off again every year at the same time to remember that day. And in March 2024, the sirens screamed across Gernika to remember the victims of Israel's destruction of Gaza.

The fall of Gernika was part of the Nationalist conquest of the Basque Country and the rest of Northern Spain. Although the Basque army put up dogged resistance, it was only a question of time. Franco's army had taken Gernika by 29 April, and Bilbao fell on 19 June. It would now continue with the remaining regions to the west of the Basque Country: Cantabria and Asturias, much of which was still in loyalist government hands but fatefully separated from the rest of the Republic.

International impact of the bombing

Gernika was not the first locality to be destroyed by bombing raids by Franco's allies. Apart from the bombing of Spain's major cities, plenty of smaller places had already been targeted. The town of Durango was attacked four weeks before on 31 March, a few hours after Mola's statement that he would raze the Basque Country. Some 250 people were killed. Another example is the shockingly underreported destruction of the agricultural community of La Sauceda in the province of Cádiz on 31 October 1936 by Nazi planes. Many of the survivors were then massacred by ground troops, and the settlement of some 1,500 people was almost razed. If you're in the area, have a walk around the few sad remains of the buildings standing among cork trees and visit the Casa de la Memoria La Sauceda in Jimena de la Frontera, which has an excellent permanent exhibition on the atrocity. Unlike these cases, the bombing of Gernika soon entered the world's consciousness. Initially, this was because a group of eyewitnesses reached the town on the night of the bombing, including the journalist George Steer, whose account of the bombing, published in both *The Times* and *The New York Times*, is widely regarded as one of the greatest pieces of war reporting ever written in English. More articles denouncing the destruction of Gernika soon appeared in all the world's non-fascist press, including a remarkable 7,000 reports published in the US press between 27 April and 12 June. The name of Gernika was now very much in the minds of the European and American public, coming to symbolise the war in Spain, but also a focus for wider fears of aerial bombing of cities.[1]

On 28 April, Steer's article was translated by *L'Humanité*, the French Communist Party newspaper. This is probably where Pablo Picasso, a regular reader, learned about the atrocity, its black and white newsprint and photos reflected in the monochrome of the work *Guernica* (the painting has always been known by the town's Spanish spelling). In January, he had reluctantly agreed to paint a large mural (349 centimetres × 776 centimetres) for the Republican government's pavilion for the upcoming Paris Exposition. He was, however, uncomfortable about a direct political commission, whatever his sympathies for the Republican cause, and was unsure how to proceed, sketching without enthusiasm for a piece that was intended to depict his work as an artist in the studio. After reading the news and Franco's subsequent lie about Basque responsibility, he attacked the canvas with vigour and anger, creating the huge mural in just six weeks, incorporating themes and motifs that had occupied his recent art—the bull, the weeping woman—now putting them to new use in a stark, frightening hellscape.

It certainly took my breath away the first time I saw it at the Reina Sofía in Madrid, where it hangs on permanent display. The work is unrelenting and monstrous; the only theme is war. Black and white angular figures with severed limbs and heads. There is no relief, and, if you allow yourself to fall into the painting, it is actually quite frightening. All is pain and suffering. The new, disturbing images by the corps of brilliant photographers in Spain influence the work. It documents the development of air warfare, which filled people's nightmares in the 1930s, as nuclear war did to my generation's dreams in the 1980s. The distinction between the soldier and civilian is gone. War is now indiscriminate. You are now a target, and it's coming to your home. Many consider it the greatest painting of the twentieth century. It is certainly one of the most moving and powerful anti-war paintings in history, and perhaps the work most open to different interpretations. The scream of the mother with her dead child limp across her arms reaches out to every atrocity since.

Coming down from the Casa de Juntas, we stumbled on a full-sized tiled mosaic of the work. An information panel explained it was created in 1997 to commemorate the sixtieth anniversary of the massacre. Underneath, it reads "'Guernica' Gernikara". The Basque suffix "ra"—Gernika*ra*—means "to" Gernika (see Fig. 6.3). It calls on the onlooker to consider that although the painting has been in Madrid since 1981, its real home should be here, not that Picasso ever indicated this.

Context: an international war

In the summer of 1936, desperate for weapons, the Republic turned first to its natural allies: the Western democracies. It was rejected. France, governed by a similar Popular Front government under the socialist prime minister Léon Blum, was initially not unresponsive, but the British Conservative government, more sympathetic to Franco, threatened to renege on the security pact between the two countries if the French supplied arms, leading to the so-called Non-Intervention Agreement, signed by every European state except for Switzerland. The signatories agreed not to supply weapons to either of the warring parties, thus depriving the legal government of the Republic of its rights under international law to purchase arms. The agreement was widely broken by Germany and Italy, who blatantly provided supplies to Franco.

In desperation, the legal Republican government was forced to turn to the Soviet Union, which, also breaking the Non-Intervention Agreement, provided large amounts of aid—at a price. In October 1936, a secret operation covertly shipped from the naval port of Cartagena to Odessa 70 per cent of Spain's gold reserve, at the time the fourth largest reserve in the world. This metal didn't come from Latin America—that had long run out—but rather came from the huge profits Spain made selling to both sides as a neutral power during the First World War—Barcelona itself became an industrial metropolis thanks to this.

All of this almost certainly saved the Republic in late 1936. It also gave the PCE much greater influence in the Republic than their pre-war support merited, leading to an extraordinary growth in party membership, and enabled the party to dictate military strategy and, in some cases, murder its opponents. The Republican government looked the other way. None of this is to say that Stalin was in a position to take over in Spain. This was not an option without the presence of the Red Army, and the Republic remained a plural institution to the end of the war, which probably would have quickly ditched the USSR had the Western democracies changed policy and provided support. The extent of Soviet influence in Spain has been greatly exaggerated, particularly during the Cold War. However, it is clear that in the Republican zone there was an understandable atmosphere of fear and suspicion in which it was impossible to know whom to trust, whether within the army, the police or the administration, and that this was significantly increased by Stalinist influence.

However, Soviet shipments were in much lower quantities than Hitler and Mussolini provided to Franco. Stalin's commitment was always half-hearted, probably preferring to avoid a Republican defeat if only because a continuation of the war distracted Nazi

Germany. The clearest example of this was how few military staff the Soviets sent to the Republic: just 1,800 to 2,000. This figure stands in stark contrast to Franco's side. Mussolini sent some 75,000 troops, the Corpo Truppe Volontarie, along with huge amounts of war material, all of which almost bankrupted the Italian state, draining its resources and severely undermining its ability to wage the Second World War. And the Italian forces learned little from the experience (see Fig. 6.4).

Nazi Germany, by contrast, did well financially from their involvement, for example through concessions on mining rights and exports of food and other goods during the Second World War. They also learned valuable lessons, testing out twenty-seven types of new planes, new tanks, new tactics. The German military contribution involved the infamous Condor Legion, organised from Berlin by Hermann Göring, the head of the Luftwaffe. A total of 19,000 so-called technicians served in Spain, including tank drivers and pilots (see Fig. 6.5). As Göring admitted at Nuremberg, he wanted "to test my young Luftwaffe in this or that technical respect".

Thus, although the Spanish Civil War was fought out on the battlefields of Spain, its outcome was also decided in London, Paris, Moscow, Rome, Berlin and Washington. In that sense, it can be seen as a prologue to the Second World War. You can see this reflected in the postcard printed in 1937 to aid the Basque Front. Many in 1936 understood that another war was coming to Europe. They couldn't, of course, foresee the absolute horror of Auschwitz. But they did know horrors were coming. I think it really helps us to understand why so many people took the cause of Spain to heart in the 1930s. I have the tail fin of a German B1 incendiary bomb (see Fig. 6.6), which I bought in an auction. It was found on the Madrid Front and is the same type used to help destroy Warsaw, Coventry, Leningrad, and all the rest, but also in the attacks on the cities of Spain and the destruction of

Gernika. When I pass it around on the tour, some people don't want to hold it, as if it still is imbued with evil power.

By April 1937, the revolutionary euphoria in Barcelona had evaporated. The war was going badly, and food supply and shortages were becoming serious issues, leading to long queues for the most basic of items, which inevitably increased tensions. Fights were breaking out between supporters of the Republican order and revolutionaries. Many supporters of the CNT and the POUM argued that their concessions to the Republican authorities had gone far enough. Others believed in the need for a strong state, arguing that this was the only way to win the war. Barcelona was a tinderbox; it was only a question of time before the situation exploded into violence, the tragic infighting known in English as the May Days ("Hechos de Mayo" in Spanish, "Fets de Maig" in Catalan).

Context: the May Days

The fighting and ideological complexities have been covered and argued over in numerous books. I gave my own tuppence in *Forgotten Places*, and I do not want to cover the events in any detail again here. To cut an extremely complex story shockingly short, here's a quick summary. Some form of confrontation was perhaps inevitable, given the fragmentation of power on the anti-Francoist side emerging from the defeat of the military coup in Catalonia in July 1936. In this sense, the fighting was a logical conclusion of the CNT's refusal or inability to consolidate the revolution in the summer of 1936 and the desire of the Republican and Catalan governments to regain the power they had lost, stoked by Stalin's obsession with crushing Marxist dissidence represented by the POUM. It was also fed by pre-war, sometimes violent, tensions already existing between the CNT and UGT unions, and also between the parties of the

Catalan left. The events can also be seen as a reckoning between a working-class Barcelona, frustrated by the power it had gained in July 1936 slipping away, and a middle-class Barcelona wanting to regain its traditional sway over the city.

The events tumbled out of control on 3 May 1937 when a group of Republican Assault Guards attempted to take over the Telefónica, which had been in the hands of the CNT-dominated worker's committee since July 1936. The telephone workers resisted, and anger spread like wildfire across the working-class districts, which saw the attack as an assault on their revolutionary gains. Once again, cobblestones were pulled up to build hundreds of barricades, erected to block streets and control key buildings and neighbourhoods. Fighting broke out chaotically between forces in favour of the Republican state—broadly speaking, the Soviet backed communist party the PSUC, the Catalanist ERC and the police—and those in favour of defending the 1936 revolution (also broadly the anarchist unions of the CNT/FAI and the Marxist POUM), although it should be stressed that no organisation on either side issued any official instructions to take up arms. Over the next five days, some 400 people were killed and more than 1,000 wounded in this absolute breakdown of trust between different leftist factions in the city. Orwell, who had returned from Aragon on 26 April himself, was caught up in the events and defended the POUM headquarters in La Rambla from a vantage point in a theatre across the street, although he never fired a shot.

In 2023, Eli Pastó, a Catalan friend of mine, gave me a huge stack of several hundred newspapers from the war that her father had collected over the years. They form a veritable archive—a bit daunting in some ways as there is just so much stuff to organise and digest—which I have only begun to dip into at the time of writing. I'll probably end up donating most of them to a proper archive at some point. There are a couple of dozen issues of the biggest selling newspaper in wartime Republican Spain: the anarchist flagship *Solidaridad Obrera*. Several cover the infighting, including one dated 6 May 1937, which prints on the front page a joint statement released by the CNT and socialist UGT calling off the general strike and the infighting in the name of anti-fascist unity. It reads: "Comrades: the bitterness and competition that leads to hatred and disaster must be buried. The workers are brothers; not enemies ... fascism is the enemy of all."[2] It's a real museum piece that illustrates the importance the CNT's leadership, and probably most of its membership, gave to the war effort over the revolution by this stage of the war. After five days, an exhausted city awoke to news that this apparent compromise between the different factions had been reached. However, it quickly became apparent that the Republican order had emerged victorious over the revolutionary groups.

Alex Gabriles

Some years ago, I was given a fresh perspective on the ideological mess of the May Days when I received an email from an elderly man called Alexander Gabriles from Texas, who was kind enough to share his story with me. Alex was born in Barcelona in 1930 to a Greek-American father and a Catalan mother. He celebrated his sixth birthday on 18 July 1936 (the day before the military rose in the city) and remembered the first bombing of Barcelona on 13 February 1937 when the Italian fascist cruiser *Eugenio di Savoia* shelled the Catalan capital, killing eighteen people. "We lived on the fourth floor of a new apartment building right on the shore of the old fishing quarter of Barceloneta, facing the sea," he wrote. "We were at home when the cruiser attacked and could hear the whistling sound of explosive shells flying over our area, and the loud explosions that followed. Looking out towards the horizon were the flashes of the ships' cannons firing." He went on to describe the aerial bombing by Mussolini's planes in the coming months, but I was most struck by his memories of the May Events:

> Two days, maybe longer after the fighting began, my mother, being very curious, and her friend Catalina, took me to see the damage around Plaça Catalunya. There were burned-out vehicles, blackened buildings from fires and bullet pock marks on the sides of buildings. It would have been around 11 a.m., and shortly after we arrived, all hell broke loose, with gunfire, explosions and all the civilians running into the bushes which surrounded the square. My mother threw me under a shrub, and then jumped on top of me. We lay there till dusk as we listened to shooting and blasts for hours. Finally, as it grew dark, a truce was called, and civilians waving white handkerchiefs were allowed to leave the square. We went down to the Metro station, but of course there were no trains (nor buses, taxis or trams), so we walked, together with the multitude, along the tracks to the next station where we went back up to ground level. There was no fighting, but the streets were dark and no vehicles were running, so we had to walk several miles to our home in Barceloneta.

A few days after the May Events, their American passports allowed Alex, his brother and mother to cross the border into France. A train took them to Marseille, where they were reunited in mid-July 1937 with their father and boarded a small ship, *The City of Joliet*, bound for the United States. The email then took an interesting turn:

> BUT ... surprise! The ship's first port of call was Sevilla, up the Guadalquivir river, which was in fascist hands. Our passports allowed us to go ashore, where I saw a parade of Franco's Moroccan troops. That was a frightening sight. But we also witnessed something else: the unloading of the green metal barrels with a white circle, red star, and the name "TEXACO" in the middle of the star. These were lubricants and motor oils, all destined for Franco's military.

Alex concluded:

> Over the years I've got to know many exiles in Mexico, the US and
> South America. And through my maritime work I met a former
> fighter from the Dabrowski battalion on a Polish ship, and another old
> International Brigader on a Dutch vessel. We never knew the "rebels"
> as "Francoists". That's a decaffeinated name for "fascist". It seems to me
> that the Western media began labelling the rebels as "Francoists". For
> us, they were always fascists.

While I'm doing tours in the square, I often tell the story of
Alex, six years old, hiding under his mother in the shrubs and
their long walk home.

I showed Alex's emails to Mònica. They reminded her of her
father's stories of the war. José Navarro was born in Barcelona in
1929. The memories he wanted to share were of fun and freedom,
of playing about on barricades, exploring bombed-out buildings
and robbing fruit and vegetables from the urban farms—he was
always hungry.

Context: the May Days; consequences

The consequences of the May Days were, like much of the
political background of the Spanish Civil War, complex. Broadly
speaking, they marked the formal end of revolutionary power
in Barcelona. Some, though not all, of the larger industrial
enterprises, collectivised in the summer of 1936, were now
nationalised in the name of the war effort or even returned to
their former owners, if they were not suspected of supporting the
military rebels. Others, such as public transport, continued in
the hands of the trade union committees until the fall of the city
in January 1939. In the context of an ongoing anti-fascist war
with worsening prospects, most CNT militants and workers—
and its leadership—were not prepared to support offensive

action against the state by May 1937. The CNT and the rival socialist UGT were left out of the new government under the moderate socialist Juan Negrín formed on 17 May 1937. Both unions returned to Negrín's second government, formed on 5 April 1938. Elsewhere, the Regional Defence Council of Aragon was disbanded at gunpoint by Republican troops in August 1937 and its collectives broken up.

The POUM was accused of military rebellion and effectively declared illegal on 16 June. Much of its leadership was arrested, including its leader Andreu Nin, while others went into hiding. As far as the wider war is concerned, the Republican government was now firmly back in control and able to concentrate on continuing to rebuild its army and state administration, which had collapsed at the start of the war.

The Stalinists, however, went a bit further against the leaders of their Marxist rivals. This had been going on for some time. Another newspaper Eli gave me dates from December 1936, five months before the events. *Juliol* was published by the youth section of the PSUC, the pro-Stalinist communist party. The front-page article does not yet explicitly mention the POUM, but the message is loud and clear. The headline reads in Catalan: "Anybody who does not explicitly support the USSR should be treated as a traitor" (see Fig. 6.7). After the May Days, they really upped the ante. An infamous poster appeared showing a POUM mask, behind which is revealed a leering Trotsky with a swastika stamped on his forehead, while in June 1937 the British Communist Party's *Daily Worker* thundered on its front page: "Spanish Trotskyists Plot with Franco".

Whether the May Days were deliberately provoked as part of an orchestrated Stalinist attack on supporters of the revolution, as has been claimed by some on the left, is very much open to doubt, and if it was, it was certainly badly planned and half-hearted. Whatever the case, the communists certainly took full advantage of the aftermath to destroy their dissident Marxist rivals, weaken the anarchists and defeat their social revolution once and for all. The most flagrant case is that of Nin, who disappeared after being taken to Alcalá de Henares near Madrid. POUM supporters (and Orwell) believed he had been killed by the NKVD, the Soviet secret police, while the communists claimed he had been rescued by Nazi agents disguised as Republican police and escaped to Berlin. The true story didn't fully emerge until the Moscow archives were opened in the 1990s, demonstrating that he was indeed abducted from a Republican jail by Soviet NKVD agents and murdered, probably on 22 June after being horribly tortured. His body has never been found.

Other POUM leaders were arrested by the state and put on trial in Barcelona in October 1938, which took place in the wider context of the Moscow Trials and generalised communist hysteria against left dissidence. Referring to the case, the prominent communist Dolores Ibárruri, better known as "La Pasionaria", declared in a public meeting in Valencia:

> If there is an adage which says that in normal times it is preferable to acquit a hundred guilty ones than to punish a single innocent one, when the life of a people is in danger it is better to convict a hundred innocent ones than to acquit a single guilty one.

Despite these pressures, the trial followed due process, and in the end and much to the disgust of the communists, the POUM's leaders were absolved of treason and espionage, which would have carried the death penalty. Instead, they were convicted of the lesser offence of having publicly supported an illegal rebellion and sentenced to long terms in prison.[3] The Spanish Republican state also exploited the failure of the Catalan republicans to govern the city's streets in order to suspend the region's statute of autonomy. It would seem the underlying causes of the May

Days were quite distinct from how the events themselves were capitalised upon by those who emerged victorious.

Orwell's wounding and escape

After the May Days, Orwell no longer wished to—nor could— enlist with the International Brigades as he had fought on the opposing side to the communists, and he went back, somewhat disillusioned, to his old POUM unit in Aragon on or around 10 May. Ten days later, he was shot through the neck by a sniper and almost killed.

After passing through a series of hospitals, he returned to Barcelona on 29 May to convalesce. Two weeks later, he made his way to see Eileen in the Hotel Continental. As he walked into the lobby, Eileen approached him and hissed in his ear "Get out!" The POUM had been banned, and the police were looking for him, she explained. Orwell spent the next three nights sleeping in bombed-out buildings, a fugitive from the Republican government for whom he had come to fight. On 23 June, the couple managed to catch a train and escape into France. With Eileen's help, he had completed the manuscript for *Homage to Catalonia* by New Year 1938, but his old publisher Victor Gollancz wouldn't touch it due to his denunciation of communist policy in Spain and the book's wider criticism of the Republican government. Eventually published by Secker & Warburg, it sold very few copies until the 1960s, long after Orwell's death in 1950.

Today, *Homage* is probably the most widely read book in English about the Spanish Civil War and often the only book on the subject anyone reads. This is problematic because Orwell saw very little of the war: a small amount of fighting in Aragon and some important events in Barcelona. He also wrote it as he understood things in 1938, overplaying the role of the Soviets in the Republican government and defending the POUM's revolutionary line as a way of winning the war. Few historians today would agree the latter was possible, and Orwell himself modified his understanding of the war in *Looking Back on the Spanish War*. However, *Homage* is a superb memoir by a man who was prepared to risk his life fighting fascism. He conveys what it felt like both to experience a revolution and to be bored in the trenches with little of the necessary equipment. The writing is beautiful and measured, evoking the sights, sounds, and smells, and shows great empathy for those around him.

Georges Kopp wasn't so fortunate. He was arrested, and despite Orwell's brave attempts at getting him released, he was left languishing in atrocious conditions in a makeshift prison. After undergoing a series of prisons and camps, including interrogation by the NKVD, who thankfully didn't realise he was Russian, he was released in December 1938. On arrival in England, he weighed 44 kilos, his body was covered in scars and he had blood poisoning and scurvy. He died in 1951, a year after Orwell, from a blood clot, probably arising from his experiences in Barcelona's jails and his war wounds from fighting with the French in the Second World War.

7

BELCHITE AND THE FALL OF ARAGON

We are now in the summer of 1937. The war is going badly for the Republic. The Basque Country has fallen, and Franco's forces are closing in on Cantabria and Asturias. In an attempt to stop the Francoist onslaught, the Republic launched a major push north towards Zaragoza in Aragon on 24 August. All this achieved was to slow things down, with Franco merely pulling out some planes to defend positions before continuing with their final attack on the Cantabrian capital of Santander, which fell on 26 August. Asturias would be next. Meanwhile, Republican forces surrounded the small town of Belchite before continuing towards the Aragonese capital. The offensive soon petered out, so they turned their attention back to the town as a consolation prize.

Back to Aragon

A white bridge takes us across the wide Ebro. If you look at a satellite view, the river is a painting of a green serpent winding through a dry land. But modern agriculture, supported by

EU subsidies, heavily irrigated, fertilised and ugly, has arrived, the artificial green vividly contrasting with the pastel hues of uncultivated areas, dotted with clumps of shrubs. Monster machines stand by, ready to water the parched ground, while solar and wind farms bring money to a poor region.

The road now rises and winds into wilder farmland and uncultivated steppe lands. Wildlife suddenly seems to be everywhere: rabbits flit, and partridges scuttle across the road, griffon vultures circle overhead, a hen harrier quarters low over a stony field, and we all admire the bushy-tailed fox as it scrambles up the rocks and away from us. It feels as if we have driven into an arid paradise. Around 70 per cent of the steppe has been lost, but most of the remaining 30 per cent enjoys some form of protection. There's now a plan to turn what's left into Spain's next National Park, providing a haven for its unique flora and fauna, including the possible reintroduction of the endangered Iberian lynx into these lands. We stop at El Planerón, a bird reserve run by SEO (Sociedad Española de Ornitología), set up to protect this unusual habitat. It's a magnificent rolling plain, framed by low hills and decked now in spring wildflowers. I've walked around here before and singularly failed to see its star species: stone curlews, pin-tailed sandgrouse and the incredibly rare Dupont's lark, luring Spanish and foreign naturalists to catch fleeting glimpses. Scarce birds and old wars both bring tourists from the north to this out-of-the-way corner of Aragon.

Then, in the late afternoon, we arrive at Belchite. Here more than anywhere in Spain, you can imagine the sheer violence of war and the killing unleashed by the military coup (see Fig. 7.1). It is written in stone. Walking around these ruins, unique in Europe, you can perhaps feel what the dictatorship represented for all those who lost the war. But, in truth, nor did the Republic's military commanders have much to be proud of for what they did to this place. Decades of abandonment followed the devastation wrought by two offensives—one Republican, one Francoist—destroying an urban fabric 1,000 years in the making.

In July 1936, Belchite was a sizable, bustling town within an Aragonese context with a population of around 7,500. It boasted two substantial churches, two convents and a monastery all built in the Mudéjar style, common in much of southern Aragon. The Mudéjares were the Muslims who had stayed after the Christian conquest. Over the years, many converted but maintained their traditions, including construction methods influenced by Islamic architecture, which involved employing ornamental motifs and patterns, often using ornate brickwork, to decorate public buildings, particularly churches.

The right defeated the Popular Front in the wider Belchite district in the February 1936 general election, although the town council itself was won by the socialist PSOE. Tensions were rising, as elsewhere in the country in the following months. The attempted coup of July unleashed a murderous response by the town's right against the left. There were mass arrests; 300 people were shot, many against the cemetery wall. Others managed to escape across Republican lines. In contrast, as the front was so close, many families identified as supporters of the military coup had by 1937 left their homes and moved to towns farther away. However, more than 2,000 civilians remained, mainly women, children and the elderly.

The first battle

Belchite was defended by 2,000 well-armed and bunkered men. This was a strategy developed during the colonial wars in Morocco, where the Spanish military concentrated their efforts on strongholds as their lack of resources prevented control of the wider territory. On 1 September 1937, Republican forces began their assault with a heavy artillery bombardment supported by

Soviet-built Polikarpov I-15s, nicknamed *chatos* (snub noses). They were flown by the first young Spanish pilots to graduate from the Soviet training school at Kirovabad in Azerbaijan.[1] At Belchite, dog fights raged overhead, while a bloody battle ensued street by street. The final onslaught was carried out by the XV Brigade, including English-speaking volunteers and the predominantly Balkan Dimitrov battalion. Their losses were appalling.

We are taken around by local guide Juan Carlos Salavera. Today, he lives in the New Belchite, built by the Franco regime after the war. He tells us he used to play in the ruins as a child. I'm sure I would have very much liked to do the same: a massive unsupervised playground for him and his friends to explore (see Figs 7.2 and 7.3). Over the years, Juan Carlos became drawn to the history. "As I learnt more, people started asking if I could guide them around and the tours took off." Later, he became head of tourism for Belchite town council under the PSOE. In 2015, the conservative PP won back control, and he was replaced by a more politically comfortable appointment, something, for that matter, that is standard practice among all political parties in Spain. The council didn't close the site—too many people were visiting—but Belchite is now sold simply as a historical site and as a "monument for peace". When I booked online again for another visit, I was confronted with a short insipid text in Spanish at pains not to offend anyone: "Walk the streets of Pueblo Viejo learning about the events that took place during the days of the Battle of Belchite." Every time I've been, the narrative craves to appear as "impartial" to either side as possible. Would we expect such "even-handedness" about a visit to a battle site from the Second World War? This apparent non-partisan approach seems absent from the official narrative around the Ebro battle, as I would learn.

Since the local council fenced off the site in 2013 and started charging for guided tours, demand has grown. They do twenty to forty tours a week. More than 40,000 people visited in 2023, making it surely the most visited Spanish Civil War site by far (if we discount the art rooms dedicated to the conflict with Picasso's *Guernica* at the Reina Sofia in Madrid and Barcelona's MNAC). In one sense, visiting the ruins has lost something. I had more feeling of the horror of war walking silently around on my own. But turning it into an organised visit was the right thing to do. It brings visitors and gives work to the guides. Depopulation and unemployment are issues in the area. And it provides a stage allowing the story to be told.

We walk along the main street. No bustle, shops, children playing. Just rubble piled here, a pock-marked house still standing sadly there, beams pitted with woodworm strewn on piles of broken bricks, window frames in lone walls, everything else that was a home gone, streets blocked with ruin forever, all witnesses of violence and fear and loss. Poppies, ox-eyed daisies and other wildflowers grow among the old stones, nature slowly covering up the crime. The signs of any modern war you care to think of are all here. Sarajevo, Kandahar, Aleppo, Gaza, of course ... There are fifteen of us: a couple from Barcelona, a group of French tourists and our carload.

Juan Carlos also tells us about the battle waged here in June 1809, when Napoleon's Polish-French troops took Belchite. The town's name, he says, is inscribed on the Arc de Triomphe in Paris, one of 158 battles listed that commemorate French victories during the Revolutionary and Napoleonic Wars. He also explains it was one of the most important towns in the province in the 1930s, second only to Zaragoza. But most of his story is centred on the Civil War. Again, he's careful to seem impartial. He sticks to the bare facts. The fighting was brutal, waged house to house, room to room, using modern artifices but also with bayonets and knives. Goya's ghosts come to me, leering through gaps in the walls, drawing cruel deaths. He was born barely 20 kilometres to the west at Fuendetodos. It's well worth a visit to his house and the museum that exhibits prints of his *Disasters of War*. Here in Belchite, the shells of some buildings are gaping holes, knocked through from outside by Republican troops. American brigader Bill Bailey described how it was done: "We would knock a hole through a wall with a pickaxe, throw in a few hand grenades, make the hole bigger, climb through into the next house, and clear it from cellar to attic. And by God, we did this, hour after hour."[2]

In the Second World War, this technique came to be known as mouse-holing. Lessons learned in battles like Belchite and above all in the earlier defence of Madrid would be applied to great effect by Soviet troops at Stalingrad, while some units of the British Home Guard were initially taught guerrilla warfare techniques learned in Spain by Tom Wintringham, who had commanded the British Battalion at Jarama, and who, incidentally, was wounded in the same offensive farther north at Quinto.

The defenders fought incredibly bravely. Many were ideologically hardened Falangists and Guardia Civil, but many others believed that the Republic automatically shot all Nationalist soldiers, as their officers had told them. This was not an unlikely fate for their commanders, but Republicans generally looked on Franco's rank-and-file troops as either forced to fight against their will or having been duped by propaganda. Some of the defenders were recently recycled Republican prisoners who could not be trusted and were forced to take off their footwear to prevent them escaping. In some cases, they appear to have helped the attackers by shooting their commanding officers at key moments. The resisters would have folded more quickly had it not been for the support of planes flying in supplies. However, despite promises given by radio to desperate commanders, there was no relief column. A few airdrops aside, Belchite was the only town allowed to fall by Franco during the war, something certainly absent from the later regime propaganda surrounding the battle.

By the time the surviving defenders surrendered on 6 September, 5,000 or 6,000 (nobody knows the true figure) of the dead from both sides—including women and children—lay in the summer heat, the stench drifting for miles around the surrounding countryside. Bailey continued: "The dead were piled in the street, almost a storey high, and burnt. The engineers kept pouring on gasoline until the remains sank down. Then they came with big trucks and swept up the ashes. The whole town stank of burning flesh."

We needed to get away from the town. It was early December, so we drove south to the Laguna de Gallocanta. Windmills were busy on the horizon; you're never far from a turbine these days in Spain. We arrived just in time at sunset as the continental cold swept in. Wrapped in scarves, hats and gloves, we headed to a viewpoint. Above our heads, first a few, then dozens, then thousands of common cranes flew home to roost in the safety of the water after feeding in the surrounding farmland. As many as 60,000 stop off every winter at the lagoon, one of the largest saline lakes in Europe, on their migration between Northern Europe and their wintering grounds in Extremadura. Their collective calls, deep and resonant across the darkening sky, is a sound you'll never forget; it is one of the most evocative wildlife experiences anywhere in Europe. It was an invigorating moment of wildness to wash away the horror.

Context: the loss of Northern Spain

The Republic had taken Belchite. A town of scant importance, a few villages and a few hundred square kilometres of cereal steppe and olive groves had been won, but the offensive had lost its steam. Thousands had been killed or wounded on both sides, and the Republic had lost valuable tanks and planes. Meanwhile, the Nationalist assault on Northern Spain continued unabated. By 1 September, almost all of Cantabria was in Francoist hands. The offensive then moved into Asturias. On 21 October, Gijón was captured, bringing to an end the conquest of Northern Spain. Franco now controlled the industries of the Basque Country and Asturias, 60 per cent of Spain's coal production and all of the country's steel output. He was also able to re-deploy around 100,000 troops from the Republican army, who were either conscripted or used in forced labour battalions. The war was now firmly tipping in Franco's direction.

Context: the Battle of Teruel

For strategic reasons, the Republic launched a major offensive against the provincial capital of Teruel in southern Aragon on 15 December 1937. This remote, mountainous province is today the heartland of what is now sometimes called "Empty Spain" (España vacía), a land with one of the lowest population densities in Europe. It is also the coldest region in Iberia, where temperatures regularly drop to -10ºC in winter. That year, though, was worse. It was the coldest winter in decades, with the thermometer dropping to below -20ºC. Both armies' inadequate clothing and footwear was made worse by the difficulties of supplying the troops in an isolated area with such harsh terrain, resulting in 25,000 casualties from frostbite. The town itself was taken by Republican forces on 8 January 1938, after an incredibly dogged defence by the small Francoist garrison in some of the bloodiest fighting of the war—the only provincial capital ever won by its army. Franco's counterattack was not long in coming, and, after a series of terrible clashes in frozen expanses, the Nationalists recaptured the town on 22 February.[3] The losses on both sides were appalling: 40,000 dead and tens of thousands wounded, in addition to the frostbite. The Republican army was exhausted, had lost huge amounts of material, especially tanks and planes, and was ill-prepared for the large-scale offensive in Aragon that Franco now launched.

Context: the collapse of the Aragon Front

On 6 March 1938, shortly after taking Teruel, Franco launched a surprise, massive offensive along the Aragon Front, backed by almost 200 planes, an equal number of tanks and thousands of trucks. The Republican army, severely depleted materially after Teruel, was soon routed across the region. Belchite, where the Francoist defenders had held out for two weeks, seven months previously, now fell to General Yagüe in a day and a half on 10 March after a short, desperate resistance by the same XV International Brigade that had initially helped take the town. The demoralised Republicans panicked and fell back chaotically to Caspe.

Belchite again

Part of the destruction you see as you walk around Belchite today was wrought in this second battle as Franco's Condor Legion ally bombed the town in wave after wave. Juan Carlos now led us to perhaps the most dramatic ruin, La Iglesia de San Martín de Tours, standing there as a cavernous shell, its roof long gone, ugly holes in its scarred walls. This is often the image shown of the old town in the media. When I first visited in the early 1990s, a large flock of sheep with clanking bells around their necks grazed around the ruined church, accompanied by their shepherd, an attractive Romantic pastiche if you want. Now, we wander around San Martín's cavernous ruin. Ugly, violent holes are blasted through its walls, a gaping blue sky shows where the roof once stood. One of the wooden doors bears the words in large painted letters, "Pueblo viejo de Belchite, ya no te rondan zagales, ya no se oirán las jotas, que cantaban nuestros padres" ("Old town of Belchite, boys no longer ramble your streets, the *jotas* sang by our parents are no longer heard"). They are the words of a *jota*, the song and dance style strongly associated with Aragon, written by Natalio Baquero, who was born on the very first day of the offensive. Melancholy for their lost town is not far below the surface of every local I've heard speak.

Volunteers from Ireland and a trip to San Pedro

Irish Brigader Bob Doyle, aged twenty-one, fought that day in 1938 in Belchite. He remembered defending one of the town's churches with a Russian machine gun, which jammed. "I threw it down and picked up a rifle. I stood up and started firing till it got too hot. I don't know how I wasn't killed, because the bullets were flying everywhere." Captured by Italian fascists two weeks later in the chaotic retreat, he was sent to the hell of San Pedro de Cardeña, a Francoist concentration camp in the disused monastery near Burgos 350 kilometres to the northwest, where hunger, humiliation and beatings were everyday staples.

A few months after my visit to Belchite, I managed to pay a visit to the old monastery. The guided tour around the ancient buildings was led at some speed by a Trappist monk. He explained it was founded around 900 CE by the Benedictines from Cluny in France. This was once the most powerful ecclesiastical centre in Castile and represented a key stopover on the Camino de Santiago in the Middle Ages. He emphasised with some pride that it was also the resting place for the Castilian mercenary hero El Cid, who died in 1099, until Napoleonic troops sacked the abbey during the Peninsular War—his remains, the monk told us, now lie in Burgos cathedral. We also learned that Babieca, El Cid's legendary horse, was buried in the monastery, as is remembered in a memorial bust at the front of the complex. All interesting I'm sure, but when I asked the monk at the end about the use of the building as a concentration camp during the war, he quickly sniffed that it was elsewhere in the abbey, and anyway, it was best not to talk about such things, before turning away. A defaced, fading information panel put up by a previous Burgos town council outside the monastery is the only reminder of what happened here.

Doyle records his experiences in his moving, stoical and at times humorous memoir *Brigadista: An Irishman's Fight against Fascism* (2006), which charts his life from a harrowing childhood in Dublin church orphanages to Spain and trade union activism in Britain. He died in 2009 aged ninety-two, the last of some 270 volunteers from the Irish Republic to take up arms against Franco. Sometime later in Barcelona, I met Irish historian David Convery, who has researched their role. He explained over a coffee their attitudes towards the Catholic Church:

> They would have grown up with Catholicism. For most Irish families at the time it was a very strong cultural tradition and even if they were anticlerical or did not believe, they were still greatly influenced by the culture. It was also a very different sort of Catholicism from that of Spain at the time. The Irish Church had been underground or oppressed for centuries under British rule so it was more of a grassroots religion for the masses rather than one aligned to the state, the military and big landowners as it was in Spain. The Irish brigaders, even if they didn't personally believe, were uneasy when they saw the levels of anticlericalism, particularly the desecrated churches with imagery and icons shot through by bullets. They also didn't like having lunch in mess halls in converted churches. They'd write home to their families to convince them that it was not a war against Catholicism, that rather they were there to fight fascism.

The Irish volunteers are remembered in Moore's "Viva La Quinta Brigada", which I'd heard sung with different lyrics in Huesca during the Orwell ceremony. Recorded in 1999, it's my favourite contemporary song in English about the war. There's a great version on YouTube of Moore's song played live at the Barrowland in Glasgow. The partisan crowd know all the words. There is also a stirring rendition belted out by Celtic fans waving Spanish Republican flags at Parkhead at the Champions League game against Real Madrid in September 2022. Madrid won 3–0.

Moore also name-checks the Irishmen who fought on the other side. Their leader Eoin O'Duffy had been chief of staff of the IRA and by 1936 was head of the fascist Blueshirts, a 40,000-strong paramilitary organisation in Ireland. Perhaps 2,000 volunteered for the so-called Irish Brigade, of whom around 700 made it to Spain, docking at Ferrol in Galicia in December 1936. Many were young conservative Catholics who believed press reports of priests' heads being on sale in Barcelona's La Rambla. David explained further to me:

> O'Duffy was an out-and-out fascist as were many of those who led the Irish Brigade, but most of the volunteers were simply taken in by the propaganda that it was a war to save Catholicism from a communist uprising. Franco was seen as its saviour. It was in every local paper in Ireland. It was on the newsreels. It was everywhere. However, once O'Duffy's volunteers got here, there was a lot of disillusionment. They saw how the portrayal back home differed from the reality. And their deployment was less than distinguished, and some were killed in a confused action at Jarama when they found themselves mistakenly fighting against a Falangist unit. Most came home in June 1937. Only a few died, while a handful stayed on because they were committed to Franco's crusade.

In 1939, Franco sent O'Duffy a message thanking him for his support in "the victory of the Spanish Army in defence of

Christianity, occidental civilisation and humanity, over the forces of destruction and disorder".[4]

Memorial

Two days after his forces had taken Belchite, Franco paid a visit. Standing on the balcony of the Falange's headquarters in front of his troops, he proclaimed: "I swear to you that once the war is over ... on these ruins of Belchite a beautiful and spacious town will be built as a tribute to its unparalleled heroism." Whether he was lying or he changed his mind is not known, but a few months later a different plan was announced. New Belchite would be built not on the ruins but a few hundred metres away, while the old town would be left purposefully to crumble as a permanent monument to the heroic resistance of the defenders and a physical reminder of the Republic's barbarity (see Fig. 7.4). Across Spain, as I learned time and time again, Francoism was in part a cult of the dead, and Franco and his ideologues saw the power that lay in these ruins.

Similar ideas were considered for Gernika and the university campus in Madrid, although neither were enacted. Stéphane Michonneau, professor of contemporary history, has written that Belchite "represents the first large-scale attempt at conserving war ruins in Western Europe".[5] There are several examples of buildings or walls left purposely after the Second World War: Coventry Cathedral, maintained as a ruin to symbolise the Luftwaffe's bombardment of the city in 1940; Frauenkirche in Dresden, left as a memorial to the Allied destruction in 1945 for fifty years until its reconstruction after German reunification; Gerhardt's Mill in the former Stalingrad, kept to remember the building's vital role in the heroic Soviet defence of the city between 1942 and 1943. On a different scale is Oradour-sur-Glane in France. After the Second World War, Charles de Gaulle instructed that the village never be rebuilt but rather remain as a memorial to Nazi barbarity. On 10 June 1944, four days after D-Day, the beginning of the Allied invasion of Normandy, in reprisal for the capture of a German officer, a Waffen-SS company entered the settlement and murdered 643 human beings.[6] Their number included nineteen Spanish women and children aged between one and fifteen from six families, two of whom were from Aragon, who had gone into exile in 1939 escaping Franco.[7] Their fate epitomises the awful destiny of so many Republican refugees caught up in the Second World War.[8] But what is unique about the ruins of Belchite is their sheer size. This was a whole town. Discounting camps, they remain the largest war ruins anywhere in Europe outside of Ukraine. And its residents were forced to live in sight of the ruins as a reminder of the war to this day. It saw two relatively minor battles. It did not see complex troop movements with counter-offensives accompanied by the terrible protracted slaughter of Teruel or the Ebro. Its story lies not so much in its military importance but in its legacy.

Belchite not only witnessed violence during the fighting over its streets. First, as already mentioned, there were the 300 who had been shot by the Francoists by the time of the Republican offensive. A further 100, mainly Francoist officers and local Falangists, were executed by the Republicans in the area around the town after they took control in September 1937. And then a further wave of murder saw 200 more executions of people accused of leftist sympathies by the Franco regime, both after taking the town and in subsequent years. In all, this adds up to 10 per cent of the population, many of them among the most educated, talented and enterprising, who were murdered judicially or otherwise. In addition, the Franco regime used its new legal framework to confiscate 300 pieces of land and homes in and around the town out of a total number of confiscations of some 4,000 for the whole of Aragon.

Akin to much of Aragon, Belchite suffered a huge economic and social cost from the war and the post-war dictatorship, draining its economy and shattering its economic structures. Other factors such as the harsh climate and poor farmland added to the mix, leading to the migration of so many talented people to elsewhere in Europe and to Madrid and Barcelona. Has it ever recovered? Some 15 per cent of people born in Aragon live outside the region, half of whom are in Catalonia. Many settled in my own Barcelona neighbourhood of Poble-sec, including Ángeles Teresa, the mother of one of its most illustrious sons, the singer-songwriter Joan Manuel Serrat, a household name across Spain. There's a plaque on the wall of the apartment block where he was born in 1943 at Carrer del Poeta Cabanyes, 95, a couple of minutes' walk from ours. In a newspaper interview in 2012,[9] he explained that Franco's rebels—mainly Falangist militia—murdered his grandfather and thirty more family members in July 1936. When Franco's army entered Belchite for the second time in 1938, Ángeles, a young teenager, was sent by her parents to warn her uncle and aunt. By the time she got there, they had already been shot. She ran back in terror to tell her parents, only to find they had also been murdered. Ángeles managed to escape from the village under fire, trekking for days across plains and mountains until she reached Republican lines.[10] Years later, she married a Catalan anarchist called Josep Serrat in Barcelona. Their son Joan Manuel has written hundreds of love songs, but in "Cançó de bressol" (1967) he also sang the words:

> The lullaby that already spoke to me
> of my grandfather who sleeps at the bottom of a ravine,
> of a dusty road, of a white cemetery,
> and of vineyards, wheat fields and olive trees.

Of a virgin on a peak, of lanes and paths,
of all your brothers and sisters who died in the war.

At the end of the tour, Juan Carlos sprang a surprise. Much of the desolate panorama of ruins we walked through is not the direct result of war. Photos in particular after the Republican offensive and to a lesser extent after the Francoist assault testify to a town that while damaged was still largely standing. In the 1940s and '50s, Belchite's residents had nowhere to live except for the old town, so they made homes here, as best they could, in the houses that were still standing. As the new town was built and people were moved out, residents returned and pirated their old homes for materials to build the new town. Most of the destruction we see now is the result of buildings, weakened by war, collapsing through years of abandonment—as far as I can remember, there's a lot less standing now than when I first visited in the 1990s.

Caspe

The Francoist offensive continued unabated across Aragon as Republican lines all along the front collapsed. It was a rout, with troops fleeing in disarray. A week later, the rebel army, having swept through all those villages where the libertarian dream had briefly shone, reached Caspe, which had until August been the headquarters of the Regional Defence Council of Aragon. The town fell to Franco's forces on 17 March after a bloody three-day fight. Among the numerous casualties was Alfred "Chick" Chakin, the US People's Olympiad coach, who had joined the International Brigades in June the previous year. He never made it back home, disappearing in the retreat from the town.

I was making this stage of the journey with a couple of historian pals: Alan Warren, fellow Civil War guide and probably the biggest expert on the International Brigades on the ground anywhere, and Ulrich Eumann, who has since sadly passed away. Ulrich was working as an archivist at the ex-Gestapo headquarters in Cologne, now a museum and record centre for Nazi atrocities in the city. It was Ulrich's trip really. He was following the steps in Spain of Willi Remmel, a German communist and International Brigader from his home city. An hour out from Barcelona, we stopped for a quick break in a layby next to an abandoned textile mill. There must be hundreds of these decaying old factories scattered across Catalonia, vestiges of a nineteenth-century industrial past that had earned it the nickname of the Lancashire of Spain. We were soon greeted by a tall, handsome young man with a wispy brown moustache hiking along the road with a gigantic red rucksack, unperturbed by the lorries thundering past. We all noticed the large wooden cross swinging around his neck—it's just not something that young people in any numbers at all wear in Catalonia today. Kacper was from Łódź, Poland, and told us he was walking from Barcelona to Santiago de Compostela, a journey of well over 1,000 kilometres and not a form of the pilgrimage I've ever heard of anyone else doing. He was paying homage to his grandfather, who had taken up arms against the Nazis in the liberation of Warsaw in 1945. Unsurprisingly, perhaps, he knew nothing of the 5,000 Poles who fought in the International Brigades. Their history, as I would learn, is ignored when not vilified in today's Poland, and if we had told him, Kacper might have been uncomfortable hearing about our journey following a German communist. Still, this chance happening felt like an auspicious start as we too were on an anti-fascist historical pilgrimage of sorts, albeit of a different ilk.

As we drove, the subject came up of how we first became aware of the Civil War. For Ulrich, it was the songs by the German singer Ernst Busch, but Alan had the best story:

My father knew an old man in County Cork who had been a member of O'Duffy's Blueshirts, the Irish fascists who had fought for Franco.

He missed the boat to go and "fight for Christ" and ended up in Victoria Station in London trying to get to Spain. There he met two Irishmen who were also heading there, but to fight in the International Brigades so he tagged along, even though they were going to fight for the Republic. He ended up joining the Brigades and it must have changed his outlook as I remember him being incredibly left wing. I met him when I was about twelve. I was very curious why he had had a "Road to Damascus" experience. Years later I asked my father what his name was, but he couldn't remember. He'll be dead of course by now, and I could probably find his name in ten minutes, but if he wants to be found, he will probably appear by chance in a book I am reading. Then I can quietly thank him for inspiring me!

We parked by the empty roadside and walked the few metres up to the top of the ridge. The scent of thyme and rosemary was pungent in the spring breeze, while larks rose vertically in the air, performing their bubbly songs. To the southwest, the low rise looked back across a sloping plain towards Belchite. To the northeast, we looked down on Caspe. I have fond if very hazy memories of the small town from my first year in Spain back in 1988. I spent some rather alcohol-infused weekends in the bars and disco with Luis, the friend from Zaragoza, and his mates. They liked to describe their village as "el Wild West". Having recently arrived from England, it felt a bit like a frontier-land: people drove drunk without seatbelts, and the young, middle-aged and old danced in the all-night disco. Looking back, it seems like a microcosm of 1980s Spain, a country swept by an apolitical, hedonistic culture after the slab of the dictatorship had been lifted.

Willi Remmel

On the ridge above Caspe, Ulrich and I came to a trench. It had been hacked into the hard stony ground, and ran 300 metres, zigzagging along the ridge to stop the track of enemy shrapnel. It must have been back-breaking work, but it's so shallow you'd have to crawl on your hands and knees to avoid getting a bullet. There'd have been sandbags, Alan had pointed out, and it was probably a bit deeper then, but not much. Several information panels erected by the Aragonese government inform us that the line was built by the Republican army as an advance defence of the town. As we sat in a concrete bunker, looking down over the plain and watching the skylarks, Ulrich filled in details of Remmel's life. Born in Cologne in 1906, as a young man he worked at the huge Klöckner Humboldt Deutz car factory. A communist and active anti-Nazi, he was arrested in 1935 and taken to the EL-DE Haus, Gestapo headquarters in Cologne, where he was tortured and imprisoned: this is Ulrich's workplace now, and the reason why he became interested in Remmel's story. After seven months of torment, he was conditionally released and on New Year's Eve 1936 managed to slip across the border into the Netherlands. On 29 May 1937, he boarded a ship called the *Ciudad de Barcelona* in Marseille bound for Spain, one of some 3,000 anti-Nazi Germans to fight against Franco, most of whom, like Juan Guzmán (Hans Gutmann), author of the famed Marina Ginestà photograph, fought in the Thälmann Battalion of the International Brigades.

Remmel was one of 250 to board that day. On the evening of the next day, 30 May 1937, it was spotted by an Italian submarine sold to Franco's navy. The captain desperately tried to bring his ship as close to the shore as possible to save its passengers. After the first torpedo missed its target, a second hit the stern full-on. The ship went down in just four minutes near Malgrat de Mar, 70 kilometres northeast of Barcelona.[11] More than sixty brigaders drowned, but Remmel and some 150 others managed to swim the 400 metres to the shore. "So," smiled Ulrich, "Willi swam to Spain. He was a good swimmer, he'd been a member of a club in Cologne."

Wounded in the leg near Brunete on 17 July 1937, Remmel was evacuated to the English hospital in Huete, Cuenca, run by the British Medical Unit. Here, he was cared for by New Zealand nurse René Shadbolt, who described him as "elegant, eloquent and wispy bearded."[12] The two soon fell in love. Remmel was back to the front by October, fighting at Teruel, Quinto and Belchite, before his unit fell back to the line here outside Caspe. As Ulrich talked, I tried to imagine the atmosphere among his comrades in this exposed trench a few minutes before General Yagüe's troops attacked. Outnumbered and facing far better weaponry, the German 11th Brigaders resisted for two days until 17 March 1938. Exhausted and hungry, Remmel and the survivors managed to get back to Republican lines and two weeks later crossed the River Ebro.

Remmel came back over the river in July 1938 as part of the Republican army's Ebro Offensive—we'll come to this—during which he was wounded again, this time hit by shrapnel in his back. He was brought to a hospital at Mataró on the Catalan coast on 20 August and reunited with René a month later. They were soon married in a civil ceremony in the hospital grounds. After the International Brigades were disbanded in October, René tried to take her husband with her to New Zealand, but her country's authorities refused to recognise their Republican marriage certificate. They never saw each other again. Like many brigaders, after crossing the border into France in February 1939, Remmel was held in a series of internment camps, where the severe conditions were eased by the money René managed to send him. After the Nazi invasion of France in May–June 1940, he was arrested and deported to Sachsenhausen, Buchenwald and then Mauthausen, where, as we'll see, he would have encountered Spanish Republicans. In 1946, having survived the camp system,

Remmel chose to move to the Soviet occupation zone of Germany. Ulrich pointed out that while other former brigaders played a key role in building the new communist state of East Germany,[13] Remmel himself was very much an object of suspicion and was soon sidelined for being "independently minded". He died in Leipzig in 1970. Shadbolt passed away in Auckland seven years later.

We left the bunker and headed back to the car, Alan driving us in the same direction Remmel and his German comrades had retreated from as they avoided strafing by Nazi planes and fought a rear-guard action before reaching the safety of the opposite banks of the Ebro.

Lleida

The road took us east out of the Aragonese steppe into Catalonia and the fertile Pla de Lleida, a vast agricultural plain, much of it covered in apple orchards and famed for its freezing winter fogs when temperatures regularly fall to -10°C compared to summer highs of 40°C plus. Franco's forces took a great chunk of the province as their offensive progressed into April 1938. We continued past the city of Lleida, the old cathedral standing on the steep hill surrounded by apartment blocks. On 27 March 1938, the town was heavily bombed by the Condor Legion, causing an estimated 400 deaths and a mass exodus of civilians across the River Segre into the Republican hinterland. By the time Lleida fell after fierce fighting on 3 April, perhaps a couple of thousand of the 40,000 residents remained. Hundreds had been killed earlier in the war in air raids, including on 2 November 1937, when up to 250 died. The crime, committed by the Italian fascist air force, was immortalised the next day in a photograph taken by Centelles. You see a wife's inconsolable grief as she kneels over her husband Gabriel Pernau i Sans' outstretched corpse in the city's cemetery. Maria Riu i Esqué's expression is a universal symbol of pain and loss.

Gandesa

It was an hour's drive south from Lleida. Alan's instructions by phone sent us to a dirt track flanked by a low embankment at the top of which stood an almond orchard in full blossom. The air was alive with birdsong, and white petals lay scattered across the bare winter soil. I was now travelling with local historian Andreu Caralt, who has written several books on the conflict and who with his partner Maite runs "Terra Enllà", which specialises in tours in Catalan on the Ebro battle.

"I think this is the spot," Andreu said, looking at his mobile. We stared, silent now, down at the track below. On 2 April 1938, fifty American volunteers were captured as Gandesa fell, a few kilometres from the safety of the Ebro River. The next morning, stripped to their underwear, they were marched here and machine-gunned, one by one, on the embankment's edge. A single man, wounded, managed to crawl away.[14] On the other side of the village, we came to a field of gnarled vine stumps overlooking the cemetery. Somebody had inserted a wreath of flowers, now long dead, into the single almond tree (see Fig. 7.5). White petals—from the almond—again decorated the ground. Then, Andreu and I turned towards the vines: there was a semicircle, perhaps 10 metres across, of bare, toiled ground where no vines grew. "Farmers often do this in the Ebro if they know *something* is underneath," Andreu explained. It was here the Americans were probably buried. There seemed to be an absence of two kinds: of crops but also of recognition.

Alan told me he'd been shown the sites by Antoni Blanch, a pioneering local historian. Blanch had interviewed an old man who'd been forced to dig the grave as a sixteen-year-old boy.

Blanch had worked the area with a metal detector and found nothing, but if the account of the Americans being unclothed is true, this is hardly surprising. Blanch died in 2014, and the American survivor of the massacre is surely long gone. The threads of memory are snapping one by one. "Perhaps one day they'll do an excavation," says Andreu.

We leave the field of vines, driving along a back road of life-affirming beauty, which I would never have found: a narrow, low, intimate valley of tidy little fields, shimmering with a thousand almonds in blossom that brought us to the edge of the old village of Corbera, lying in ruins since 1938, as I would learn. We got out of the car. Beside a pomegranate tree, the shrunken balls of last year's fruit still on its branches, is a memorial to American commander Robert Merriman. He had retreated close to the village with his men on 2 April and passed over the hills to the vineyards not knowing that it had already fallen. Merriman is thought to be among those executed, although his body has never been found. Months earlier, Hemingway had met the tall American communist in Madrid and was impressed. He is widely believed to have inspired the character Robert Jordan in *For Whom the Bell Tolls*. A ceremony held here in April 2018 unveiled the plaque where Marcus Mandojana, the US consul general soon to be replaced by the first Trump administration, insisted on having himself photographed with the flag of the Abraham Lincoln Battalion, paying homage to an American communist. It reads in Catalan "Robert Merriman: Per la vostra llibertat i la nostra" ("For your freedom and ours").

Context: Franco holds back

Against the advice of German and Spanish commanders who recommended keeping up the drive all the way to Barcelona to finish Catalonia off, Franco, despite the evident disarray of the enemy's troops, decided to hold back and continue his offensive farther south. The Nationalist forces reached the sea at Vinaròs in the Valencia region on 15 April 1938 and within a few days held a stretch of 64 kilometres of the Mediterranean coastline, thereby splitting Republican territory into two. Again, the Republic had lost millions of tonnes of valuable equipment, thousands of troops had been killed and 12,000 had been taken prisoner. Moreover, the loss of the hydroelectric plants in the Catalan Pyrenees almost stopped industrial production in Barcelona. Meanwhile, the Republican army, licking its wounds, managed, in a fashion, to re-establish defensive positions behind three interconnected rivers: the Noguera Ribagorçana, the Segre and the Ebro. These were defended by a line of fortifications, trenches, bunkers and machine gun nests that stretched for 300 kilometres from the French frontier down through Catalonia to the Ebro Delta.

8

THE BATTLE OF THE EBRO

Context: background to the Ebro battle

By the spring of 1938, two years into the conflict, Franco was clearly winning the war. As a result of supplies of modern military equipment from Germany and Italy, Franco's forces were slowly but surely grinding the Republic down in a war of attrition.

With Catalonia separated from the remainder of Republican territory following the rebel army's spring offensive and with Franco's forces moving south to threaten the capital of Valencia, the Loyalist high command conceived a major offensive back across the Ebro. Apart from relieving pressure on Valencia, and, hopefully, reconnecting Catalonia with the rest of Republican Spain, this was also seen as a way of gaining a victory to improve beleaguered morale. Another aim was to try to convince the Western democracies that the Republic was not finished and could sustain the conflict until what it and many others saw as the inevitable great clash between fascism and democracy.

A new fighting unit, the Army of the Ebro, was established in the spring of 1938 under communist officer Juan Modesto. Large shipments of weapons including artillery had arrived from

Czechoslovakia and the USSR when France, briefly under a new Popular Front government, had opened the border in March. The Republican air force had also been considerably bolstered by the arrival of new Soviet planes. However, the military lacked reserves of arms, equipment and artillery after the collapse of the Aragon Front. The fall of this more sympathetic government in France in April 1938 and intense British pressure led to the renewed closure of the frontier in June. On the west bank of the river, Franco's lines were commanded by General Yagüe, notorious for his role in the massacres at Badajoz in 1936. He had ignored intelligence reports detailing Republican preparations as he believed the Republic was incapable of launching a proper offensive. Yagüe's forces included hardened Legionnaires, Falangists, Carlists and Regulares, although many were young, untested recruits.

The Ebro River

Faraway, in the Cantabrian mountains of Northern Spain, rises a small stream. Quickly growing into a river, it makes its way across País Vasco, La Rioja, Navarra, the drylands of central Aragon, engorged by Pyrenean rivers on the way, and into Catalonia, where more than 900 kilometres later it finally empties into the sea, forming the Mediterranean's second largest delta, dwarfed only by the mighty Nile. The Ebro is also the longest river entirely in Spain, second only to the Tajo in the Iberian Peninsula. Its importance is perhaps reflected in the name of the peninsula itself, which, according to a widely accepted theory— others exist—comes from the river, known to the ancient Greeks as the Iber, which may ultimately derive from the Basque *ibai* (river) and *ibar* (valley). Once navigable as far as Zaragoza, 200 kilometres inland, the 3,000 dams and weirs along its journey and its tributaries have sapped its flow, meaning you wouldn't get far today in a boat. Most were either built during the Primo de

Rivera dictatorship or the Franco regime to irrigate the drylands. Before this tamed Ebro reaches the sea, it cuts through a series of rugged limestone hills including Els Aüts, the Serra de Cavalls and the Serra de Pàndols. The Republican plan involved crossing to the western bank, occupied by Franco's forces, and attempting to take the heights of these sierras and the strategic villages in the valleys.

My drive down from Barcelona took me past the shining chemical works of Tarragona before cutting inland across precipitous sierras. Then, a winding road took me through the intimate vineyards of El Priorat, growing impossibly steep on terraces and producing some of the finest wines in Europe, and into the Terra Alta—the High Land—where most of the fighting took place. Outside my window, a mosaic of olive and almond groves and vineyards grew on the better soils, the former producing superb oil, the latter strong red wine. Thick Mediterranean scrub and wood have encroached on the expanses of marginal, rocky and scarped land. Elsewhere, many steep slopes have been tamed with impressive dry-stone walling. The limestone bedrock emerges everywhere. I stopped at a layby to look at some black and white photos on my phone. Back in 1938, it was different: almost all of the land that could be farmed was cultivated. The poorer plots can hardly have provided a living in the dry, stony ground, with scant groundwater as any rain drains quickly through the karst bedrock. Aside from the short siege of Gandesa in 1838 during the First Carlist War (see Appendix for Carlism), not much history outside of its own concerns had ever happened here. There wasn't much to fight over. There's a dozen or so villages, the largest of which today is Gandesa with just over 3,000 inhabitants, about 10 per cent fewer than in 1936. This was the landscape in which the Battle of the Ebro was waged.

As I wound my window down, the scent of rosemary and thyme immediately swept in, expelling in a second the stale Barcelona air. The Battle of the Ebro was the longest and bloodiest of the war and perhaps the biggest ever fought on the Iberian Peninsula, involving some 200,000 to 250,000 troops between both armies and lasting 115 days. Looking out across a peaceful orchard of peach trees, it was all so hard to conjure. Estimates vary, but as many as 35,000 men were killed and more than 130,000 wounded—around half of those involved.[1] They were slain by the bombs, shells, bullets, grenades and bayonets aided by heat exposure and thirst. Most were terribly young. Thousands lie in mass graves buried under a thin mantle of earth. The Ebro was also the largest battle—in terms of troops, casualties and ordnance—fought in Europe in the twentieth century outside the two world wars. The world's press and attention were focused on this little corner of Catalonia for the first and only time in its history, with daily reports from newspapers such as *The Times*, *The Manchester Guardian*, *The New York Times*, *L'Humanité*, *Paris-Soir*, *Pravda* and the *Völkischer Beobachter*, the chief mouthpiece of the Nazi regime. People read about it and understood that it was a harbinger of what was to come. For many around the world at the time, and for some ever since, the river became associated with this battle. It is part of the long, tragic list of places most of us would never have heard of (Srebrenica, Mosul, Darfur, Bakhmut ...) but that enter the world's common geographical knowledge because of the killing that takes place there. Lark song drifted through the wild herbs as I started up the car and headed for my hostel.

Crossing

The Moorish castle, rebuilt by the Knights Templar as a fortress-monastery after its seizure in 1153, clings high above the village of Miravet, on the west bank of the Ebro. I walked down to a beach, just past the last of the houses. It was a hot night, the cicadas calling as they did in 1938, the dark water barely stirring at the river's edge. On the opposite bank from the reeds, the Republican army was able to wade across, as the water level is low just here. I checked my watch. It was 12.15 a.m. It was 25 July, the anniversary of the crossing.

The battle plan had been swiftly and meticulously drawn up under the command of General Vicente Rojo, a liberal Catholic who had chosen to remain loyal to his oath to the Republic. There was, however, a serious hurdle: how to launch a major offensive across a river, something that military manuals to this day advise should not be engaged in lightly. Numerous boats and the sections of the pontoon bridges were built in Barcelona. Troops were given swimming lessons and trained in river crossing without their knowing the objective. Meanwhile, commandos were sent over the river to learn from sympathetic peasants about the location and strength of Francoist positions. The moonless night of 24–5 July was chosen. At 12.15, swimmers stripped down and slipped into the dark water, clenching a knife between their teeth as they made for the reeds on the opposite bank. They surprised the relatively few Nationalist defenders, cutting their throats.[2] Once the advanced positions had been secured, hundreds of little boats and barges were pushed out across the dark river. In the coming hours, tens of thousands of men traversed the 100-metre-wide river at sixteen points, and by early morning the first pontoon bridges were up, soon to be strafed by the enemy's planes, now alerted to the magnitude of the offensive.

The Republican troops quickly gained positions in the nearby Els Aüts hills. Their forces, including the British Battalion of the International Brigades, then moved on to the town of Corbera, which was taken by the Polish-speaking XIII Dabrowski International Brigade on the evening of the 25th. From here, they were ordered to advance on to Gandesa, from where they had retreated in April, just 5 kilometres down the road. However,

Franco's forces had by now regrouped and managed to bring up reinforcements to defend the town and were able to repel the attack. The Republican offensive began to run out of steam and was soon answered by the first of six gruelling Francoist counter-offensives. The Republican army was now trapped in a pocket of rugged and militarily useless terrain, with the Ebro to its rear not only hindering its supply lines but also a quick retreat. It became a battle of attrition, a battle the Republic was incapable of winning since it did not have access to new supplies of weapons or men.

Corbera d'Ebre

We walked around the ruined streets of Corbera past the ghosts of houses (see Fig. 8.1). The scale is much smaller than Belchite, but the language of violent destruction wrought house upon house is the same. On the evening of 25 July, Republican troops regained control of Corbera, where Merriman and the other American brigaders had been shot in April. Republican troops now took back the village. In response, it was ceaselessly bombed by the Condor Legion and Mussolini's planes. American brigader Alvah Bessie passed through here on 7 August, writing in his diary: "[A] horrible shambles (planes and shells). The smell of the dead rotten-sweet through the dead streets, the shell-like houses, the very trees torn to shreds—nothing is left of the town."[3] Bessie himself had volunteered shortly after watching a newsreel of the destruction of Gernika with his wife at a cinema in New York. I wonder how many others came after seeing those images.

Corbera fell again to Franco's forces on 3 September. It was practically destroyed during the fighting. After the war, what was left of their homes around the hilltop and church were abandoned by the locals—unlike Belchite, the ruins weren't left on purpose as a reminder by the Franco regime: it simply provided no money for a new village. Corbera's residents set about haphazardly rebuilding a new settlement a couple of hundred metres down the hill, salvaging what materials they could from their old homes, itself a genuinely dangerous occupation given the amount of unexploded ordnance lying about. As at Belchite, as you walk around Corbera today, it is difficult to know what was destroyed by war and what is the result of decades of abandonment. The Spanish Civil War is a minefield of myths that are so easy to step on. Some years ago, I posted on Facebook that the ruins had been left as a form of punishment by the Franco regime. A contact, Ferran Cacho Zamora, who is from Corbera, corrected me:

> During the dictatorship, the old village was forgotten by everybody. Life only took place only in the new Corbera. The old ruins were almost a taboo, they simply stood there, but nobody talked about them and what they meant, as for many they represented the still painful symbol of the defeat in the war. With the return of democracy, little by little the feeling grew that we needed to preserve the ruins as a monument to the whole Ebro front.

These days, you pay a small admission charge to walk unhindered through the remains, which goes towards its upkeep. The high ruined church stands dramatically to one side, its roof recently restored. Inside, there are frequent art exhibitions with works related to peace and war. As you walk around the streets, you'll come across the artistically fashioned letters of an *Alphabet of Freedom* created by twenty-five different artists that appear here and there among the ruins. Each letter represents a humanist ideal. *P* for example is for *pau* (peace), *S* is for *solidaritat*. There are several memorials near the church. One is to the International Brigades, but the one that struck me most is a small plaque to the six men from Corbera d'Ebre who were deported to the Mauthausen concentration camp in Austria in 1941. Five were murdered. Six men from this little Catalan village ending up in a Nazi nightmare.

Hill 481

A group of us huff up the steep craggy path through an aromatic scrub of lavender, thyme and rosemary. Alan Warren tells me a story about an old Welsh brigader who for the rest of his life couldn't stand the smell of roast pork at Sunday lunch back in his homeland because the cooked flesh infused with rosemary brought him straight back to the horrors of the Ebro. Veterans from both sides often remembered how these Catalan hills stank of death. Bodies lay decomposing just a few metres from the lines. Men at the front were often given camphor balls to hang around their necks to hide the smell. Veterans also often remembered that the birds stopped singing. The cicadas didn't. They'd start up with their sawing no sooner had the shelling stopped.

An hour or so later, we reach the top of Cota or Hill 481 (most of the hills in the battle are named after their height). As the main Republican offensive ground to a halt outside Gandesa, the British Battalion was ordered to take this craggy knoll occupying a strategic position overlooking the town. Locally, it is called "Punta Targa". The Brits nicknamed the hill "The Pimple". There's a heck of a view, but in the scorching sun of 1938, it must have been hell for defenders and attackers alike. And there are quite a lot of trees and scrub today that would offer a semblance of cover. Back then, there was hardly a bush. The men, accompanied by many very young Spanish recruits, sustained appalling losses as they were mowed down by the machine guns fired on them from above and from shells blasted from Francoist positions. The battalion called off the attack on 3 August. Hundreds had been killed or wounded.

Among those who died was Lewis Clive, an Old Etonian and gold medal winner in rowing at the 1932 Olympic Games. He'd led the British troops, heroically by all accounts, in successive waves to try and take the hill. Alan later took me up a steep, winding wooded path to see a small concrete monolith erected during the battle near where he fell. Because of its secluded location, it is one of the very few Republican memorials to have survived the Franco dictatorship anywhere in Spain. It lists the names of Clive and thirty-four other officers of the International Brigade killed during the battle. I was struck by the incongruity of naming just the officers in the memorial rather than the rank and file, but perhaps I shouldn't have been, as the International Brigades were a conventional military force in terms of their structure, if not in their origin. Post-Francoist memorials to those who died in the battle are scattered across the landscape of the Terra Alta, including one at Hill 705 listing all of the British Battalion who died in the battle. It details their place of birth: Stoke, Manchester, Belfast, Glasgow, Rhondda, London, Dumbarton and so on. A high percentage came from working-class communities, their lives often scarred by the Great Depression. Included in the wounded at Hill 481 was young Liverpool volunteer Jack Jones, who became one the most powerful figures in British trade unionism in the 1970s as the General Secretary of the Transport and General Workers' Union. He remembered that day in Catalonia:

> There were many casualties and I became one of them. Once more I had clambered up the hill with my comrades, taking cover where we could and firing at the enemy wherever he appeared. The bullets of the snipers whizzed over, grenades and shells were striking the ground, throwing up earth and dust and showering us with shrapnel. Suddenly my shoulder and right arm went numb. Blood gushed from my shoulder and I couldn't lift my rifle. I could do nothing but lie

where I was. Near me, a comrade had been killed and I could hear the cries of others, complaining of their wounds. While I was lying there, to make things worse, a spray of shrapnel hit my right arm. The stretcher bearers were doing their best but could hardly keep up with the number of casualties. As night fell I made my own way, crawling to the bottom of the hill.[4]

The fight at Hill 481 is evocatively remembered in the song "Over the Ebro" by Teesside folk group The Young'uns. It forms part of a remarkable musical and theatrical project, *The Ballad of Johnny Longstaff*, which tells the story of the British brigader Johnny Longstaff, charting his journey from depression-era North East England, via the fight against Oswald Mosley at Cable Street in London, where he first heard the words *no pasarán*, before coming to Spain and crossing the river. The album has seventeen tracks, including a humorous tribute to Lewis Clive. Each song tells a story and is interspersed with recordings of Johnny's voice, at times on the edge of tears, recorded by the Imperial War Museum in the 1980s. "Over the Ebro" begins with Johnny's words: "Hill 408: There's a limit to any man's endurance." He died in 2000.

Franco's forces held on to Gandesa, and the Republican advance ground to a halt. On 6 August came the first of the six Francoist counter-offensives. The Republic was forced on to the defensive in trying to defend these rocky hills. Slowly, their resistance was worn down by more firepower, more planes, more tanks, more trucks, more Texaco oil, more and better-equipped and fed men.

On our way down, the frenzied electricity of cicadas fills the air. You can tell the temperature by the frequency with which they stridulate—by rubbing their forewings together. The hotter it is, the faster they rub. It was the incessant soundtrack for the men who fought here in 1938. Suddenly, the boom of a Spanish fighter plane thunders past, an F-18 I'm told, breaking the sky, manoeuvring spectacularly close to the crag edge. It feels like it is desecrating a wild place, reminding me of the British air force jets ruining the peace of the Cumbrian fells. Except, I've read it completely wrong. My companions tell me it's the grandson of a Republican pilot who returns here every year to pay homage to his grandfather who died in these skies in 1938. We are overcome. He banks and twists, and we imagine him returning to the past decimating Franco's command position with ultra-modern weapons. All a bit boyish and childish on our part. He turns and salutes us with a wave of the wing... Except later, we find out it's not true. It's an urban myth. The jet is a homage by the Spanish air force to those who fought and died on both sides. They send a plane every year on 25 July from Zaragoza. By my calculations, it's a seven-minute flight at 1,500 kilometres an hour to get here. My feeling is that it's fair that the state remembers the individual men and women who fought, suffered and died on both sides. To remember how they suffered, but not, I hope, at least, to equate both sides or honour the ideas that inspired the insurgent leaders and caused the conflict.

The enemy planes' arrival would strike fear in troops defending rocky outcrops with hardly any shelter in which to hide. The shout *avión* would cry out in warning when a plane was spotted. Every International Brigader knew this Spanish word, however poor their language skills. Aerial warfare was a major feature of the Ebro, with terrible dogfights fought in the skies over these limestone hills. Some of the most modern killing machinery then in existence was employed, including some of the latest models of planes, tanks and artillery, giving the idea of a battle equivalent to those waged in Western Europe during the Second World War. The Nazi Stukas, for instance, first used their screaming banshee sirens, a sound of the Blitzkrieg of the

Second World War, over these Catalan hills to sow terror among the Republic's soldiers.

While modern artifices were employed to deadly effect, on both sides much of the common soldier's kit would have been familiar to their fathers and grandfathers fighting in Cuba in 1898 in the Spanish–American War: the same rope sandals—the *alpargatas*—the same primitive 5-round, bolt-action Mausers, the same leather cartridge cases. For that matter, some of it would have been familiar even to those who took part in the Carlist Wars that ravaged the country earlier in the nineteenth century. Unlike the generally well-equipped armies on the Western Front in the First World War, the Spanish economy was less able to produce supplies of basic equipment for the front. Aid from Germany and Italy, and oil from Texaco, meant this was less of a problem for Franco's forces, especially after their occupation of the manufacturing and mining centres of the Basque provinces and Asturias in 1937. The rebels also benefitted from controlling the major food-producing areas of Spain. By contrast, the Republic struggled to supply equipment and, as the war dragged on, even to feed its forces.

Later, we walk down into the shade of a steep wooded valley. At the bottom, the ground under the pine trees is uneven, marked by little hummocks. Alan tells us it's a mass grave. "We know because local children saw it being dug by Republican prisoners. They had been forced to collect and bury the dead from both sides." There's an ex-British soldier called Len with us. Later, in the restaurant, he pulls out a plastic bag from his haversack and empties the contents on to the table. Shards of burnt metal and what turns out to be a Soviet anti-tank shell fired by a T-26. You can tell from the copper ring, he says. He collects the stuff and gives the best pieces to the museum in Gandesa. I ask him what he thinks about the British volunteers. "Brave bastards. Should have given up on the second day. Didn't stand a chance. Brave bastards."

La Quinta del Biberón

After the hike, we head down to Gandesa for a big meal. It's been organised by the town council to pay homage to surviving fighters from the Ebro battle (see Fig. 8.2). One is an old Falangist who seems popular even though almost everyone else in the restaurant is a Catalan Republican. The rest, half a dozen, were ageing recruits from the Republican army. Five were members of the so-called Quinta del Biberón. I'm introduced to one. He shakes my hand. His skin is wrinkled, but his grip is firm. Joan Guasch was called up aged eighteen to strengthen the ranks of the Republican army for the offensive. "I saw friends die looking for water," he told me. "We were so young, many cried, friends dying next to me, their last words asking for *mamá*. I lost this," he nodded downwards at his prosthetic leg, "when a mortar hit. That was the end for me. I'll never forget." After the fall of Aragon, the Republic was beginning to run out of men of fighting age. Moreover, its territory was split in two, so it was unable to count on many of its best troops in Central and Southern Spain. This led the army to conscript some 27,000 young men, aged between sixteen and eighteen—almost half of whom either evaded the call-up or were declared unsuitable—and to deploy most of them on the Ebro and Segre Fronts. Hardly men—boys really—boys sent to kill men. Even a few fourteen-year-olds somehow ended up in the army. They became known colloquially as "La Quinta del Biberón"—the "Baby's Bottle Draft"—after anarchist leader Federica Montseny heard about the conscription and exclaimed "[s]eventeen years old!—But they still are sucking baby bottles." For most, the only weapon they'd ever fired were pop guns at fun fairs. They were told to turn up with *alpargatas*, a metal plate, cutlery and a blanket—as if they were turning up for a school camp. The Republican industries could no longer supply these items, such was the desperate state of things.

Much of their training had involved marching with fake wooden rifles and doing rowing exercises on the ground in pretend boats. Although most were probably anti-fascist and sympathetic at some level to the Republic, most were not politically motivated, their first concern being to survive. Some of course went willingly, excitedly. Many others were scared out of their minds. Alvah Bessie reported in his notebook about their presence in the International Brigades:

> The kids are more like children than men or soldiers—this a.m., feeling better they sang, shouted and danced in the school rooms like children younger than 15–16–18. It is doubtful if they have any conception of what they are going into—more doubtful if they could be held in the event of hot action and attendant panic. These aspects of the moment make an older man sad for them and the losses they will inevitably suffer in the next action. It is shit that such babies should have to know this sort of thing—as it is shit that anyone should have to know it. But as we pity the young for their helplessness, we feel worse about their pain and death.

For its part, Franco's army never needed to call up men younger than eighteen. But, on both sides, most of those on the front line were very young. Wars to this day are typically fought by the young under the command of the old. After the war, almost all of the surviving *biberons* who remained in Spain either ended up in Franco's camps or were drafted again for three years into Franco's army. The survivors often felt that their youth had been stolen from them.

Today, the Quinta del Biberó (Catalan usage) forms an important element of the historical memory of the war in Catalonia. There are a number of plaques to the *biberons* in their home villages and on the fronts on which they fought. Books and documentaries tell their story, along with a movie produced in 2016 by the main Catalan public channel TV3, *Ebre, del bressol a la batalla* (Ebro, from the cradle to the battle). I frequently meet people who tell me their grandfather was a member. The *biberons* are often portrayed, in addition to being a lost generation, as a symbol of the stupidity of war and a lesson not to be repeated.

Another group included in the same desperate call-up, but far less documented, were men between thirty and forty years old, many of them married and with children, who carried the added anguish of not knowing what would happen to their wives and children if they were killed, wounded or captured.

Vilanova de la Barca

In the late afternoon, we arrived at the village of Vilanova de la Barca on the east bank of the River Segre, an hour's drive north of the Ebro. After a huge *entrepà* of pork loin and roasted green peppers, we walked over to the riverbank. On the other side of the water lay Franco's lines. In August 1938, the Republicans launched an assault from the village back over the water. The attack was a diversionary tactic to relieve pressure on their beleaguered forces on the Ebro to the south. It failed, and the Republican attackers were massacred. Many were those *biberons*. Some were swept away when the Francoists opened the dam gates of the Camarasa reservoir 50 kilometres upstream in the Pre-Pyrenees. This thunderous, frightening wall of water, trees and detritus continued for 100 kilometres downstream into the Ebro, wrecking the pontoon bridges built by the Republicans. The Francoists called their weapon "hydraulic artillery".

We'd come to Vilanova de la Barca to see a tank (see Fig. 8.3.) It sits on an esplanade on permanent display, minus its turret. It is a Soviet T-26, possibly the best in the world in 1936 and certainly the best to see action in Spain. The USSR sent 281 to the Republic, handsomely paid for in Spanish gold. Most were manufactured in Leningrad, but some were eventually made at the Stalingrad Tractor Factory, which came to world fame during the German siege of the city in 1942. The T-26 was based on a British Vickers model bought by the Soviets in 1930 and became the most widely manufactured tank in the world during the 1930s, with 12,000 units produced. The first fifty vehicles, together with their Soviet instructors, arrived at the Republican port of Cartagena in Murcia on 12 October 1936. Two weeks later, they entered into action at Seseña outside of Madrid, helping to slow the Francoist advance on the capital. Franco also received several hundred tanks from Mussolini and Hitler, but these were much lighter and only armed with machine guns, while the T-26 also came with a cannon. This seeming advantage was not generally pushed home by the Republicans. The rugged terrain, inexperienced drivers, their poor tactical use and frequent technical breakdowns meant they were rarely effective in battle, perhaps only achieving some success at Seseña and Brunete in the war around Madrid. To top it off, by the end of the war, the Francoists had managed to capture and re-service around 150 of the Republic's T-26s: more than half of those sent by the Soviets and more tanks than Nazi Germany sold to Franco. Indeed, it could be said that, inadvertently, Moscow was a major supplier of tanks to Franco's army.

The information panel explained that our T-26 was pulled out from the river in 1986 after a flood had brought it to the surface several years earlier. It had been involved in action along with around twenty other tanks in the afternoon of 9 August. By the time Republicans had retreated across to the east bank a week later, they'd lost most of them, some to the "hydraulic artillery". This corroding hunk of metal stands today as a memorial to the 2,000 soldiers, principally Republicans, who lost their lives in a few days that August. A miniature garden of fungi, ferns and lichens grew inside, supporting a little world of millipedes and woodlice. I sat on its rusting edge and tried to imagine the fear of young men—whatever side they were on—nerves calmed with brandy, or *kif* if Moroccan, harangued by their officers, as death sped towards them from the reeds.

There's not much else to see in Vilanova de la Barca—its Wikipedia page in Catalan lists the parish church and the T-26 as the only attractions. The old village was almost completely destroyed by Hitler's and Mussolini's planes in August 1938. A photo depicts three soldiers making their way through a ruined street. Piles of rubble and burnt timber lie on either side. It could be any ruined village from any modern war. The photo was taken by Francesc Boix, the young photographer born 30 metres from my home. By June 1937, Boix was working for the communist youth magazine *Juliol*. In late 1937, he joined the 30th Division of the Republican army, still seventeen years old. As he knew how to use a camera, he was assigned as the unit's photographer. After retreating from Aragon, he was stationed along the Segre Front and visited Vilanova de la Barca shortly after its destruction in August 1938. Many of the images he took depict Republican soldiers resting behind the lines. There is also an image of Boix himself with a goofy smile playing at firing a machine gun. I'll pick up his story when he crosses into exile in France in 1939.

At the front

We drove up a low hill overlooking Gandesa. Cistus and wild asparagus grow between rocks strewn on the ground among the young pines. Andreu explained this was a command post for the 35th Division of the Republican army, which included several battalions of the International Brigades. They'd held the summit (Cota/Hill 402) in the first weeks of the battle in their attempt to take the town. Low trenches crisscrossed the hilltop, cut shallow into the hard Iberian ground. They'd been dug out by the archaeologists working on the site, said Andreu, then pointing to vague impressions in the ground, half hidden by pine needles and undergrowth, marking the trenches yet to be excavated. As at Caspe, the thin soil on a hard substrate made it impossible to dig deep trenches. So soldiers had to build low parapets, piling up rocks—or sandbags, when they had them. Again, the pines give a misleading sense of protection today, as at the position at Hill 481, it would have been completely exposed back in 1938, vulnerable to everything Franco and his allies threw at it. The evidence is there to see. The site is pock-marked with pits from the artillery shells and bombs that rained down here. It wasn't only the shrapnel that killed. When the projectiles hit the rocks, they shattered into shards, often wounding or slaying. I picked up a jagged piece, the size of my hand, that I found in one of the holes, running its cutting edge along my finger. I later showed it to Isa Cacho, a friend of mine and a professor of geology at Barcelona University. She confirmed that limestone does not cleave like this. "Something violent happened to your rock," she said.

Limestone, the dominant rock type in the Terra Alta, does not retain water, as it filters through its fissures, resulting in scant surface water during the year and virtually zero in the summer. Compounding this were the scorching daytime temperatures of more than 40°C during most of the battle. This meant that water was a constant necessity. At home, I have a metal water bottle that a friend once found in these hills. The old cork stopper is still there, but the bottle is battered, perhaps by something explosive. I imagine a young man from my street, crouched in a hole, dripping the last drops into his mouth, hoping the mule carrier will arrive soon. Or perhaps he was from Oslo, from Glasgow, from Madrid. Or the bottle could have belonged to one of Franco's soldiers. The troops in both armies suffered from terrible thirst, although the Republicans had it worse as they were faced with the added problem of supplying front-line troops across the river. I've never seen a statistic, but many succumbed to dehydration, exacerbated by the burning sun with scant shade. A brigade of close to 4,000 men, Alan told me, needed 6,000 litres of water a day just to keep going.

Cova Hospital de Santa Llúcia

In the heavy rain, Mònica and I had to dash from the car to the cave, more of a large overhang really. La Cova de Santa Llúcia has been offering shelter from the elements for thousands of years (see Fig. 8.4). The Republican authorities also recognised the protection its geology offered from enemy planes and assigned it as a field hospital 50 kilometres behind the lines during the Ebro battle. It was set up by the British Medical Unit,[5] which attended to some of the thousands of men who received horrific wounds during the fighting on the other side of the river. I must confess we got a bit car-sick on the winding road to the cave, but it must have been sheer hell for the wounded men to reach here, carried first from the front on stretchers and the backs of mules, and then bumped and bounced in lorries along potholed roads. Here, they were relatively safe and attended by an excellent, dedicated team of doctors and nurses. More than 100 beds were arranged on the uneven, rocky floor on two levels along the 50 metres of the overhang. There were two operating theatres, lit by a generator.

The rain stopped, and suddenly the fluting song of blackbirds filled the overhang, punctuated by thunder booming through the little valley. We wandered around, studying the information panels. The memorialisation is excellent. Reproduced black and white photographs help the visitor imagine the cave in 1938. They were taken by Alec Wainman, a Quaker and British ambulance driver whose images of his time in Spain form one of the most interesting photographic records of the war.[6]

One information panel talked about Reginald Saxton. Born in Cape Town, Saxton qualified as a doctor in the UK in 1935 and was one of the first to volunteer for the British Medical Aid Unit. He helped set up the hospital in Grañén in Aragon where Australian nurse Agnes Hodgson was based in September 1936. Saxton was one of several doctors who helped develop a ground-breaking blood transfusion service for front-line Republican hospitals. Most notable among them was the Canadian surgeon Norman Bethune, who realised the importance of administering transfusions directly on the battlefield and helped develop the world's first mobile medical unit. Saxton himself worked closely with Bethune in creating these units and in organising the early provision of blood at field hospitals. Key to the system was the work done behind the lines by the Barcelona haematologist Frederic Duran i Jordà, who recognised the crucial importance of large-scale blood supplies at the outset of the war. This became the world's first blood transfusion service, which by the summer of 1938 counted on some 14,000 donors in Barcelona.[7] Duran was able to test blood for syphilis and malaria and even acquired an X-ray machine to screen people for tuberculosis. In 1939, the British medical journal *The Lancet* praised the "magnificent blood transfusion centres in Republican Spain ... a great advance on any system that has been advocated in this country". Duran and Saxton later played a key role in developing blood banks in the UK during the Second World War.

The war placed an immense strain on medical infrastructure and resources. Hospitals at the front and in the cities were overwhelmed with casualties, and medical supplies were often inadequate, particularly on the Republican side, as most of the doctors at the start of the war had sided with the Francoists, and most of the nurses were nuns. However, while medical science on Franco's side saw few developments, the more liberal atmosphere on the Republican side saw other advances in battlefield surgery and the treatment of traumatic injuries. The latter is patent particularly in the work of Josep Trueta in Barcelona, a response to the large number of civilian casualties caused by the bombing of the city. These innovations were published in scientific publications around the world and were also adopted by the Allies during the Second World War, saving large numbers of lives.[8]

The Republic managed to supplant the relative lack of medical staff by attracting more than 1,000 foreign medical staff, often based in nationally organised units such as that of the British, and within the International Brigades, where an estimated 70 per cent of the doctors were Jewish. As many were from Central and Eastern Europe, the language often used in the operating theatres was Yiddish, the historical language of the Ashkenazi Jews. Aside from Barcelona's Raval, which, in the early 1930s attracted considerable numbers of mainly Polish Jews, this is the only time when Yiddish has been used as a vernacular language in Spain.

I wonder if some of the objects in my collection helped to fund the cave hospital's work. There are several badges from the United States and Sweden, a matchbook from New York, a Cinderella stamp from Denmark sold to raise "[m]ilk for the Spanish children" (see Fig. 8.5), a 1-franc sticky bandage from the Belgium Socialist Youth. There is also a Spanish Republican army medical box containing forceps, vials, bandages and such. Movingly, secreted in the box is a toy ambulance, used, I speculate, to calm children who had been admitted with shrapnel wounds. I also have a spiral-bound collection of Spanish children's drawings entitled *They Still Draw Pictures*. The images depict pre-war scenes but above all events from the war: of tanks firing, burning buildings, bombs dropped by planes. It was published in New York in 1938 by the Quaker American Friends Service Committee for Spanish Relief with a foreword by Aldous Huxley. Children, as ever, victims in war. Mònica reminded me that her father José had told us he'd been kept alive, aged eight or nine, by what he called "American tinned milk" shipped to Barcelona, I strongly suspect, by the Quakers, who performed remarkable humanitarian work in Republican Catalonia.

Before we left, Mònica called me over to see the visitors' book (see Fig. 8.6). There were short tributes to family members who had died at the Ebro and appeals for us to never forget, but there was one dedication that really caught her eye: "Hola, I'm from Syria. My name is Nasr. I also know what a war is and know how it feels. I'm very sorry."

La Fatarella, Joan Sambró

Joan Sambró drives us off the road and up a bumpy track, metal clanking about in the boot. "Sorry about that, it's just an old German bomb I'm re-building—just the shell, mind," he chuckles in his gently lilting southern Catalan. Huge new wind turbines stand to our right, part of a park of 250 of these monsters, but we drive left into a grove of pines on the top of a low rise above the village of La Fatarella, 10 kilometres west of the River Ebro. I half hear somebody mention the name "Charlie", but it doesn't really register. Outside the car, Joan, who helps run a local association, Lo Riu, which works in recovering the memory of the battle, stoops and picks up an unidentifiable piece of burnt metal. Shrapnel from a killing instrument. He gives it to me. I thank him, feeling its weight and texture before putting it in my pocket, momentarily pleased to have acquired a piece of history, but very soon I'm not sure what I'm doing with it. It weighs more than it should in my pocket. I still have it, sitting ugly and misshapen on the shelf in front of me as I write this book, this nondescript piece of iron made to enter our bodies and maim. Below us, the ground slopes down into Joan's smallholding of neat rows of almond and olive trees. It's spring, and poppies and other wildflowers grow in profusion. A jay caws as it flies across this timeless Mediterranean scene.

We clamber into the trench that Joan, his son, friends and archaeologists from the University of Barcelona have dug out and restored. I hear the name "Charlie" again. Joan leads us through the trench as it runs zigzag into a concrete bunker. "In the 1950s, I used to play shop here when I was just a kid," says Joan. Like Juan Carlos back in Belchite and my father in the blitzed Manchester of the 1950s, his natural playground was the scene of war. He tells me about his father, Ramon, who passed to Franco's lines after his wife Teresa warned him that the Republican army had crossed the river. Ramon was fortunate not to have been killed by anarchist gunmen in the notorious "Events of Fatarella", an ugly, murky affair that saw radical militants, extremist elements in what was a very broad movement, murder thirty-four men in a village of some 2,500 people on 25 January 1937. Most were like Ramon, poor smallholding peasants who had opposed collectivising the villages. "My father fled through fear for his own life, not because he supported the other side. He couldn't see the difference between those particular anarchists responsible for the events and the Republican army," explained Joan.

Given Franco's now massively superior firepower and resources, it was just a question of time before the battle was lost. It's remarkable perhaps how long the Republican resisters held out against all the odds in these hills. The front was broken in early November. Faced with the inevitable, all the Republic could do was try to get as much of its equipment and men back across the river. It should have done so long before, but, having committed so much, it was difficult for those who had ordered the offensive to accept failure and defeat. On 14 November 1938, the order was given to retreat secretly back across the river. Lieutenant Colonel Manuel Tagüeña, the brilliant young commander in charge of the remaining troops on this side of the Ebro, ordered a line to be established along the heights around La Fatarella shortly after the Republican army had crossed the Ebro in July. Now they would be used to delay Franco's army for as long as possible. Volunteers stepped forward. It was a suicide mission involving a few hundred men strung out along kilometres of trenches and in bunkers to hold back an army. Some were internationals who had adopted Spanish citizenship to stay to the end after the disbandment of the Brigades. But Franco's troops were unaware of how few the defenders were and so moved forward slowly. The Republican army was also fortuitously aided by a thick dawn fog through which Franco's troops had been unwilling to advance into unknown territory. That didn't help those brave defenders. Out of 1,000 volunteers, most would fall over the next two days.

In the bunker, Joan tells me, with a hint of pride in his voice that this is his land: "This was the last trench of the Republican army in the Ebro." While the line stretched along the ridge for kilometres, the height of Joan's farm means that it is a reasonable candidate for a last stand. From here, he explains with a sweeping arm, the troops managed to escape down to the river. In the distance, he grimaces as he points to a hill in the opposing direction that had been the command post of General Yagüe, now on the verge of victory.

"This is where they found Charlie," Joan sighed, signalling to a spot on the ground. In 2011, University of Barcelona archaeologists excavated the trenches and came across a body, one of the last defenders. "He was still holding a grenade in his hand. They think he was probably killed by shrapnel. We decided to call him Charlie because of his height: 1.8 metres was tall for a Spaniard back then. We thought he might be a Canadian or an American." The archaeologists also said his dental work seemed too modern to be from Spain. They also found thousands and thousands of cartridges, which gives you an idea of how fierce the fighting was. Most of those attacking were the 82nd Division Tercio de Montserrat. Catalans, but from the other side. They died in large numbers too. Many would have been right-wing Catholics who had escaped to France or Italy from the revolutionary violence of the Barcelona summer of 1936 and had returned to fight for Franco. Twenty bodies of the defenders were also found when the wind farm was built in 2009.

Later research has revealed that Charlie was probably Spanish or Catalan and was probably middle class. So he'd be a Carlos or a Carles. I guess we'll never know his name, but whatever the case and wherever he was from, he was one of those brave few who held back an army for a few hours so his comrades could escape. By the time the fog had lifted, the 25,000 troops of what was left of the Republican army and its remaining tanks and armoured vehicles had crossed to the left bank of the river, many over the bridge at Flix. Sappers laid charges on the bridge that were set off at 4.45 a.m. on the night of 16 November. The explosion, sending shards of iron crashing into the water, announced, after 115 days, the end of the Ebro battle.

The Republican offensive across the Ebro, involving such unsuitable troops, was part of Prime Minister Juan Negrín's wider war strategy, encapsulated by the slogan "To Resist is to Win." Not that he had many other men at his disposal. He had concluded that the Republic and its armed forces must keep going against all odds until the Western democracies realised they had to come to the Republic's aid—or until they were drawn into a war against the fascist powers and so would make common cause with the Republic. The illusory nature of this hope was shattered when Neville Chamberlain returned from Munich on 30 September 1938, two months into the Ebro battle, fluttering his useless piece of paper on arrival and claiming to have achieved "peace in our time". Britain and France agreed that Nazi Germany would be free to annex the mainly German-speaking part of Czechoslovakia called the Sudetenland. As it was clear at the time to those who fought Franco, it was a futile act in the attempt to appease Hitler.

If Britain and France would not come to the aid of Czechoslovakia, they certainly wouldn't help the Spanish Republic. Negrín's military strategy was now in tatters. If defeat was looking likely before, now it was just a question of time. Munich also indicated that Stalin's foreign policy aiming at a common front with Western democracies against Nazi Germany had failed, further weakening his support for the Republic and leading to the infamous Molotov–Ribbentrop pact of 23 August 1939.

Fig. 6.2: Installation in Gernika Peace Museum recreating in dramatic fashion the fate of one family home during the town's destruction.

Fig. 6.3: Full-sized mosaic of Picasso's painting *Guernica* on Allende Salazar Kalea, Gernika. The mural was created in 1997 to commemorate the sixtieth anniversary of the massacre. Underneath it reads "'Guernica' Gernikara". The Basque suffix "ra" (in Gernikara) means "*to* Gernika", calling for the work to be brought from Madrid to the town.

Fig. 6.4: Fascist Italian photo magazine *La Domenica del Corriere*, 10 April 1938, showing Savoia-Marchetti SM.81 planes routing the Republican army in Aragon.

Fig. 6.5: Special issue of the Nazi military magazine *Die Wehrmacht*, which reads, in German, "We fought in Spain", and includes memories of Germans in the Condor Legion. This issue was published on 30 May 1939, two months after Franco's victory—and four months before the Nazi invasion of Poland which began World War Two.

Fig. 6.6: Tail fin of a German B1 incendiary bomb found on the Madrid front.

Fig. 6.7: *Juliol*, the weekly newspaper of the youth section of the PSUC, the pro-Stalinist communist party. The headline reads, in Catalan, "Anybody who does not explicitly support the USSR should be treated as a traitor." December 1936.

Fig. 7.1: The ruined town of Belchite. The remains of the sixteenth-century Iglesia San Martín de Tours can be seen in the background.

Fig. 7.2: The ruinscape of Belchite. Of the 1,200 buildings before the war, 30 per cent were destroyed and 40 per cent were damaged by the fighting, while only 30 per cent were still habitable. Eighty years of abandonment, the *cierzo* winds and the poor quality of the buildings made of adobe bricks put paid to the rest.

Fig. 7.3: La Iglesia de San Agustín in Belchite. Out of the picture is its characteristic Mudéjar tower, embedded into which is a Republican 105mm shell which the guides will invariably point out, should you visit. In 2022, the Guardia Civil removed and deactivated it, before allowing it to be re-embedded into the wall.

Fig. 7.4: Belchite's Iglesia de San Martín de Tours in the background. Franco's presence is stalking Spain again.

Fig. 7.5: A red ribbon tied around an olive tree near Gandesa, left by a family member of the Americans executed here. The ground in front is tilled but uncultivated.

Fig. 8.1: The old village of Corbera d'Ebre, destroyed during the battle of the Ebro. Sant Pere church is in the background.

Fig. 8.2: Some of the last members of Quinta del Biberón on 22 July 2018. They are standing in front of the Peace Monument at Hill 705 in the Serra de Pàndols. In 2024, for the first time, this annual homage featured no survivors.

Fig. 8.3: Remains of a Soviet T-26 tank on permanent display at Vilanova de la Barca. It is accompanied by a helpful information panel produced by the Catalan government's Memorial Democràtic, part of its Espais de Memòria programme.

Fig. 8.4: Santa Llúcia cave hospital just outside the village of La Bisbal de Montsant. Many wounded International Brigaders and Republican soldiers from the Ebro battle were brought to this field hospital run by the Spanish Medical Aid Committee.

Fig. 8.5: A 1937 Danish fund-raising stamp reading "Milk for the Spanish children". It was produced by the Matteotti Foundation, which was set up to aid political refugees from fascism and to remember socialist politician Giacomo Matteotti, who was murdered by Italian fascists in 1924.

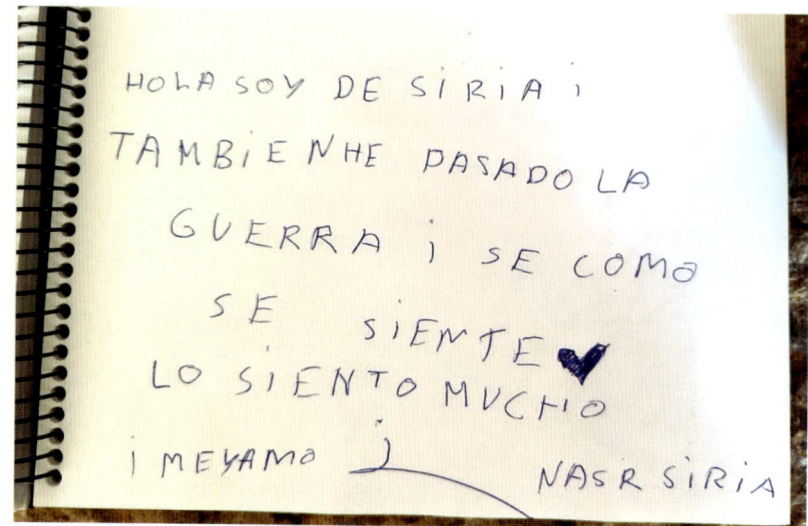

Fig. 8.6: Visitor book at the Santa Llúcia cave hospital, 2023.

Fig. 9.1: A 2023 mural on Les Masies hostel, painted by the artist Roc Blackblock, recreating a famous Robert Capa photograph of a farewell event of the International Brigades here on 25 October 1938.

Fig. 9.2: Ink bottles by Nonex found in the Ebro battle site. They could have been from either side. One still has ink; the other contains soil from Terra Alta.

Fig. 9.3: Soap shaving stick by Colgate, New York. Found in the Ebro battle site. I can't prove it, but I like to think it belonged to one of the 2,800 Americans who fought in Spain. I bought this at an auction.

Fig. 9.4: Cigarette lighter found in the Ebro battle site, damaged by a bullet. The Austrian brand was apparently common in Spain in the 1930s. It could have been from either side. I bought it at an auction. Did it save somebody's life?

Fig. 10.1: Sant Ferran fortress in Figueres. This is the largest castle in Europe outside of Russia and was the mustering station for the International Brigades on their arrival from France.

Fig. 10.2: Monument to the Exile, La Vajol. It recreates a 1939 photo of Mariano Gracia and his daughter Alicia, mutilated by a Nazi bomb, and was taken 60km to the east. Erected in 1999, it is one of the first monuments to remember the Republican exile anywhere in Spain.

9

ECHOES OF THE EBRO

Farewell to the International Brigades

On the drive back to Barcelona, I stopped at an old spa at Les Masies de Poblet, a fine collection of buildings 20 kilometres north of Tarragona, now run as a hostel by the Catalan government. On 25 October 1938, it was used to host the first farewell event to the International Brigades. A month earlier, on 21 September, the Republican government had announced its decision to disband the Brigades in an attempt to put pressure on the Western democracies to somehow persuade Hitler and Mussolini to withdraw their troops and lift their arms embargo on the Republic.

Whatever the case, by this stage of the war the Brigades were a spent force. So many were dead or maimed, as we've seen in the appalling casualty rates. By the time of the Ebro battle, the depleted battalions were filled with a large number (often a majority) of Spanish recruits.

I walked around the nineteenth-century porticoed courtyard of the hostel decorated with a permanent photo exhibition documenting the farewell event of the brigaders. A number show the volunteers dancing with local women and with each other, having a good time, the war now seemingly behind them. For those from the Western democracies, their journey home now might have seemed a relatively easy one, although this was often not the case. For those from the dictatorships of Central, Eastern and Southern Europe, their path must have felt impossible. Many of this latter group decided to stay in Spain. They took out Spanish citizenship and elected to fight until the end.

Quite a few of the photos are by Robert Capa. Some of them are relatively mundane shots of the parade and of Spanish Prime Minister Negrín and Juan Modesto, commander of the Army of the Ebro, making speeches, but others offer more personal narratives. One, among the most powerful and iconic that Capa took in Spain, shows a youngish-looking man holding his fist against the side of his head in the anti-fascist salute. It's an image full of grim determination and heroic resistance but pathos too. Capa manages to make us want to look at the man and empathise with his life and fate.

There's a beautifully colourised version online by an artist called Julius Backman. It's so good that it has revealed what looks very much like smallpox scars over the man's face, something I for one had never noticed before. It reminds us that its scourge was still not uncommon, particularly among the poor in 1930s Europe. The man's identity is not known. Perhaps, like Capa, he was Hungarian, and, like the photographer, he had fled the authoritarian dictatorship of Miklós Horthy. Another famous Capa photo in the same reel shows a young volunteer with the newspaper *Il Legionario*, which was published by Italian volunteers in Spain, nestled under his arm, also doing the anti-fascist salute. His name is not known, but it's a safe guess he was an exile from fascist Italy.

Before leaving, we went outside the hostel to admire a magnificent mural covering the front façade of the building that recreates this latter photo (see Fig. 9.1). It was painted in October 2023 by the Catalan artist Roc Blackblock and is one of a number of works he has created remembering those who lost the war. That this homage to the brigaders has been so prominently painted on a government-run building and was paid for by public money is a reminder that in Catalonia at least the memory of the International Brigades enjoys official recognition. This is also true of the wider struggle against Franco, as is demonstrated by all those museums, panels and plaques in the Ebro.

Back home

When the brigaders returned to their countries, they were often not treated very well. Many volunteers from Switzerland and the Netherlands were imprisoned when they arrived home. Indeed, historical knowledge of Swiss brigaders is among the most complete due to the thorough police records of interrogations made in 1939. The few Dutch volunteers to survive their later involvement in the resistance and the roundups by the Nazis—aided by Dutch police and their records—didn't get their passports and civic rights back until the 1960s. The Swiss weren't pardoned until 2009. In contrast, although the British government invoked the 1870 Foreign Enlistment Act—which still prohibits British subjects from enlisting in foreign armies at war with countries with which the UK is at peace—returning brigaders were not prosecuted.

We'll later discuss the role of the brigaders in the resistance movements of the Second World War. When the Brits arrived home, they were treated as heroes by a huge crowd at Victoria Street Station in London, which included future Labour Prime Minister Clement Attlee and future Conservative Prime Minister Edward Heath.[1] In contrast, they were the object of great suspicion by the British security services. Most, however, were allowed to enlist in the Second World War, although whether their experience in Spain was valued (and therefore their rank in the British army) depended on local commanding officers. Several played an important role in the formation of the Home Guard, most notably as we've seen with Tom Wintringham.

When the Americans got back, there were 3,000 people to greet them in New York, but they were equally suspect in the eyes of the American government. That said, some 900 enlisted in the American army during the Second World War, most of whom fought in some of the worst battles of Southeast Asia. On their return to the US, they became victims of McCarthyism, accused among other things of being "premature anti-fascists".

Over the years, I've met the descendants of dozens of American brigaders. They often know little about their relatives' experiences in Spain, but many are aware of and even remember first-hand the hard years of McCarthyism when many veterans were prosecuted and then hounded from job to job for having fought against Franco. One story that hit me was told by an elderly American whose father, Chuck, a communist and a pacifist to boot, had served in the International Brigades as an ambulance driver. His son Jack told his father's story to a captivated group one day on my tour.[2] Chuck became frustrated with hard-line communist doctrine in the Brigades and, after returning to the US, left the party. He was now ostracized as a traitor by his old comrades, but he was also an object of great suspicion by the American government and was rejected as a driver by the US army. Jack remembered the difficult years of the 1950s when every time his father found a job, the FBI would knock on his employer's door: Chuck slowly fell into alcoholism, dying in the late 1950s. Moving forwards to the mid-1960s, Jack and his brother, now young adults, felt they needed to clear the family's name, and so both tried to volunteer for the army. Jack was spurned on several occasions. Many years later, he learned through the provisions of the Freedom of Information Act that this was because his father had volunteered in Spain. His brother was successful at the third attempt and was sent to Vietnam. As a university graduate, he should have been enlisted as a non-commissioned officer. Instead, he was sent as a radio operator, among the most dangerous jobs in the army, the first man the snipers want. He lasted barely a week. Chuck also learned that his brother was given this post because of his father's time in Spain. Jack, now breaking up with emotion, ended his story to the group with the words "the Spanish Civil War cast a long shadow on our house".

International memory

Among the most well-known songs of the Spanish Civil War is "¡Ay, Carmela!" As a folk tune, it dates back to the 1808–14 struggle against Napoleon's invading army. It is also the title of a film by Carlos Saura, one of the very first films I saw at the cinema in Spain back in 1990. It tells the story of a trio of travelling players who perform bawdy variety shows for Republican troops near the front. On a foggy night en route to Valencia in March 1938, they lose their way—a regular feature of the war—and inadvertently drive across the lines into Francoist Spain. They are soon captured and sent to a makeshift prison in the local school, all the grimmer in the pouring rain, in Belchite, which has just fallen to General Yagüe's troops. The co-protagonist Carmela—played by Carmen Maura—befriends a fellow prisoner: a Polish brigader. They look at the map of Europe on the wall and point to his homeland. He calls the foreign land he had come to fight for "Hiszpania". She teaches him to say "España". He and his Polish comrades will all be shot. I won't spoil any more of the plot for those who haven't seen the film, but you are taken to an inevitably tragic conclusion, a personal tragedy also symbolising the defeat of the Republic. The film is based on the 1986 play of the same name by José Sanchis Sinisterra. After numerous productions around Spain and the rest of the world, it was performed for the first time to a packed audience in the presence of the playwright in Belchite in 2015.

I was also interested to learn from a friend from Sarajevo that a highly successful version in Bosnian has been playing in a theatre in the city and beyond since 1999. The play features a stirring recording of the song "¡Ay, Carmela!" in Croatian by Darko Rundek—have a listen online. It seems strange that this very Spanish work has proven so popular in another country—it is the most successful play in Bosnian history—but somehow audiences have been attracted by its direct anti-fascist message, finding common cause with the events in Spain and their own more recent history, associating the play's story with the defeat against the Nazis and the resistance during the Bosnian war. The play and song also connect to the 1,700 Yugoslav volunteers who fought against Franco and their later prominent role in the partisan resistance during the Second World War. It has been used in recent years as an anthem during anti-corruption protests in Belgrade and pride parades in Zagreb. There's also a really beautiful version on YouTube by the Bosnian choir Mješoviti hor Seljo, performed remotely from thirty little screens during the COVID-19 pandemic in and around Sarajevo in May 2020. The video begins with the Second World War partisan cry "Smrt fašizmu"—"Death to fascism."

Another rendering of "¡Ay, Carmela!" was "Viva la Quince Brigada" (not the same song as Christy Moore's track about the Irish), made famous in the English-speaking world by Woody Guthrie and then in Pete Seeger's 1940s rendition in praise of the 15th Brigade, which both singers had learned from old American brigaders. There was also a Francoist version, but the song is overwhelmingly more associated with the Republicans. It would be sung together with other songs around the world in the coming decades, marking the memory of the anti-fascist struggle, initially often clandestinely we can imagine, by veterans from the Civil War in basements from Paris to Prague, by partisans in the mountains of Italy and Yugoslavia, and later on the other side of the Atlantic in marches against the Vietnam War and the Pinochet coup, but also more problematically in Soviet and East German schools as part of their officially imposed anti-fascist culture.

The Republican offensive and resistance in the Battle of the Ebro came to represent an episode in the international memory of the left. Another version of "¡Ay, Carmela!" is called "El Paso del Ebro". The 1958 Polish film *Popiół i diament* (Ashes and diamonds) by Andrzej Wajda, considered a masterpiece of world cinema, narrates the events after the liberation of a Polish town in 1945. In a key scene, two Polish communists wonder what the future might hold. In the background, a gramophone plays "El Paso del Ebro", evoking memories of the Spanish struggle. Szczuka, one of the film's heroes, asks: "Do you remember? That's where it all began." Wajda purposely used a brigader veteran because, as he explained in an online interview, he was someone

> who was ready to risk his life ... out of a need of the heart to defend democracy and freedom that had been taken from the Spanish people. We saw these communists as people with ideals, far more than those who had brought freedom impaled on the bayonets of the Soviet Army.

Back in Barcelona, I met Jeremi Galdámez. Born in Warsaw to a Polish mother and Chilean father, a communist who had escaped Pinochet's police (his grandfather is one of the disappeared), Jeremi is the spokesperson for Stowarzyszenie Ochotnicy Wolności (SOW), the Polish International Brigades' memory association. He had been travelling for several weeks around Spain researching his book on the volunteers from Poland. Over lunch, he sketched out their details. "As many as 5,000 Poles fought here. In the main they were miners working in France and Belgium. We could say most were economic migrants but they were also often political exiles. Poland was a military dictatorship, not a democracy in 1936 and for most of the interwar period," he reminded me. Most fought in the Dabrowski Battalion, which was named after Jarosław Dąbrowski, the commander-in-chief of the 1871 Paris Commune who was killed fighting the French army on the barricades. Although people from the English-speaking world tend to focus on the presence of volunteers from their own countries, Poles, and other Central and East Europeans, were certainly more numerous.

Around 30 per cent of the Poles were Jews, who, in addition to economic and political concerns, had fled from the antisemitism of their homeland. About 100 Polish women also came to Spain, mainly medical workers. Jeremi estimates as many as 3,000 Poles died or disappeared. This is an extraordinary figure even in the context of the terrible attrition suffered by the International Brigades, and, if true, it would mean that one in three brigaders to fall in Spain were Polish—possibly explained by the fact that many elected to stay to fight to the bitter end after the Brigades were disbanded. "One thousand more were killed during the Second World War," said Jeremi: "In every resistance movement and in every camp, you always find Polish veterans from Spain."

In truth, we'll probably never know the real figures. If it's hard enough to get exact estimates of the numbers of British volunteers, it is surely impossible for those from Eastern Europe. Many came to Spain under false identities or were registered as French or Belgian. And so many of these men and women and their names disappeared in the hell of the Second World War. Of the 1,000 or so of the Poles involved that were still alive by 1945, many would fall victim to the Stalinist repression in Poland of the late 1940s, although others would also play prominent roles in the new state.

Since 1989, attitudes in Poland towards the Poles who served in Spain have varied. The distinction Wajda made between these idealistic young Poles, many of whom were communists, and the country's later Stalinist repressors was lost on the Polish ultra-conservative government led by the Law and Justice Party between 2015 and 2023, which renamed streets that once honoured Polish brigaders and attempted to remove memorials. This is in contrast to the former East Germany, where street names of Spanish fighters have so far generally been maintained without controversy. Jeremi's organisation successfully fought a legal battle to protect the name of a street (Ulica Dąbrowszczaków) in Warsaw named after the Dabrowski Battalion.

SOW also helped organise an exhibition on the Spanish Civil War at the Independence Museum in Warsaw using material brought back by veterans from the war. It was called "Jeśli dziś padnie Madryt, jutro padnie Warszawa"—"If Madrid falls today, Warsaw will fall tomorrow," the prescient cry of Polish brigaders to defend the Spanish capital. Six months to the day after Madrid's fall, the pilots of Göring's Luftwaffe, many trained in Spanish skies, began the carpet bombing of Warsaw. Despite an attempt by the Law and Justice government to close it down, the exhibition proved to be one of the most successful at the museum in recent years. "After the end of the communist period, the Poles who fought in Spain were completely forgotten. Their memory was only kept alive in families," Jeremi told me. Now, thanks to the work by SOW and others, this past is being brought back into the light.

After the Spanish Civil War, the conflict continued to reverberate militarily, politically and culturally beyond Spain's borders. Over the years, I've built up a small, eccentric if you will, collection of novels, movies, theatre flyers, documentaries, vinyls and other cultural products from countries ranging from the UK, the German Democratic Republic (GDR), France, Italy, the United States, Poland, Czechoslovakia and Bulgaria. I used them for a pop-up exhibition at our local library in 2019 on the war's cultural impact. Most commemorate the Republican defeat and/or condemn the Franco regime, but they can also be seen as a broader commentary on the society in which they were created.[3] Several are focused directly on the Ebro. The novel *Yfir Ebrofljótið* (Across the River Ebro, 2001) by Álfrún Gunnlaugsdóttir narrates the experiences of an Icelandic brigader. As the years pass by, he looks for records of friends who took part in the battle. The book is dedicated to three Icelanders who went to Spain and was nominated for the Icelandic Literature Prize in 2003. Another example is the acclaimed 1960 East German movie *Fünf Patronenhülsen* (Five Cartridges—available on YouTube), which narrates the story of five German brigaders who volunteer to defend the line on the same day in November 1938 as "Charlie", while the rest of the Republican army retreat back across the Ebro.

I sit on dry earth, my back to a carob tree. A Sardinian warbler, its brilliant red eye shining through a jet-black head, is bravely performing its scratchy song on a thorn bush just to my left, but instead of listening, I connect the speaker to my mobile. It's a recording of "¡Ay, Carmela!" made in the late 1940s by the US folk band The Weavers with Pete Seeger on vocals bashing out the banjo. A cormorant fishes in the quiet water below. "One night we crossed the river, / ¡Ay, Carmela, ay, Carmela!"

Objects tell stories

I have acquired a few pieces from the Ebro battle sites that I use on my walks in Barcelona. There's a corroded Adrian helmet, a 1926 design I'm told. It's the same type used by the French police into the 1970s—think of the images of Paris 1968—with its leather inside long gone. They were bought in large quantities from France as helmets did not contravene the arms embargo and were worn widely by the International Brigades, as numerous photos attest. I like to invite people on the tour to put it on. They often comment that it looks a bit like a toy fire brigade helmet with its small visor at the front and ridge running along the top. I'm told it was useless against all but the most glancing of shots.

I also have a pair of ink bottles (see Fig. 9.2). They could have been used by either side. Ink bottles are frequently found in trenches and battle sites from the war. One still has the top and brand label (Nonex), the other is full of the earth from the Terra Alta. In an age before WhatsApp and video calls, letters were so important for the troops at the front as they were the only way they could stay in contact with home. Most were addressed to the women in the men's lives: wives, girlfriends, mothers, sisters, friends. The arrival of the post, *el correo*, was a moment of joy on both sides amid so much fear and pain and death, connecting soldiers with the world they had left behind and reminding them it still existed. It also reminds me that although at the start of the war, the young revolutionaries went eagerly to the front, the numbers of volunteers for the militias were never enough. As early as October 1936, the Republican government had introduced conscription, mobilising all able-bodied men aged between twenty and forty-five, although this decree was not initially enforced. Gradually, however, the call-up became more rigorous and was firmly established by 1937.

Another item is a tin of shaving soap, evoking the everyday concerns of the troops (see Fig. 9.3). It says on the front that it was made by Colgate in New York. I can't prove it of course, but I like to think that it belonged to one of the 2,800 Americans who fought against Franco. Aside from military strictures, keeping clean-shaven was a daily ritual for soldiers, a way of maintaining some semblance of normality. Did our hypothetical brigader buy it in New York before boarding a ship, or was it sent as part of an aid package from Chicago, along with chocolate, cigarettes and thick socks? There's also the old cigarette lighter in Fig. 9.4, crumpled by the bullet still embedded in the groove it made on impact. Again, it could be from either side as the Austrian make of Regens was commonly sold in Spain in the 1930s. Did it manage to sufficiently stop the bullet's journey to save the owner or not? Whatever the case, it represents a dramatic moment in one man's life, whatever his politics. When you hold it in your hand, it tangibly takes you to one violent moment in the war. Then there's a condensed milk can with the words "El niño. Con toda su crema" ("The child. With all its cream") stamped on its base. The top has been punctured twice to pour out the liquid, perhaps into hot coffee served to soldiers being readied for a dawn attack. There's a jagged, gaping hole in one side, looking like shrapnel, indicating a terrible end.

I sometimes hear from descendants of the brigaders on the tour about objects their family members brought home. One American, Daniel Torres, told me about his grandfather Mac Krauss, who was possibly the last member of the Abraham Lincoln Battalion to leave Barcelona, one day before the city fell in January 1939. For many years, the family kept two items from his time in Spain. The first was a burnt Spanish–English dictionary that his grandfather said had caught alight during a bomb attack while his boat was crossing the Ebro. The second object, the wings of a butterfly he had collected on a forgotten hill, was kept inside a book. I thought it would be interesting to have a photographic record of these items, and both would seem powerful objects in their way for someone to use in an exhibition, but, after a search, Daniel was sorry to inform me the family had lost track of them over the years. I was left to imagine the species of butterfly. Perhaps something colourful and spectacular like a two-tailed pasha, whose dragon-like green caterpillar feeds on the leaves of strawberry trees (*Arbutus unedo*), a common species in the Terra Alta, which he had found dead on a path and had slipped, marvelling at his beauty among the horror, into his brigader identity card.

I also have a rusted sardine tin with a key opener. *Norge* is printed on the back. A friend found it somewhere in the Ebro battlefields. I often show it together with a photo of a group of Danes from the same battle. A dozen or so are resting, eating out of mess kits and cans. They look like they've been through hell, dazed with "thousand-yard stares", an expression I learned from a Vietnam vet who found parallels between the image and his own memories. I like to think my tin was sent by the Norwegian trade unions, who certainly sent a lot of aid to the Republic. The Spanish archaeologist Alfredo González Ruibal, author of the excellent and original *Archaeology of the Spanish Civil War* (2020), wasn't so sure when I asked him: "We have found identical tin cans marked Norway in fascist outposts in Ethiopia, so my impression is that Norwegians were selling fish cans quite indiscriminately. But there might be a story like the one you tell behind this one."

The Delta del Ebro and Tortosa

Andreu and I met an old mutual friend Armand Duch in the Ebro Delta, his homeland. The first time I came here, I felt I had entered another world. As we drove in, the sky opened up a vast canvas, the flooded land appearing to merge with the sea. Not Catalan or Spanish, the green, watery expanse of paddy fields seemed almost Southeast Asian in its exuberance. Looking back landwards, you saw the rugged white limestone massif of the Serra del Montsià marking out the delta's flatness. And so many birds. Terns flitted lightly past the car. Egrets and herons were everywhere.

We drove through the agrarian landscape to Poblenou del Delta (New Village). It's a rather attractive place to spend the weekend—if you can cope with all the mosquitoes in season. Palm trees stand outside little whitewashed homes, giving the village a more southern feel. In the restaurant, Armand insisted on ordering an array of delicious local specialities to impress the Barcelonan: cockles, frog's legs, *suc d'anguiles* (eel stew) and *ortigues de mar*—"sea nettles", which are, in fact, snake lock anemones, the ones with the long wavy tentacles found in rock pools all around Europe's coasts. They were fried in tempura batter and left a spicy tickle in my throat. After lunch, we wandered around the neat little streets reminiscent of touristy villages in the south of Spain. They also bring to mind New Belchite's streets—for the origins of this pleasant little settlement is also Francoist to the core. The village was inaugurated as Villafranco del Delta, named after the dictator, in 1957 to provide better housing for the rice farmers.

The Franco regime built from scratch some 300 of these model agricultural settlements (*pueblos de colonización*) for tenant farmers across the country between 1940 and 1971, usually constructed in a standardised architectural style intended to evoke Southern Spain, ignoring local traditions and the unsuitability of the local climate. Tenants were provided with irrigation, infrastructure, machinery and housing. The aim was to repopulate areas and to foster a prosperous countryside with a class of self-sufficient, compliant farmers as a counterpoint to the industrial cities and their "untrustworthy" workers. Some 55,000 people moved voluntarily to these villages. Large families were often given precedence, while people associated with the losing side in the war had no chance of being offered a place. In return, residents were expected to work hard to repay the loans they were given by the state and to live within the authoritarian strictures imposed. Each little "rural utopia" would be centred around a main square (*plaza mayor*) with its village hall, representing the state, and with its church: the twin pillars of civic life under national Catholicism. The Guardia Civil were also on hand should anybody step out of line. Many of the *pueblos de colonización* failed and have been abandoned over the years, although some have become productive villages or dormitory towns. In 2003, the Catalan government renamed Villafranco as Poblenou del Delta. Very slowly across Spain, almost all the other surviving settlements have also removed their Francoist epithets. At the time of writing, there are still a handful that have resisted, most strikingly "Llanos del Caudillo" in Ciudad Real, named in honour of the dictator.

On the edge of the delta, Andreu brings us to a rise overlooking the river. A plaque explains that the Bataillon Commune de Paris of the International Brigades crossed the Ebro here on the first night of the battle. "It was a diversionary tactic to deflect attention from the main thrust of the offensive. Across there hiding in the reeds," he explained, pointing over the river, "were machine guns manned principally by elite Moroccan troops." There was a massacre. Few of those 1,200 who crossed that night of 25 July survived. The political commissioner of the brigade, Henri Tanguy, was wounded but managed to swim back to the Republican shore. He later became a prominent member of the French resistance, in which he took the *nom de guerre* of Colonel Rol, after friend and comrade Theophile Rol, who had died in the crossing, and in June 1944 he took command of the Paris region. I'll pick up his story and that of a band of indomitable Spaniards on my visit to the French capital near the end of my journey.

The road led us back up the river to Tortosa, where Armand wanted to take me around a new Civil War route the council had laid out in his town. The panels cover themes such as the revolutionary violence that descended on Tortosa in 1936 and, above all, the bombing raids by the Condor Legion. One panel showed photographs taken by Ernest Hemingway, who described visiting Tortosa—"a city almost demolished, evacuated by civilians and no soldiers"—on 4 April 1938 to cover the defence of the River Ebro before the advance of Franco's troops. He wrote:

> Above us in the high cloudless sky, fleet after fleet of bombers roared over Tortosa. When they dropped the sudden thunder of their loads, the little city on the Ebro disappeared under a mounting yellow cloud of dust. The dust never settled, as more bombers came, and, finally, it hung like a yellow fog all down the Ebro Valley. ... There were many reasons impelling us to leave Tortosa and go towards Barcelona, these include life, liberty and the pursuit of happiness.[4]

On the pedestrian bridge across the river, Armand showed me the holes ripped in the bright red iron girders. Andreu explained they might have been caused by the Republicans who blew out the centre of the bridge that used to carry the Barcelona–Valencia railway line in April 1938 to slow Franco's army. Or, he added, they might have been caused by the ravages of the Condor Legion. I imagined the violence needed to twist metal like this and shuddered at the thought of what it would do to human flesh. He pointed out the memorial upstream. It stands on a pillar in the middle of the river, which used to form part of the main road bridge that was destroyed in the air raids. Two narrow metal spires rise 26 metres into the sky, crowned with the Cross of Saint James. They are meant to represent the steeples of a Christian church, but they look like missiles. On a later visit, Mònica shuddered, saying the structure looked like the gateway to Mordor.

Inaugurated by Franco himself in 1966 in memory of the regime's dead, the memorial is today among the largest Francoist memorials left in Spain. In 1986, the inscription "To the Caudillo of the Crusade and the twenty-five years of peace" ("Al Caudillo de la Cruzada y de los veinticinco años de paz") was removed. The imperial eagle—a symbol the regime adopted from the heraldry of the Catholic kings—was, however, kept, although the symbol meaning "Victor", that is, Franco, was removed from its talons. "So," said Andreu, "they got rid of the nastier bit of the memorial referring to Franco and his claim of peace, but kept the rest. It is a neat analogy of the Transition and the Pact of Silence." The fate of the memorial divided Tortosa. In 2016, a referendum was held in the town. One side wanted to keep it. They argued for its artistic and historical value, reasoning that it should simply be re-signified as a commemoration to the dead on both sides. The other wanted it dismantled and removed to a museum somewhere else. To the great dismay of many people in Catalonia, the good people of Tortosa voted overwhelmingly to keep the monument. Tortosa is also among the most conservative and Catholic of towns in Catalonia, where Francoism grew deep roots. I was as disappointed as my Catalan friends in Barcelona by this failure to remove a triumphalist monument to fascism. But Armand, anti-fascist to the core, didn't agree. "It's important not to erase the past," he argued: "[T]he monument has been re-signified. It's part of our history." He might be right, but, looking at this huge shard of metal seemingly stabbed into the river, I couldn't agree. The referendum and its result were heavily criticised in the rest of Catalonia and were ruled in court to be legally invalid. At the time of writing in mid-2025, the memorial is due to be removed.

The Ebro battle area is the most heavily memorialised space of the war in Spain. There must be around 100 plaques and memorials. Around 20 sites have been restored and signposted, including trenches, command posts and hospitals. At the time of writing, there were ten small public and private museums. Corbera's new village is home to the largest—the 115 Days

Interpretation Centre—named after the battle's duration. It's a good enough place to start a trip and provides an overview, a bit staid perhaps, of the battle and its consequences. The centre also has maps and leaflets of the different sites. Andreu explained to me that the idea and the money for all this came after a group of local politicians belonging to Convergència i Unió (CiU) went on a fact-finding trip to Normandy. CiU was the centre-right Catalan republican party that governed Catalonia almost uninterruptedly from the restoration of Catalan self-government in 1980 until it split apart in 2015 over disagreements as to whether to support the push for independence. The politicians were extremely impressed with the work done remembering the history of D-Day in terms of memorials and museums. And they were also very impressed, Andreu winked, with the large numbers of Americans and other tourists spending lots of cash. Sadly, despite the investment, few foreign tourists visit La Terra Alta. The number of local tourists isn't huge either. Catalan school children do, however, often visit. It's part of the educational strategy of the Catalan government's "Memorial Democràtic".

Local memory

Whatever the international memories of the fighting, it is in Catalonia and above all in the Terres de l'Ebre where the battle is most remembered. When I ask anyone in Barcelona about their grandparents' role in the war, there's a good chance they'll tell me they have a family member who fought here, many of them young men from the Quinta del Biberón.

On the drive back to the village, Joan told me more about his father. A day or so after the battle, Ramon Sambó returned to La Fatarella, but he could no longer recognise his land, such was the destruction wrought upon the farm. Nor could his neighbours; the topography and walls dividing the land had all been blasted away. Almost all the olives and almonds, Joan explained, had gone. I imagined the scene he looked upon that day. A blackened, birdless Somme-like place, where ruined stumps stood in hopeless, shattered fields, all desecrated for Franco's lousy new world. Nature defiled often stands as a symbol of the horror of war. The last words of Irish poet Charles Donnelly came to me as he crouched behind a tree during the Battle of Jarama. According to a Canadian brigader at his side, he picked up a bunch of olives from the ground, squeezed them, and in a lull in machine gun fire exclaimed, "Even the olives are bleeding." A few moments later, he was cut down.

At first, Ramon and his wife Teresa had no furniture, as Republican troops had burnt everything to cook and keep warm, and a gaping hole from a bomb stood in place of a roof in their home in La Fatarella. This was remedied when he came across an abandoned Republican supply centre hidden away in a valley. Loading his mule, he brought uralite and bags of cement to repair the roof and walls and to restock the house with military mattresses, tables and chairs. Others from the surrounding villages also took advantage of what the armies had left behind to rebuild their ruined homes as best they could. Many had lost all their possessions. Now they used plates and cutlery abandoned by soldiers. "I came along in 1945," Joan smiled:

> When we were harvesting (almonds twice, once in late spring and again in September; olives a month later) we slept in a small building at the farm for a few weeks. Until I guess I was about ten we used an old threshing board as a dinner table. It was stained with blood which formed shapes like the continents on a map.

They had to make do.

Most of Terra Alta's farmland was ruined, its fruit trees charred, its farm equipment destroyed. Many had fled into exile; many others were dead or languishing in Franco's huge network of camps and prisons. It would take years to re-establish the vineyards and the fruit, nut and olive orchards that had been the mainstay of the local economy. There was, however, an awful lot of scrap metal. During the battle, 40,000 tonnes of shrapnel had rained down on these hills; it was a giant open cast mine. So, if they couldn't harvest almonds and olives, they could gather iron and steel. *Metralleros* (shrapnel pickers) even came from the rest of Spain. They'd sell the scrap to merchants—Francoists, of course, as nobody else could get the licence. The merchants made a fortune selling it to the state, which sent it to Germany in the early 1940s to help pay for Hitler's aid. Iron paid the least, followed by steel, lead, tin, copper, brass and, the highest of all, aluminium. Many were maimed by unexploded bombs looking for metals. Some were killed. Hazardous pieces are found to this day. One of the scrap dealers still operates between Corbera and Gandesa. It used to have hulks of Soviet and German tanks rusting in its yards, but they're long gone now.

Joan was sent out after school to look for stuff. His parents kept most of it to sell, to pay for food. Hard times. Once, he managed to find ten old bullet casings for which he knew the dealers paid well and instead of taking them home traded them for a packet of twenty Peninsulares. The ten-year-old boy promptly smoked the lot and fell ill, intoxicated by nicotine poisoning. "I've never touched a cigarette since," he grimaced. "I can still taste them. Even the smell makes me sick." We joked that the packet had added a couple of decades to his life. "I also used to go looking for shrapnel for the fiestas so I could buy drinks. We used long tongs to pick up the most dangerous pieces. There was always someone in our class missing a finger or a hand."

I asked Joan why he felt the need to dedicate part of his free time to helping preserve the memory of the war. "In part, it's because it happened in my land—not just my little farm but everywhere around here. It's part of our heritage. But I also do it to remember my father, Ramon." One day in the early 1940s, Ramon went to a town to sell some scrap metal the family had collected. While having a drink outside a bar, he was approached by a hungry man. Ramon gave him food and thought nothing else of it. Later that evening, back in La Fatarella, he was arrested and accused of having given support to a *maquis*, an anti-Francoist guerrilla. Ramon had already had a run-in with the village mayor over the latter's refusal to pay him money that he owed. Now the mayor instructed the local Guardia Civil to deal with him. They beat him to within an inch of his life. Joan isn't prepared to forget that. It is also a reminder of the immense bullying power wielded at a national but also at a very local level in every village across the country by those who won the war.

10

THE FALL OF CATALONIA

Barcelona Zoo

We go to the zoo quite a bit with the kids. It is layered with so many family memories: their first experience of monkeys and meerkats, the goats nibbling at their little fingers in the petting farm. Without Albert and then Iona, it would probably feel a sad place with all the animals living out enclosed lives, but I'm engrossed in my children's experience, so I tend to close my mind to the fate of the inmates. One June, I went back on my own to meet Josep Garcia, resident zoologist. The pine tree in front of our bench was packed with dozens of grey herons and egrets, wild birds that make their home above the captive pelicans and flamingos. But on this occasion, we hadn't met up to talk about birds. Josep had something to show me and pulled out an old letter he'd literally saved from the bin when someone was clearing out their office the week before. It was sent by the zoo's director to the Catalan government on 18 September 1938, detailing the death of a camel from shrapnel wounds during an Italian bombing raid thirty days earlier. The document was a graphic reminder of the fate suffered by Barcelona for almost two years during the war, one of the first cities in the world to be systematically attacked from the air. Some 2,700 people were killed and thousands more seriously wounded in almost 200 air raids. People slept in their beds in fear, not knowing if their home might be hit that night.

Beginning in March 1937, Barcelona was bombed principally by the Italians from their base on Mallorca, which Franco had granted to Mussolini to bomb the Catalan coast. There was no radar and no land from which to telephone a warning of their approach. Folk typically had about three minutes to get to an air-raid shelter. Often, they didn't know the planes were coming until they were heard or even seen above the city. Despite this, the death toll was comparatively low. In part, this was due to medical advances. Many of the victims were treated by Professor Josep Trueta, head of trauma services for the city, who developed the use of a ground-breaking plaster cast method for the treatment of open wounds and fractures. More important, though, in saving lives was the building of a dense network of some 1,400 air raid shelters. Initially, the work was done by the local population, who set out to dig as soon as the first bombs fell. As the war continued, the authorities, through the remarkable work of the Junta Local de Defensa Passiva de Barcelona, built larger, more secure shelters and improved the self-built ones. Without the collective effort of a large part of the population, this herculean task would have been impossible.

Previously unknown shelters are found in Barcelona every six months or so. They came across a new one while doing building work a few streets from where we live in Poble-sec at the end of 2023. The designated shelter for our building, had we been living there in 1937, was just a few metres across the road from the front door. On the night of 22 June 1938, a bomb hit the building. It pierced most floors but didn't explode. Thankfully, nobody was injured, although my elderly neighbour Sra Rosa, then just a little girl, told me that everyone, asleep in their beds, had the shock of their lives. I regret now not asking her more about her memories of the war before she passed away. The bomb had its structural impact. Our apartment has wooden beams supporting every ceiling, while the central part of the apartments across the landing are supported by thin metal girders, installed after the bomb hit. All the flats in our building have seen large cracks open in the back façade, probably, I'm told, the result of the stress caused by the bomb crashing through the floors. Many were killed in raids on the neighbourhood. Indeed, the first aerial bombs to hit Barcelona on 16 March 1937 fell on Barceloneta and Poble-sec itself. One hit the corner of Carrer Creu dels Molers and Carrer Anníbal in Poble-sec. In all, six people were killed and thirty-nine injured. I walk past the rebuilt homes most mornings with my daughter on the way to school. As yet, no plaque has been erected, although this would seem a matter of ignorance rather than wilful omission on the part of the city council, as it has put up numerous plaques and memorials related to the war and the dictatorship.

The zoo was hit several times, killing a number of animals: a giraffe, a porcupine, a kangaroo, a polar bear—their meat very probably eaten by famished Barcelonans. I'd brought a few photographs along with me to show Josep. In one, taken on 16 September 1938, two Barbary macaques—not baboons, he corrected me—stare down at the camera from the top of a ruined building. It seemed a fair assumption, we discussed, that they were taken from Spanish colonial Morocco.[1]

I couldn't work out the location of where the macaques were perched, but Josep had an inkling: thinking he recognised the cornice, he took me out of the back entrance to the buildings across the road. He was spot on. Today, it's part of the Pompeu Fabra University campus, but in 1938, the complex was taken up by the Karl Marx barracks, headquarters of the International

Brigades in Barcelona. The macaques had presumably escaped after their enclosure had been hit and had found refuge on the roof. In another shot from the same reel by Carlos Pérez de Rozas, a monkey, maybe a vervet, its tail curling behind, picked its way across a desolate scene of rubble and masonry. Another photo by the Hungarian exile Kati Horna shows a dog lying slaughtered among rubble, a victim of the 18 March 1938 bombing of the city. Horna's lens often focused away from the epic towards the back scene, often on women and children, and, here, this poor animal, its black eyes seeming to still look into us today.

Josep and I talked about how the animals must have suffered from hunger. In his memoirs, the Abraham Lincoln Brigader Alvah Bessie related the story of a captured young Francoist soldier somewhere at the front who pleaded, "I will die, but please shoot me; don't feed me to the lions in Barcelona Zoo." This, of course, was the result of pure propaganda. The animals had very little to eat during the war. I took out another photo. Nine emaciated lion corpses and, as Josep pointed out, one hyena, are laid out on the ground, their keepers kneeling distraught behind them. They had to be shot: there was no meat left in the city for wild beasts. Whenever I see the photo, it always makes me think of the city's kids not having enough to eat.

By 1938, malnutrition had become a serious issue for the human population of Barcelona. The lack of food from farmland still controlled by the Republic and the difficulty of paying for imports was compounded by huge numbers of refugees arriving in the city fleeing Franco's army. The figures are dramatic. By the end of 1938, there were 400,000 refugees in Barcelona, which had a pre-war population of 1.2 million. It would have been much worse if not for the tens of thousands of tons of crops grown by the urban agricultural collective and allotments.

Júlia the elephant, a beloved pre-war celebrity, died on 12 August 1938. The Catalan Republican daily *La Humanitat* reported she had been killed by shrapnel, although it was probably starvation, the former story put out as a more politically acceptable account. Better it was a fascist bomb than publicly admitting the city could no longer feed her. Not that this failure would have come as any surprise to anybody living in Barcelona. According to a 1931 account, Júlia's daily diet consisted of between 30 and 40 kilos of straw, 60 kilos of beetroots, 20 kilos of oats and 5 kilos of carobs. Where would a hungry city that couldn't even feed its children find such quantities of food?[2] In the end, things must have been truly desperate for the surviving animals. Irish poet Louis MacNeice, who was in Barcelona just a few weeks before it fell in January 1939, described the zoo as "macabre—a polar bear 99 per cent dead, a kangaroo eating dead leaves". Josep sighed: "Stress might not have killed them directly, but hunger would have first broken up the structure of the groups. That would have caused aggression and infanticide. They would have lost considerable muscle mass. It would have slowly killed them."

Context: the final offensive on Catalonia

The Republic still had large armies in Central and Southern Spain in late 1938, but it could not transport them across Francoist lines, and although it could still nominally count on 250,000–300,000 troops in Catalonia, most were completely demoralised, unarmed and had no front-line experience. A Republican general estimated the army had just 17,000 rifles. Franco waited until 23 December to launch his final offensive on Catalonia. His 350,000-strong army, supported by hundreds of tanks and planes, quickly smashed through Republican lines.

As Franco's army approached in January 1939, Barcelona was also attacked by the Condor Legion, including forty incursions between 21 and 24 January 1939, principally in the form of a series of deadly raids by Stukas on Barceloneta. Like Mussolini, Hitler saw the city as a murderous testing ground, the results from which would later be put into widespread use with deadly effect on Warsaw, London, Leningrad and all the rest.

When Barcelona finally fell without resistance on 26 January, Franco's forces turned north towards the French border.

Fleeing from Barcelona

The traffic is heavy on Barcelona's ring road as it always is on a Monday morning, but the driving is comfortable enough in the disciplined traffic. Soon, we slip on to the A-7 Autopista towards Girona. Tens of thousands of refugees came this way as the Catalan capital fell in 1939. Within a few days, the figure had swollen to hundreds of thousands. It was a desperate flight to the French frontier. Many soldiers had given up by now. Large numbers went into hiding at the earliest opportunity. Some were caught and pressed back into service or simply shot. What was left of the Republican army fought a brave and desperate rear-guard action along a crumbling front to allow as many civilians to reach the border as possible. I can hardly imagine what it would have been like for these families, almost all of whom fled on foot with scared, hungry, exhausted children. And I can hardly imagine our own kids being put through such a fate, bombed and strafed all the way to the frontier.

We're now 30 kilometres northeast of Barcelona. The industrial sprawl of Granollers moves past our window to the left. I'm feeling a bit warm, so Mònica switches on the air-conditioning. Mussolini's planes flying in from Mallorca had hit the town on the morning of 31 May 1938. They were supposedly targeting its electricity power plant and war industries but missed, whether purposely or not. Instead, a murderous load of sixty bombs was dropped in the one-minute raid on the centre. It was at 9.05

a.m., peak time as locals made their way to work and school. Some 224 people were killed, including thirty-three children, and 165 injured. Many women were hit while standing in a long food queue in the market square. Food queues were always long in Catalonia by that stage of the war. In 2008, commemorating the sixtieth anniversary of the atrocity, a route was created by the town council marking the point where each of the sixty bombs struck. Dozens more were killed in bombing raids on the town in January 1939 as part of the widespread campaign to attack the routes followed by the refugees. An untold number died on the way, killed by bombs, shelling, strafing, exhaustion and hunger. Towns were also hit to block the Republican army's escape, a tactic Nazi Germany later used in the Second World War. They tested it first in Spain. Granollers fell on 28 January.

Half an hour more, and we're past the medieval city of Girona. Franco's forces captured it on 4 February after several days of heavy bombardment. The Republican territory was shrinking day by day. The motorway now strikes into the fertile Alt Empordà, today a playground for Barcelona's wealthy and the last county before France. The rebel army reached here on 7 February. *La Vanguardia Nacional* called it "the Little Red Zone". Republican resistance in Catalonia was crumbing. We take the exit for Figueres.

Figueres

Foreign visitors who head to Figueres for the Salvador Dalí Museum are often disappointed by the lack of old buildings. It used to have a lot more. Located far from the front, the town had been relatively unaffected by the war, but all of this changed in early 1939. As hundreds of thousands of refugees and soldiers streamed through, Figueres was repeatedly hit by Nazi and Italian airstrikes. Its streets soon became clogged with frightened humans, the dead and rubble. According to the figures in Enric

Pujol's book *Figueres, la Gernika catalana* (2019), 400 people were killed, although he admits the true figure could be higher. We'll never know because so many of the victims were refugees. Years later, they were still pulling out bodies from the rubble. More than 500 houses were destroyed. The town that Franco's troops entered on 9 February 1939 had a grim aspect as photos attest. But what is most striking about this horror is that it was never talked about. When I lived for a year in Figueres in 1990, my friends and my students made vague references to the damage done but never to people being killed or to who was responsible for dropping the bombs. And I must confess that I didn't ask questions either. Pujol explains that this amnesia has continued to the present—not only do most Catalans not know about the destruction of the town but neither do (or at least did) most Figuerencs. His book is part of a wave of publications across Spain that is helping to address this absence in memory.

On Sunday evenings, I'd sometimes hike up the hill to the Castell de Sant Ferran (see Fig. 10.1). Built in the mid-eighteenth century to defend the frontier against the French, it is the largest fortress in Europe outside of Russia. I learned long after my time in the town that the castle was also used during the war as a mustering station for the International Brigades who had hiked across the Pyrenees before being sent to Albacete. As such, it was often among their first memories of their time in Spain. Jack Jones, the twenty-two-year-old British volunteer who, as we saw in Chapter 8, was later wounded in the Ebro, arrived here in March 1938:

> In the light of the morning, we could see Spanish territory. After five hours or so, stumbling down the mountainside (I found it almost as hard going down as climbing up), we came to an outpost and from there were taken by truck to a fortress at Figueras. This was a reception centre for the volunteers. The atmosphere of old Spain was very

apparent in the ancient castle. For the first day or so we felt exhausted after the long climb. The food was pretty awful. We ate it because we were hungry but without relish.

The castle has been open to the public for some years, and in 2017 I finally got around to visiting with my son, then aged five. A group of us were taken around the huge moats in Land Rovers. They gave us yellow helmets to explore tunnels, and for a short while we were paddled eccentrically in a little dinghy around the dark cisterns deep underground, the highlight of the whole day for Albert. The Catalan guide did a good job keeping the mixed group of adults and children happy and was fun and knowledgeable in explaining the military architecture and earlier history. But it all went a bit strange when he touched on the topic of the Civil War. He claimed that the retreating Republicans had tried to blow up the castle's arsenal as they retreated from the town because they were following Stalin's orders, who, he also claimed, was "the inventor of scorched earth policies", which would have been news to the Romans and other ancient empires. The picture became all the clearer when he explained: "The terrible explosion shattered every single window down in Figueres." Apparently, they had all been undamaged by the carpet bombing of the previous two weeks, which he somehow neglected to mention. He was also unforthcoming on the presence of the International Brigades, and when I asked about a tiled memorial to the Brigades that I knew was somewhere in the castle, I was met with a lack of interest. After instructions by phone from Alan Warren, with whom I had travelled in the Ebro, I managed to locate it. It was in a sorry state, half illegible, scoured by the weather or human hand, and with the Catalan flag scratched out.

On 1 February 1939, the castle was the site of the last meeting of the Republican parliament to be held on Spanish soil. Just sixty-two of the total 473 parliamentarians were present to hear Prime Minister Negrín's final speech. The mood was funereal. *Daily Telegraph* correspondent Henry Buckley was in attendance—it was "cold and clammy," he remembered:

> There was something very like death down there. I whispered to Russian writer Ilya Erenburg who stood by me, "This place is like a tomb." He answered sententiously: "My friend, this place is not only the tomb of the Spanish Republic, but of European democracy." The awful thing about it was that I felt that he was right.[3]

La Jonquera

The N2 main road took us north into the foothills of the Pyrenees to La Jonquera, 5 kilometres short of Pertús Pass. This is one of Europe's great border crossings. Its gradual gradient and low height (290 metres) make it a logical place to traverse the range. It has certainly seen some history. The road more or less follows the route of the ancient Via Augusta, the busiest road in Roman Hispania, which ran for 1,500 kilometres connecting Gaul to Gādēs (Cádiz). Napoleon's troops came this way during the Peninsular War. Many of the tourists who came in droves to Spain in the 1960s chugged into Franco's dictatorship in cramped little cars and stuffy coaches from Northern Europe. The money they spent on the *costas* helped fuel the economic boom of the latter years of the dictatorship. Less well known are the huge remittances sent back by millions of low-wage Spanish workers who toiled in the factories of Northern Europe. Many also drove home laden with gifts and the strange accents of their children, as do Moroccan families these days on the way to and from the Maghreb.

The old town,[4] the last place in Spain, has not always been the frontier. The Pyrenees form a natural boundary and today divide the country from France, but the Catalan section of the range was not a political one until the Treaty of the Pyrenees of 1659 separated the Catalan-speaking Rosselló (Roussillon in French) from its Iberian counterpart. The mountains have in recent decades become a cultural frontier. Fewer and fewer people these days speak Catalan on the French side of the border.

It was through this little place and over the pass that the largest number of defeated Republicans crossed into France in January 1939. Perhaps 250,000 of the 450,000 who made the journey trod this way. The painter and author Max Aub described the scene in *January without a Name*:

> [T]he road to la Jonquera is like a funnel. ... full of trucks, customs police, soldiers, cars, assault guards, old people, torn newspapers, old people, petrol tankers, three cannons abandoned to my right, children, soldiers, mules, old people, wounded, cars, wounded, women, children, wounded, old people. Opposite me, a woman crouches by a fence crying, showing her legs in cinnamon-coloured stockings, and, around the top, thighs the colour of almond blossom, weeping her heart out. Nobody stops, everyone with their tiny stretch of the road on their shoulder. "The government's to blame." "The communists are to blame." "The CNT is to blame." "The republic is to blame." One child is alone, with an umbrella. "Where's your mother?" "In France." "Where's your father?" "Dead."[5]

When refugees arrived, they found the frontier closed. The French were unsure how to deal with the unfolding tragedy. People had to wait for days in the pouring rain at the different crossings. On 29 January 1939, they opened the border to women, children, the elderly and the infirm. Finally, disarmed Republican soldiers were allowed to cross on 5 February, as Nancy Cunard writing from Pertús for *The Manchester Guardian* described on 9 February:

> From nine o'clock this morning until 4.30, I have been watching soldiers pass between the two stone posts that are actually the frontier-

line. They have come by in thousands and thousands, in groups, singly, and in numberless lorries. At the posts stand the French soldiers, who immediately search them for arms. The Spanish soldiers give up their arms in an orderly fashion. The pile of rifles, revolvers, cartridge belts, dirks, and even a knife or two grow throughout the day. Two machine guns have been brought in; farther up, an armoured car. But all this is only the beginning; we are told: "Tomorrow the rearguard of the army, and afterwards—the army that has fought." On the mountains each side they come, so that the whole landscape seems to be moving. Soldiers on horseback, wounded men, women, children, a whole population, and cars and ambulances.

The exile museum

In remembrance of the tragic events in La Jonquera and its environs, the Catalan government opened the Museu del Exili in 2007. I was shown around by local historian David González. We were first confronted by two large photos covering a wall, one superimposed on the other. The first, in colour, is printed on a large transparent fabric and shows frightened life-size Bosnian refugees. David explained that day in 2016 that if they were to remake the image now, the refugees would have been Syrian—or, since then, refugees from whatever particular human tragedy was unfolding at the time. Behind this, a black and white image shows the same expressions on their faces, but in this case, they are Spanish refugees in 1939. We look through the contemporary face of a girl from Srebrenica into the eyes of those fleeing Franco's forces.

The main body of the museum inside is fashioned to represent an ocean liner, to remind us, David said, of those who crossed the sea into exile. Above us, the ceiling is taken up by a huge flat sculpture of a sandy beach covered in footprints, a dramatic reminder of the Republican experience in the French internment camps. The permanent exhibition is devoted to the Republican exile, though parallels are also made with other modern events. Most dramatically, on one wall I could hardly bear to look at the life-sized black and white photograph of young Ukrainian teenagers, with their bony chests, forced to stand to attention naked at the Mauthausen SS work camp in Austria. I avert my gaze, immediately thinking of my own son's fragility. In one of the display cases, David pointed to the donation of French medals and the beret of a Republican soldier called Bernat Olivé who had fought for the French resistance and later in the Armée française de la Libération. A single object, a bunch of dried flowers, lay on top of a glass cabinet that tells the story of Lluís Companys, who, as we shall see, was executed by the Franco regime in 1940 after being deported from Nazi-occupied France. It was left by an anonymous visitor in 2008, the year after the museum opened. The curators decided to leave it there as a memorial and an exhibit in itself. On my way out, I bought a T-shirt with the museum's motto—it's unusual for a museum to have a motto. *La llibertat viu lluny d'aquí, i això és l'exili.* It's from *King Lear*: "Freedom lives hence and banishment is here." The Catalan spells out Shakespeare's meaning and has its own poetry: "Freedom lives far from here, and that is exile."

Agullana to the frontier

With the road partly blocked at La Jonquera, tens of thousands tried their luck on the minor country roads that twist up towards the frontier. David drove along one of the routes they took, stopping at the village of Agullana. It's a handsome place, remarkable for its opulent villas built from the profits of the local cork industry and mining. A particularly grandiose house, Can Parellada, stands on the outskirts. Its huge and heavy iron gate had been fashioned into fantastic shapes by the architect Josep

Pijoan, who had clearly picked up a thing or two from Gaudí. Can Parellada was taken over by what was left of the Republican army's high command in January 1939. This was the Spanish Republican government's last seat after they had decamped from Figueres and was also the residence for a few days of Prime Minister Negrín. It was, in a sense, the last capital of Republican Spain—in a Catalan village with a population of 923 people in 2023. Information boards told us which houses were taken over by government ministries, which to all intents no longer existed in any practical sense, and by the Soviet and Mexican embassies that had also moved just before Barcelona fell. I asked an old resident if the home he was standing outside had been the Soviet embassy. "Soviets here, no. Just *Polacos*," he laughed. Meaning Polish, this is an old slur, of obscure origins, hurled at Catalans by Spanish nationalists, but one that has been claimed by some Catalans as a source of jocular pride. The man pointed with a smile around the corner to a well-appointed house, coincidentally painted in red. I peered into its lush little garden. David pointed out that relations between Spain and the Soviet Union basically ended here in this modest house and didn't resume again until the 1970s, with full recognition not re-established until February 1977.[6]

Mexico

We headed down to a more modest home at the bottom of the street. For a few days in 1939, this was the Mexican embassy. Like the USSR but only more so, Mexico never recognised Franco's government and maintained official relations with the Republican government in exile until 1977. The Latin American country was really the only state to come out well from the Spanish Civil War. President Lázaro Cárdenas supported the Republic from the outset, due to genuine ideological affinity and as part of the country's attempt to develop its own foreign policy distinct from that of the United States. It was also unencumbered by the so-called Non-Intervention Agreement, which only involved European states. Mexico sent some 20,000 mainly Mauser rifles and a large number of cartridges along with machine guns, planes and other weapons, although as the shipments were secret it is difficult to know the precise figures. More importantly, it acted as an honest broker on the international arms market, allowing the Republican government to acquire weapons it could not directly purchase itself. Along with the USSR, the country was the only reliable arms supplier to the Republic, although given the distance and modesty of its resources, this aid was always limited.

Mexico also stood out in the support it gave to Republican refugees. During the war, some 500 child refugees were taken in by the country. After the collapse of the Republic, Mexico worked to get several thousand Republicans released from French internment camps. The country accepted more than 20,000 Spanish exiles. These included large numbers of intellectuals, doctors, engineers and teachers. Several Mexicans I've met on my tours have told me it changed the country for the better. They were part of the huge intellectual diaspora that left Spain in 1939, greatly enriching intellectual life in Latin America—and above all Mexico. Spain must surely still be paying for this loss. A part of this brain drain came from Catalonia itself.

La Vajol

The road wound up through corkwoods dotted with granite boulders, as idyllic snatches of the Mediterranean appeared in our view. The Republic's leaders—Spanish President Manuel Azaña, Prime Minister Negrín, Basque President José Antonio Aguirre and Catalan President Companys—came this way, creeping in their cars, the narrow lanes clogged with broken down vehicles, horses and donkeys piled high with belongings, past thousands of desperate, exhausted women, men and children, many sick or wounded, burdened with huge bundles, all desperately trying to reach France in an ever-shrinking area of territory. Anarchist leader Federica Montseny remembered them: "Who can forget those times, that spectacle of mountains swarming with folk camped out under the trees, shivering with cold and terror?"[7] By 1 February, all four Republican figures had arrived at La Vajol, barely 3 kilometres from the French border. For a few nights, they slept in farmhouses around this quiet, tiny Catalan village. La Vajol (population of ninety-seven in 2023), like Agullana, also likes to claim it is the last capital of Republican Spain. We came upon an assemblage of fading memorials in Catalan and Spanish. It felt like a shrine to loss. One reads: "These stones are seeds of the tree of memory." Azaña, Negrín, Aguirre and Companys: each has had his own memorial put up by foundations in their name. A small plaque pays tribute to the Spanish Republicans who died in Nazi camps. Another says: "Homage to those who *suffered* exile." Of course, in English, we say "go into exile", but the Catalan verbal expression *patir l'exili* has it much better. On the early morning of 5 February 1939, the four leaders left Spain. It is said they had all agreed to meet at 7 a.m. so they could make the journey together, but, it is also claimed, Azaña did not want to be accompanied by mere autonomous regional presidents and left an hour early in the dark together with Negrín. Divided till the end, then. Their cars soon broke down. They had to hike up the last stretch along an icy path.

Monument to the exile

David took me along a short track from the village to a clearing surrounded by cork oaks. In the middle is an outcrop of granite boulders, on top of which stands a statue (see Fig. 10.2). It is perhaps the most moving memorial to the Republican exile. It gets me every time I've been back. The life-sized bronze sculpture depicts a man named Mariano Gracia. His face is gaunt, his eyes sunken, and a blanket is thrown over his shoulders. Mariano is holding his seven-year-old daughter's hand. Alicia has one leg and is supported by a crutch. The work is modelled on a famous shot taken by the French photojournalist Hélène Roger Viollet in early February 1939 and was first published in a photo report on the Republican tragedy for the French magazine *L'Illustration* the same month. It is perhaps the most iconic image of the exile, steeped in suffering and loss but also perhaps reflecting relief that they have made it across the border. Anyone with half a heart must wonder what became of those depicted. In the original photo, it's not just Alicia. Her little brother, four-year-old Amadeo, walking behind them, is also missing a leg. They both lost their limbs, along with their mother, in a bomb raid on Monzón in November 1937 as the family were fleeing the Aragonese town for the safety of the countryside to escape Hitler's planes. From here, they were evacuated to a hospital in Barcelona and then to a children's home. In 1939, with Franco's troops advancing rapidly, they made their way up to the frontier at Coll d'Ares (1,513 metres), 60 kilometres to the east of La Vajol near where the actual photograph was taken. They had to trudge through the snow as the pass is much higher than at La Vajol.

Amadeo's hand is held by a French peasant called Thomas Coll. He also has a wooden leg, replacing the one he lost fighting in the French army in the First World War. Coll had heroically hobbled up from his home in Prats de Molló on the French side to help the refugees. Behind Amadeo is Antonio, his twelve-year-old brother. He was saved as their mother had sent him back home to get a thimble, a few minutes before the bomb fell. Mariano died in France a year and a half later—from tuberculosis, as far as I can ascertain. Without parents, the children were automatically sent back on a louse-infested train to Spain, where they spent awful, awful years in hospices run by the Catholic Church; beatings, humiliations and hunger were the daily fare for the orphaned children of the defeated. In 2003, *El País* newspaper published the photo in a report on the exile. A few days later, they received a letter sent by a pensioner called Amadeo Gracia, stating: "The boy in the second row is me, and those in front are my father and sister." Some weeks later, the journalist who wrote the piece took Amadeo, now sixty-nine, back to walk the same path, but he was unable to remember anything. He also visited the memorial here in La Vajol. He had been unaware of its existence. Writing in the letter to *El País*, he said: "No, I can't forget or forgive. Have any of them ever said sorry?" Amadeo died in Madrid in 2019.

I asked David how school groups reacted when he used to bring them to the memorial. "It's what happened to Alicia and Amadeo that really connects to young people. The story creates empathy. You can see it in their faces. Then as a teacher, bam, you can connect to the wider history." It's a good lesson in how storytelling can bring history to life, whatever your age.

Mina Canta (Negrín's Mine) and El Prado

A couple of kilometres from La Vajol, we pulled up and walked along a track into a thick forest to a large concrete structure, partly concealed by the trees (see Fig. 10.3). Somebody had painted the image of Mariano and Alicia on one of the walls. "It's an old mine," David informed me. "They dug talcum here until the 1960s." I didn't even know talcum powder came from a mine, but the story of Mina Canta is a more interesting one, as David also explained. In 1937, Negrín, the Republican prime minister, ordered the Ministry of Finance to secretly build a bunker over the mine. Concealed by thick forest and protected by the shoulder of a steep hill, it would have been virtually impossible to bomb without entering French airspace, which lay just a kilometre away. All in all, an ideal place to hide things. Not all of Spain's gold had been sent to Moscow and Paris. What was left—500 million dollars in ingots along with other financial assets—were stored here. Locals call the place "La mina de Negrín". It also played an interesting role in the history of European art. By the autumn of 1936, bombs and shells were raining down on Madrid each day. The Republic decided to remove the incalculable treasures of El Prado and the city's other museums and private collections— El Prado itself was hit, purposely or not, by incendiary bombs on 16 November.

Over several months, including during the key days around the defence of the Spanish capital in November 1936, a secret operation transferred the artworks, packed into specially fashioned crates, to Valencia. It took the trucks a long day to cover the 360 kilometres along the then-dire Spanish roads, bad before the war, worse now through military traffic. They drove under the constant threat of bombardment. In all, 2,000 works left Madrid, including some 350 from El Prado, the core of one of the greatest art assemblages in the world, collected over the centuries by the Spanish monarchy. In March 1938, with Valencia seemingly about to fall, it was decided to send the trove to Catalonia. The lorries only just made it before the Republic's territory was, as we have seen, split into two by Franco's offensive, the last truck passing through Vinaròs just hours before the arrival of Nationalist troops.

It seems symbolic that among the very few works to be damaged in the whole operation were Francisco de Goya's two most famous paintings of war: *The Second of May 1808* and *The Shootings of the Third of May 1808*, both completed in 1814. The former, also known as *The Charge of the Mamelukes*, depicts an uprising in Madrid against the French occupation of Spain, one of a number of popular rebellions that sparked the Peninsular War. It shows Napoleon's Egyptian mercenary cavalry, cutting with their scimitars into civilians who fight back with knives. As the truck carrying the painting passed through the Valencian town of Benicarló, it crashed into a building previously weakened by a bomb raid by Mussolini's air force a few days earlier. A corner of the structure crashed on to the crate, tearing the painting into twenty pieces. It still bears the scars. Two fragments are missing. *The Shootings of the Third of May 1808* was also slightly damaged. It is ground-breaking in the depiction of war. We look at faceless, anonymous Napoleonic troops lining up in a firing squad to murder anonymous Spanish resisters in Madrid. There are no nobles, just ordinary people. There is a priest, desperately praying, but there seems to be no salvation, just fear as they line up. We see those already murdered. Those about to be. Those waiting their turn.

The artworks were brought to the north of Catalonia. While some were stored in San Ferran in Figueres, many were kept at the nearby Peralada castle, where restorers managed, under precarious conditions, to put back together *The Charge of the Mamelukes*. Velázquez's *Las Meninas* (1656), the most emblematic of El Prado's works, was also kept there. Others were moved to Mina Canta (no precise record exists of which works were stored at which site). With Franco's forces closing in and the escape routes being systematically bombed, Republican foreign minister Julio Álvarez del Vayo and the assistant director of the Louvre Jacques Jaujard met in secret and agreed to evacuate the treasures to Geneva, to be kept under the custody of the League of Nations. On 4 February, some seventy trucks carrying 1,842 crates left Spain, driving past women, children, the elderly and men on crutches. In some cases, the organisers stopped lorries carrying wounded men and forced them off, many of whom probably died. Seven of the lorries departed from La Vajol carrying the Republic's remaining gold reserves and other financial assets, which would be used to help relieve the plight of the refugees in France and beyond, particularly in Mexico. Local legend, almost certainly unfounded, has it that only six crossed the frontier, leading to treasure hunters periodically scouring the mountainside. The artworks and other objects arrived in Geneva on 14 February 1939. Seven days after the German invasion of Poland, the treasures returned by a specially commissioned train to Franco's Madrid. I've not been to El Prado for years, but next time I visit I'm sure I won't forget the odyssey made by many of its masterpieces—all of those Velázquezes, El Grecos, Tizianos.

Lluís Companys

Another day, Mònica and I hiked up to the frontier from La Vajol. The view behind us is stunning. The Gulf of Roses opens up, drawing a perfect semi-circular bay framed to the left by the Albera Mountains, the last gasp of the Pyrenees, and between us the Pertús Pass. It was the exiles' last view of Catalonia, their last of Spain. Antoni Rovira i Virgili, linguist and later president-in-exile of Catalonia, remembered bidding farewell along this road:

> I give my silent, heartfelt farewell to the beautiful landscape before me. I watch the fires of the last sun, these fires as red as blood. When the sun sets again tomorrow, I will be across the borderline. The star has fallen behind the mountains. I feel a cold wave of sadness pass through me. The sun has set on Catalonia.[8]

Rovira i Virgili never did return. He died in 1949 and is buried in the Cimetière de Le Perthus, a few hundred metres from his homeland.

The path takes us through cork oak woods. The trunks have been stripped of the bark just below head height. Their appearance is striking. Some are a rich orange, others ox-blood red. When mature, they are harvested every nine years for the next 150 years or so—most cork farms are passed down from generation to generation, or as an adage has it: "Eucalyptus trees are for us, pine trees for our children, and cork trees for our grandchildren." The path flattens out. We're at the top of the Pyrenees, *el Coll del Lli*, although the woods impede any view. It was sunny that day, but other times I've done this walk in the mist. That brings on a more cinematographic sense of those days of defeat. We come upon an information board about Companys, the Catalan president, who passed this way in 1939. Memorials seem to be everywhere in this landscape. His picture was hardly visible. It had been repeatedly scratched over, as you can see in Fig. 10.4. You could feel the hatred of whoever did it. The defaced version would make a good exhibit in a museum on the divided legacy of the war: a reminder of those who would want to resurrect a different narrative of the past. A few metres farther on, a modest farm gate marks the border between the two states. We passed through unaware, distracted talking about this and that. Suddenly, we hear French voices and hikers coming the other way. We might not have realised we'd crossed, but somebody had. Moments later, our mobiles beeped with messages from the Spanish Ministry of Foreign Affairs advising us to call the Paris embassy in case of emergency.

Did those leaders look back, contemplating the sure fate of Spain as a personal failure? The Republic had lifted for a few years the terrible slab of centuries of oppression. Franco was now slamming it back down again. Socialists and communists must have felt their dreams were over, as were those of Basque and Catalan republicans who'd fought in their different ways for another relationship with Spain. For most of the anarchists, that dream was probably already long gone. I thought of the thousands and thousands of others who had passed this way, their hopes and dreams now turning into a nightmare, their futures utterly insecure.

We walk on into France. The woodland was much more worked now we're on the French side, stacks of logs are neatly piled here and there, and much of the undergrowth has been cleared away. Most of the trees are young, growing over what looked like abandoned farmland—the land on both sides was much more open in 1939. We descend steeply, although the going is easy enough. Azaña, aged fifty-six and overweight, and his wife struggled down the icy path that day. Twenty minutes later, we reach the hamlet of Les Illes. A plaque on the wall of the Hostal dels Trabucayres remembers that the four leaders arrived here in the morning. It explained they had fled Spain due to "International Fascist Nazi Aggression", an unusual phrase perhaps to be written on an idyllic *gîte* in the French Pyrenees. The owner understood my Catalan—my French is a joke—but didn't speak the language. So few French people seem to these days in Roussillon. In his case, he said he'd moved from Northern France.

We had a sandwich and a beer and paid our euros. You knew you were in France because the price was 50 per cent more than on the other side, even though the Catalan Pyrenees are relatively expensive. Azaña and Aguirre would stay in France. Negrín hadn't given up yet. He was driven to Toulouse, from where a few days later, using an assumed name, he boarded a scheduled Air France flight to Alicante, which was still under Republican control, along with about 30 per cent of Spanish territory. The story goes that Companys stayed for coffee and an omelette but had no money. They still joke in the village that Catalonia owes them.

Companys settled in a village in Brittany, where in 1940 he was arrested by the Gestapo and returned by a Francoist agent to Spain. In Madrid, he was tortured and then driven to Barcelona, court-martialled and executed by firing squad in Montjuïc castle on 15 October. Catalan historians often point out he was the only democratically elected president—albeit a regional one—to be executed during the Second World War. He was tried by a kangaroo court with absolutely no semblance of legal process— one of the more than half a million people in Spain, most of whom few people have ever heard of, who were court-martialled and received the death penalty or other punishments. The principal charge against Companys and most of the others was military rebellion, which is an act of historical sarcasm given that he had opposed one. Not a single one of these cases or the sentences imposed was revoked until the 2022 Democratic Memory Law annulled all of them, including that of Companys. To put it another way, until three years before this book was published, he was still technically guilty—even though the Olympic Stadium and probably hundreds of streets and squares in Catalonia are named after him. This indicates how the Civil War and the Franco regime are still divisive issues in Spain today, which has resulted in the partial and often contradictory attempts to deal with the past. It's not that nothing has been done— on the contrary, a huge amount of work has been carried out in remembering and documenting the war and the subsequent Franco regime by historians, journalists, lawmakers, teachers, activists, cultural creators and families. But a huge amount has purposely not been done and has in some cases more recently even been undone. Another plaque, forming part of a "Chemins de la liberté route", outside the Hostal dels Trabucayres, reminds us the hostel was also used by Jewish refugees and Allied airmen escaping the German occupation in France, treading the same path but back towards Spain.

11

FRANCE

Argelès-sur-Mer

I was glad to be wrapped up as we trekked across the sand, a cold Tramontana wind whipping across our faces. A little funfair stood by the beach, looking a bit forlorn as it waited for the kids, still months away. Most of the bars, shops and apartments were boarded up for the winter. Argelès-sur-Mer felt like any other kitschy holiday place on the Costas in Spain but with a French air. Thousands of tourists come here every year. I'm sure many take home happy family memories. Few must leave knowing what happened on these sands.

In ten days in 1939, some 450,000 people—roughly half soldiers, half civilians—crossed the border into what was still democratic France. They came with their battered suitcases, makeshift bundles, casks of oil and blankets. The roads on both sides were littered with abandoned vehicles and possessions people no longer had the strength to carry. Many of them hadn't eaten for days. Many were terrified by the horrific bomb attacks from fascist planes. Many trudged along the icy roads in rope sandals. Some 10,000 were wounded. Large numbers were sick. The elderly, heavily pregnant women, children and defeated troops all came. Some carried a fistful of Spanish soil, perhaps wrapped in a red and black anarchist scarf. Or a scarf of the four red and yellow stripes of the Catalan flag. International volunteers also sometimes came home with some earth. Ken Loach employs the image at the start of *Land and Freedom*, which begins with the death of the film's protagonist David Carr, who had fought in Spain with the POUM militia sixty years earlier. Back at his Liverpool council flat, his granddaughter comes across a suitcase of mementos from the war, including the soil of Spain he had wrapped in an old red scarf. The Franco regime sealed the border on 10 February 1939.

The French state was ill-prepared for the influx. It had been expecting 150,000. The refugees had arrived in one of the poorest parts of the country. The right-wing government of Édouard Daladier had ignored warnings from their consul of the coming influx. The Spanish Republican authorities, barely functioning, were also at fault for not indicating the real numbers. Some control of those arriving was inevitable. But how they were treated was criminal. There was strong pressure in France from the right-wing press and parties to deal with people as harshly as possible so they would return to Spain and not, as they put it, "infect" France. There was also an internal political message in French politics—this chaos is what you'll get if you vote for the left. There was also a strong element of racism. The French right used to say that Africa begins at the Pyrenees. Many French villagers did a lot to help, providing food and shelter when they could, but were soon overwhelmed by the sheer numbers. Meanwhile, the French state soon militarised the zone and made such aid illegal. Others looked on in horror and disgust as these desperate, ragged foreigners traipsed through their villages. Families were usually separated. Men one way, women and children the other. They were *herded* by mounted gendarmes like *animals*—words you read again and again in contemporary accounts—on to a series of open-air makeshift camps, particularly on the beaches just across the border near Perpignan. Argelès-sur-Mer was the first and most infamous. It held more than 100,000 internees. You'll sometimes see them described as refugee or internment camps. In 1939, the French government and right-wing media happily called them concentration camps. While incomparable to the full horror of Nazi hells, these beaches and their predecessors were a step towards what was to come.

When we hear the term "concentration camp", we tend to think immediately of the SS complexes. But this emphasis conceals a longer history of camps, a distinctive feature of twentieth-century Europe, one already firmly implanted before the arrival of the Third Reich. The term itself originates from the 1890s, when the Spanish military forcibly relocated rural civilians into camps to prevent them from feeding and sheltering Cuban rebels. They called their policy *reconcentración*. By 1898, a third of Cuba's population had been moved into camps. At least 170,000 Cuban civilians perished behind their fences due to hunger, disease and ill-treatment. This was 10 per cent of the island's population at the time. There are horrible photos documenting famished children online should you wish to investigate more. The plan was implemented by General Valeriano Weyler. Until 2021, Weyler still had a street named after him in Badalona, just to the north of Barcelona.

There was no housing at Argelès. Inmates had to fashion huts from reeds from the marshes or whatever bits and pieces they could find. There was no sanitation. Hundreds succumbed under atrocious conditions: untreated war wounds, dysentery, hyperthermia and even thirst.[1] I'm sure some died simply of despair. Food didn't arrive for days. When it did, the guards amused themselves by throwing bread over the barbed wire. As the weeks drew on, guards brought in petroleum baths to combat the fleas and lice. Outside of law or protection, it was here that the defeated were held: those who believed either in the progress offered by the Republic or by the alternative society envisioned by the anarchists. For many, by 1939 it would have been an amalgamation of both. Barbed wire and guards stood on one side, the cold February sea, a natural border, on the other. More than one took their last walk into its waters. Those who tried to escape could be shot on sight or tied as punishment to a pole for days, exposing them to the elements. However, the guards were lax, and many people did manage to get away.

A year after visiting Argelès in early February 1939, the famed Catalan cellist Pau Casals, who was prominently involved in raising money for the refugees, wrote to a friend:

> There are no words to describe the horror of what is going on here. The scenes I witnessed might have been from Dante's Inferno. Tens of thousands of men and women and children were herded together like animals, penned in by barbed wire, housed—if one can call it that— in tents and crumbling shacks. There were no sanitation facilities or provisions for medical care. There was little water and barely enough food to keep the inmates from starvation. The camp at Argelès was typical. Here more than a hundred thousand refugees had been massed in open areas among sand dunes along the seashore. Though it was winter they had been provided with no shelter whatsoever—many had burrowed holes in the wet sand to protect themselves from the pelting rains and bitter winds. The driftwood they gathered for fires to warm themselves was soon exhausted. Scores had perished from exposure, hunger and disease. At the time of my arrival, the hospitals at Perpignan still overflowed with the sick and dying.[2]

Sandy beaches aren't my thing, but the kids love them. We brought Albert here one cold Easter as I wanted to have a look around at what remained. I found a couple of information panels and a small memorial. We paddled in the sea, had ice creams, made sandcastles. Sand was a constant presence in the lives of the refugees. It got into their food and every crack in their bodies. They talked about a psychosis among some prisoners called *arenitis*—"sanditis". Another time, I stood there on the sand. It was February. Eighty-five years since the first Republican refugees arrived in France. A vicious wind ripped up from the north, the Tramontana, on its way to Catalonia. While giving tours in Catalan, I've met hundreds of people whose parents and grandparents passed through these camps. They often relate how their family members had to dig holes, as Casals reported, in the wet sand to escape from the wind and the rain. They hold family memories of hunger, thirst, cold and humiliation. The lice and the scabies. The brutality of the French and Senegalese colonial guards. The sense of betrayal. The camps constitute, along with the Ebro battle, part of the collective memory of Catalonia.[3]

In March 1939, Capa was given permission to photograph part of the camp. The images were published the same month in the British magazine *Picture Post* under the title "The Forgotten Army". We see men outside the flimsiest of shacks cooking over a fire in the sand, prisoners writing letters, a mother dressed in black talking to her son behind barbed wire. The article begins: "Miguel Largo is a Catalan peasant. He thought once to have passed his life peacefully on the strip of land his family have cultivated for generations. He expected neither luxury, nor misery. Now he is living in a hole in the sand on the seashore at Argeles." It continues:

> He has no money. He has the clothes he stands up in ... He does not know where his wife and children are, except that they, too, are refugees somewhere in France. ... When he gets his food, he gulps the coffee down quickly, before the sand gets into it.

In one image taken by Capa on 18 March 1939, perhaps the most iconic of the Spanish Republican diaspora, we see a long line of ex-Republican soldiers being marched by a Gendarme across the sand. They are en route from Argelès to Camp de Barcarès on another beach a few kilometres to the north. There, at least, they were housed in wooden barracks. Some years ago, Xavier de la Cruz, a Catalan researcher in war photography, suggested the first man in the line was none other than Francesc Boix, the eighteen-year-old we'd left on the Segre Front with his camera and goofy smile. He certainly looks like him. Boix accompanied the Republican army into exile, crossing the border in February 1939, and may have been marched to Argelès, although good evidence has him at other camps. The man is smiling at Capa as if he knew him. If it is Francesc, he probably did, having worked in the photo unit for the PSUC at the Hotel Colón, which Capa had used. On his back, he is carrying a stick, which looks very much like a tripod, over which is hanging a wooden box.

De la Cruz thinks the box contained Boix's negatives, which were apparently lost in the Second World War. In 2010, an auction house put up for sale a wooden box containing 1,368 negatives taken by an unknown photographer, about half of which were from pre-war Barcelona, the rest from the Spanish Civil War. A few of the images were published by the newspaper *El Periódico* in the hope that somebody would come forward to help identify the author. To cut a long story short, people did come forward to help identify some of the subjects. The researchers connected the dots. They were aided by the handwritten annotations that accompanied some of the negatives. The images from the war—the Segre Front as it turned out, which I mentioned at Vilanova de la Barca—were by Boix. Somehow they ended up with an antiquarian in Perpignan. At the insistence of Catalan archivist Ricard Marco, they were eventually acquired by the Arxiu Nacional de Catalunya. They have since been put on show in several interesting exhibitions on Boix's work in Catalonia, Madrid and France.

We drove out of the resort past apartment blocks and pine trees down Avenue de la Retirada 1939. *Retirada* is Spanish for retreat. It was an overly optimistic term used to describe what was really a flight into exile; for many, it was a permanent one. A few hundred metres along is the Cimetière des Espagnols. It is surrounded by a low wall and fence. The French authorities buried hundreds of Spanish Republicans here who had died on the beach. There are several memorials. A granite column is inscribed with a couple of hundred names (see Fig. 11.1). In addition to Spanish and Catalan, many are Central and Eastern European. Some are Yiddish. I wrote a few down: Metsckowski, Petros, Polevoy, Popoff, Schmidt, Tugas, Winterstein. I don't know if anybody has researched them systematically, but I think it's safe to say most were wounded or sick brigaders who succumbed on the beach. Another memorial reads "Seventy children died in this camp. They were less than 10 years old." A Republican flag flies among the pines.

Collioure

Just down the coast from Argelès is the small town of Collioure. It is an attractive place. Old terraced houses with red terracotta roofs line its narrow streets as they wind down to the small harbour. Out of season, it is much quieter than the equally pretty Cadaqués on the other side of the border. There's no Barcelona on the French side to fill up the town most of the year. Its most photogenic feature is the imposing castle (see Fig. 11.2). Once a Templar stronghold, it is idyllically sited on a low promontory right on the sea's edge that splits the town's beaches into two. Castles usually have dark medieval histories that the centuries of time and romanticisation have obscured. For the Château Royal de Collioure, repression is also a more recent thing. It was used in 1939 as a disciplinary camp for some 350

Spanish exiles and international brigaders deemed to be especially dangerous by the French state, none of whom, it goes without saying, had been accused or convicted of any crime. Cold, damp, windowless, airless cells with pallets for beds, dire sanitation, forced labour, inhumane treatment and beatings in dungeons were the daily fare. The brutal guards had unlimited power over their lives. Hunger strikes were organised in protest by Yugoslav and Bulgarian ex-brigaders and Spanish exiles. The authorities responded with force-feeding. In the tight confinement of the castle's walls, anarchist and communist prisoners often found themselves crammed in together, when only eighteen months before they had been fighting each other on Barcelona's streets. As many as 100 men died in prison. The front page of the French communist daily *L'Humanité* denounced the appalling conditions with a front-page headline on 14 May 1939, "Un bagne fasciste en France" ("A fascist penal colony in France").[4] The prison was closed two months later and the survivors moved to other camps or deported to North Africa.[5]

When I last visited, the castle had recently put up a plaque remembering the history. They have since created a small permanent exhibition inside the walls. Sometime later, I met Alex Chip from Washington who was writing a novel about his communist grandfather from Zaragoza—Vicente Martín Martínez was imprisoned in these walls. Alex told me that when he visited the castle on a day of relentless wind, he'd felt the ghosts of the prisoners. He'd imagined that a rusty hook he came across was used to force-feed men on hunger strikes as if they were foie farm geese. He said the loneliness and sadness stayed with him as he left, like tobacco smoke on your coat.

Machado

A blackbird was singing on a tombstone in the little cemetery as we entered through the black iron gate. We stood in front of a grave, a shrine to the poet, decorated with dried flowers, little pebbles and pinecones (see Fig. 11.3). Republican flags were draped on the fence behind. Antonio Machado arrived in Collioure, exhausted and sick, in the late afternoon of 28 January 1939. He is perhaps the nearest thing Castilian-speaking Spain has to a national poet and one of the leading figures of the Spanish literary movement known as the Generation of '98. Although born in Seville, his words are intimately associated with his powerful evocations of the landscapes of Castile, and, in particular, Soria. I can read the verses of "Campos de Soria" ("Fields of Soria", 1912) again and again, but that would be for another book. After the arrival of the Republic in 1931, he worked for the Misiones Pedagógicas (Educational Missions). They were organised by the Republican government and helped to bring literature, art, theatre and literacy to villages around the country. The programme involved some 500 volunteers including teachers, artists and intellectuals. Machado's friend Federico García Lorca took part with his theatre group La Barraca, which performed classical Spanish plays in villages where most spectators had barely had a written word outside the Bible in Latin read to them before. More than 5,000 libraries were also established. At the start of the war, Machado was in Madrid. With Franco's army seemingly about to take the capital, he was evacuated in November 1936, not without some resistance on his part, to a village in Valencia. In April 1938, with the rebels about to split the Republic in two, he was brought to Barcelona. The ageing poet left the Catalan capital as part of a convoy of Republican intellectuals just four days before it fell, accompanied by his ailing mother Ana Ruiz. At the seaside border town of Portbou, the family were driven to the frontier, but the car, stuck in the clog of traffic, soon ran out of petrol. Ana was helped on the long, painful trek over the border by her other son José, while Antonio stumbled along, clutching a small case containing his last poems.

A Republican soldier came upon Machado and his mother sitting alone on a bench at Cerbère, the first French village after the border. Eulalio Ferrer spoke to the poet, whom he greatly admired, and wrapped his army blanket around the pair, "their need greater than mine", he remembered.[6] The family slept their first night in France in an abandoned train, before being driven to Collioure. The other intellectuals continued to Paris, but Machado insisted on staying close to his peninsula. He died in a pension hotel in the village on 22 February, wracked with grief for the fall of the Republic and the loss of many friends. He was sixty-three years old. Ana passed away three days later, aged eighty-four. She is buried next to her son, barely 30 kilometres from the border. Spanish Republican soldiers released from the camps were permitted to bear Machado's coffin to the little cemetery, covered in their flag.

What would have happened to Machado, if he had been in his beloved Soria or another provincial Castilian town on the first day of the war? Would the rebels have shot him against a cemetery wall or in a forgotten ravine as they did to Lorca? You could easily be murdered for less. He certainly had admirers high up in the Falange, but so did the Granadan poet. Many on the Sorian right hated him. The deeply conservative town, with a population of 10,000 in 1936, had experienced no revolutionary violence before the war and saw no resistance to the coup, but violence was unleashed anyway, as it was across all of Old Castile. Around 300 people were shot and dumped into mass graves around the town. After the war, the regime and the Falange appropriated Machado's work, taking its strong Spanish identity while stripping it of its political connotations.

People have been coming to Collioure to pay homage since 1939. A few days after Machado died, cellist Casals came alone to his grave and played the beautiful "El cant dels ocells" ("The song of the birds"). In the half-hour we were there in the cemetery, a dozen or so people came by to pay their respects. A father whispered to his young daughter, but I could not catch his words. A Catalan couple stood quietly before laying a flower. We spoke to an old woman from Cádiz. Carmen had accompanied her son and his family four years ago after he had lost his job. Now there wasn't enough work in France. She wanted to see his grave before they returned to Andalusia. A memorial inscribed on the tombstone reads:

> Y cuando llegue el día del último viaje,
> y esté al partir la nave que nunca ha de tornar
> me encontraréis a bordo ligero de equipaje,
> casi desnudo, como los hijos de la mar.

> When the day arrives to make the final journey,
> and the ship that will never return is about to depart,
> you will find me aboard, travelling light,
> almost naked, like the children of the sea.[7]

I picked up a yellowing piece of paper an admirer had left on top of the gravestone. It read "Estos días azules y este sol de la infancia" ("These blue days and this sun of childhood"). They are presumed to be the last words the poet wrote. José Machado had taken his brother to see the sea three days before he passed away. He found the verse in his brother's jacket pocket after he died. I hope the words were in Antonio's mind as he passed away.

We left Collioure, Machado on my mind, along the winding sea road south, through vineyards growing on steep hills, to a quiet little cove. Idyllic when looking seawards, Plage Bernardi is brutally cut off from the land by a low concrete wall. To one side, we scrambled up to two intact bunkers. Old barbed wire lay rusting around. Military-grade, my friend informed me. I took a short piece home, imagining it as an exhibit illustrating the Spanish in the camps, although it's still unused on a shelf. I couldn't work out who had built these defences. There was one other person in the cove. A sweet old German lady was collecting gravel for her potted plants. She smiled apologetically and told us it was "Us Germans." She showed us an information panel. The Nazis built the fortifications as part of the defensive line of the coast after they occupied Vichy France in November 1942, putting to an end any pretence of the Pétain regime's supposed independence. The bunkers and blocks stand here ugly in the sand, stupidly facing the Mediterranean calm. Many probably think they should be demolished. They are offensive and scar the cove. Personally, I believe it's probably best to leave them standing as a physical reminder of the past and let them decay on their own. The German woman pointed up the coast: "We also blew up the harbour and all the houses at Port-Vendres in 1944 even though the war was almost over."

Jan Geza Pošner after Spain

I'd left the story of Jan Geza Pošner, Liz Kopp's Slovak father, while I was in Aragon. After fighting in the International Brigades, he crossed the frontier with the Republican army and was interned at the infamous camp at Gurs in the Pyrenees. By July 1939, there were some 19,000 detainees from the war in Spain in the camp, of whom more than 6,500 were Basque. A number died under the harsh conditions imposed by the French government. Liz showed me a black and white photo, reproduced here in Fig. 11.4. A group of Czechoslovak prisoners are standing around an outdoor trough. "That's him there, stripped to the waist, washing himself. I visited the camp a few years ago and they helped me identify the hut he'd help to build and where he slept. That was moving."

After being released from Gurs, Jan managed to get to the UK, where he met Liz's mother Margaret. He fought with the

British army during the Second World War and then returned to Czechoslovakia with his family, where, according to Liz, "he was heavily involved with the resistance against the communists". Perhaps, like many others, he'd become disillusioned in Spain. At some point, he was betrayed—Liz strongly suspects his brother. "We were on a train. He was picked up by soldiers at a station. That was the last time I saw my father in Czechoslovakia." Jan was deported in 1950 or 1951 to the uranium mines of Jáchymov—the same mine, incidentally, where Marie Skłodowska-Curie and her husband had discovered radium in 1898. It was now run as a gulag in which many Czech dissidents perished (the Nazis had previously also used slave labour here in part of their atomic programme). Apparently about to die from the radiation poisoning, he was released. Letting out moribund inmates was also a common practice in Franco's camps and prisons and in the Soviet gulags. It makes for cleaner statistics and less mess with families. Jan managed a recovery of sorts, and after failing to escape from the country, he was eventually freed as part of a political prisoner exchange between the UK and Czechoslovakia in 1956. "But he was terribly sick," Liz continued. "He spent much of his last years in hospital beds. The uranium slowly poisoned him." He died on 14 September 1958. Quentin, son of Georges Kopp, Orwell's commander, likes to think, not too seriously, that he and Liz were two jigsaw puzzles fated to connect: both had East European fathers who had fought against fascism in Spain and had been victims of Stalinism. Both had ended up in England. Both died before their time.

Other roads

There were other routes I could have taken across the border, narrow paths clogged in early 1939 by frightened refugees. After the Nazi invasion of France, many fled the other way, including

British pilots picked up by the French resistance and brought across the hills by Spanish guides before being interned in Spain. Jewish refugees also fled this way from 1940. Among the most tragic of these stories is that of the eclectic German Marxist thinker Walter Benjamin, who, fearing deportation from Vichy to Nazi Germany, escaped on an unknown path across the border. No sooner had he arrived at the Catalan border town of Portbou than he learned that he would be deported back to France. He almost certainly committed suicide the next day, 26 September 1940, although the suspicion of murder also hangs over the tale. The mystery around Benjamin's fate is compounded by his suitcase stuffed with his last writings, which has never been found. He's buried in the lovely little cemetery above the town. His gravestone reads in German and Catalan: "There is no document of culture that is not at the same time a document of barbarism." Next to the cemetery is one of the most remarkable anti-fascist memorials in Europe created by the sculptor Dani Karavan. You descend a rusted iron chute towards the sea. Engraved in the glass at the end is a passage in Catalan from Benjamin's *On the Concept of History* (1940). It reads: "It is more difficult to honour the memory of the anonymous than that of the renowned."

My reaction to Portbou seems to depend very much on the day. In early February, with the Tramontana ripping down from the hills, it can feel oppressive, shadowed by steep cliffs, the last expression of the Pyrenees before they fall into the Mediterranean. In spring, it has a quiet charm of fallen grandeur, and unlike everywhere else on the Costa Brava, it is relatively unspoilt by mass tourism. It made its money as a border town hosting customs offices and the vast station and marshalling yards that dominate some 60 per cent of its urban area. That all closed down with Spain's entrance to the European Union and the opening of the high-speed train route from Figueres to Perpignan in 2003.

The steep road from the town took us up through scrubby hillside to the top of the Coll dels Belitres. Out of the car, we admired the Mediterranean to the right, azure and idyllic, spread out across the horizon. To the left, the Pyrenees run for 430 kilometres from here to the Bay of Biscay. We're only 165 metres high. This must be the lowest pass, at least until the Basque Country. Some 100,000 slogged up this narrow road into France. Four iron stands are arranged in a row as a memorial (see Fig. 11.5). They bear photos taken here in February 1939 by Colombian-French photographer Manuel Moros. The images depict heart-wrenching scenes of women, children, the elderly and defeated Republican soldiers who came this way. In one, a group of cold, scared and hungry-looking women and children are held back by a chain, signifying the border. In another, exhausted civilians rest on the scrubby bank as an endless stream of trucks and cars inch past along the road. The Tramontana wind was so strong that I could hardly hold my camera as I tried to capture the memorial and the landscape of mountain and sea behind. An information panel pointed us across the road to another memorial. It was erected by Franco's 4th Navarre Division to their fallen when they reached the frontier on 10 February 1939. I think the Museu del Exili is right that it should be left standing as it marks a historical moment provided there is proper contextualisation. Others won't agree. That day, it had been freshly daubed in red paint. It's hardly surprising people feel the need to interact with it. Back in the car, snug in our seats, we passed the abandoned frontier posts back into France.

12

INTO THE EUROPEAN ABYSS

Context

With the fall of Catalonia, it was just a question of time before the Republic collapsed. Papering over a series of important events involving internecine fighting on the left,[1] Franco launched his final offensive against Republican lines at the end of March 1939. In most cases, there was scant resistance. On 28 March, some 200,000 troops entered Madrid unopposed. The war formally came to an end on 1 April 1939 with the capitulation of the Republic. Something like 600,000 people had been killed violently at the front and behind the lines on both sides during the war, most of them civilians: a clear harbinger of the horrors of the Second World War.

Of those who had crossed into France, more than 100,000 had returned to Spain, voluntarily or not, by September 1939. Many would live to regret their decision. Between 25,000 and 40,000 more managed to leave France for third countries. Some managed to get to the Soviet Union, the United States, the UK, Belgium and elsewhere in Europe, but most went to Latin America. An example is Marina Ginestà of the Hotel Colón photo. She had spent most of the war working as a Spanish translator in Valencia for *Pravda*, the official newspaper of the Soviet Communist Party, which may come as a disappointment to some of today's more libertarian leftists who have idealised the image portrayed in the photo. She was captured in Alicante on 1 April 1939 and herded by the Falange into a church and forced to pray all day long. Several times a day, the Falange would take away a few women to be shot. With too many mouths to feed, many of the female prisoners were released and sent back to their own homes. Ginestà managed to escape to France. When the German invasion of France threatened in 1940, Ginestà took a boat to the Dominican Republic before later settling in Venezuela. She returned to France in 1949.

By July 1939, the population of the camps had fallen to some 95,000, not thanks to any generosity or feeling of guilt on the part of the French authorities but due in part to the expense of maintaining them. Then, with seemingly sick synchronicity, six months to the day after Spain's brutal conflict had come to an end, another even bloodier war would break out in September 1939, as Nazi Germany invaded Poland—an invasion that would suck in the rest of Europe, and the world, but also many of those Spanish exiles who crossed the border in 1939. As of late 1941, many had returned to Spain. Many would come to regret their decision. Some 150,000 still remained in France, now split between Vichy and Nazi zones. The rest, apart from the 30,000 or so fortunate enough to leave for a new life in third countries, above all in Latin America, had either been deported to French North Africa or sent east to Nazi camps.

Narvik and beyond

Within weeks of the end of the war in Spain, the international situation altered the prospects for many of the refugees. Facing the increasing likelihood of war with Germany, the French government gave ex-Republican soldiers the chance to join the French Foreign Legion. Among them were some 600 Spanish Republican volunteers in the 13th Demi-Brigade of the Foreign Legion, which embarked from Brest on 23 April 1940. They were bound for Narvik in northern Norway as part of the failed Anglo-French operation to liberate the town, which had recently been occupied by German troops. It is not known how many Spaniards were killed fighting in temperatures of -20°C, in a landscape of steep fiords and frozen mountains so far from that of their homelands, which most could hardly have imagined when they left their homes. Estimates vary, but it was more than 100. One day, I'd like to visit Narvik and see the little memorial stone to the legionnaires who were killed. It lists 118 members of the French Foreign Legion, including twenty-one from Spain who had volunteered to continue their fight against fascism in these cold lands.

Another 700 Spanish fought on the eastern front with Soviet forces. Most were communists or sympathisers who had managed to get to the USSR after the defeat of the Republic, although some had arrived earlier as teenagers, among the 3,000 children evacuated to the Soviet Union in 1937 to escape the bombing of Spanish cities, more than half of them from the Basque Country. Later, in 1941, they found themselves defending Leningrad and Stalingrad. About 300 were killed. Back in France, some 55,000 male Spanish Republicans were enlisted in labour battalions, carrying out work previously done by locals who were now being called up into the French armed forces, providing cheap labour for the French authorities and companies. Many were sent to try to complete the Maginot Line, the defensive line against Germany in Northern France. When Germany did invade in April 1940, more than 2,000 Republicans fought in French units against the Wehrmacht, while as many as 20,000 were involved in defence work: several companies, for instance, helped in the defences at Dunkirk, permitting Allied troops to evacuate. In total, some 7,000 Spanish Republicans were initially made prisoner by the Germans in 1940, in particular men building the Maginot line and those captured at Dunkirk. After an awful time in stalags, they were deported east to SS camps. Another 80,000 were used as forced labourers, whether in Vichy or Nazi-controlled France. The Vichy regime also employed them in North Africa to build the never completed Trans-Saharan railroad, where conditions were hardly better than any Nazi work camp.

Antonio Cánovas after Spain

The Trans-Saharan railway was the fate of Antonio Cánovas, whom we left, his young friend dying in his arms, during the failed offensive against Mallorca (see Chapter 1). Remarkably, although he fought throughout the war in Madrid, Aragon and at the Ebro, often as a member of Republican shock units, he was never wounded. "It was close. On one occasion a ricocheting bullet hit me here," he explained to me, thumping his chest, "but it was stopped by my thick leather jacket." After crossing the border into France in 1939, he was interned and then conscripted into a labour battalion to build the naval base at Brest. When Germany invaded, Antonio knew he had to get out and boarded a French warship as a stowaway, assuming the ship was bound for the Americas. He was soon discovered by French sailors and shackled in the hold. Some days later, the ship docked in Casablanca. "But instead of having a drink at Rick's Café," he chuckled, he was arrested by the Vichy authorities and sent as a forced labourer to the terrible concentration camp of Bouarfa to toil on the railway, where many Republicans and others died. "It was terrible. We had to work from dawn till dusk—they let us rest a bit during the hottest part of the day. And then it was freezing at night—we had to huddle together in the filthy tents to keep warm." He proudly told me about helping to organise a communist cell and managing to sabotage a train, but he was caught, tortured and sent to the maximum-security prison at Port Lyautey (today's Kenitra).

When the Americans landed and reached the prison in November 1943, he was offered his freedom if he joined a US army unit, which he refused to do, and so, it seemed remarkable to me, he had to spend another eight months in prison. Despite this, he considered that the Americans had "liberated" him, as the prison regime now was much less arduous. After his release, he moved to Casablanca, where he was taken in by a family of Republican refugees with five daughters. Antonio fell in love with one of them, Micaela, and the couple were soon married. They returned to France with their young son in 1946, where Antonio worked for a few years for the Spanish communist underground, helping people across the frontier and taking documents to and from Spain before returning with his family to Casablanca, where he played football semi-professionally for Idéal Club Marocain and took up competition swimming.

He concluded, looking at me: "As I said, I wasn't really interested in politics, but Franco and his friends made war on me, so I hit back. They destroyed my dreams of being a swimmer. They forged me as an anti-fascist. And so Nick I'm afraid I became a better fighter than a sportsman." Then he smiled: "But I still think of myself as a sportsman. I love watching water polo and I'm still a member of the same swimming club. Despite everything, I've had a wonderful life. I never thought I'd reach this age." Antonio returned to Catalonia with Micaela in 1962. She passed away in 2014, the year before I met Antonio. He died in 2018, aged ninety-eight.

Forced labour and resistance

The Nazis employed 40,000 to 50,000 Spanish Republicans as slave labourers, above all in building defensive works such as the Atlantic Wall and in the construction of the huge U-boat base at Bordeaux. Of the 6,500 men forced to work here, around a third were from Spain. Reinhard Heydrich, the infamous SS official, declared in June 1941:

> The dangerousness of this communist mob hostile to the Germans needs no further explanation. Only the labour market situation has led me not to arrest the Spanish Republicans [in France] but for the time being [to put them to work for us], to observe them closely and only to deport them to camps in the event of undisciplined or politically dangerous behaviour.[2]

Not that staying in France made their situation much better. Spanish Republicans faced among the harshest treatments. It is not currently known how many died. Even those not involved in the French resistance, or forced to work or deported, were not safe, as we have seen in the terrible fate of the Spanish families murdered at Oradour-sur-Glane in June 1944 (see Chapter 7).

Large numbers of other Spanish Republicans were sent to work in German factories. They were even deported to Nazi-held British territory, building fortifications in the Channel Islands, particularly on the island of Alderney. There is no consensus on the number of Spaniards who were forced to toil under appalling conditions on the islands. The Spanish Foreign Ministry website quotes estimates of between 1,500 and 4,000. Again, the death figure is not known. At the time of writing, after pressure from a media campaign, a study was underway to try to ascertain the numbers, and in September 2023, the Spanish ambassador laid wreaths in homage to them on Guernsey and Jersey.

Those who weren't rounded up formed a key part of the French resistance, particularly in the south of the country and around Paris, together with thousands of surviving ex-brigaders, most of them French, but also those from elsewhere in Europe who could not return to their own countries. This resistance grew organically out of solidarity networks, necessary for survival in any exile or refugee group under stress, which in time developed into commando networks. They knew for instance how to derail a train without explosives, how to use weapons and perhaps most importantly, through experience, they knew why and whom they were fighting. Women played a very important and dangerous role, collecting information, acting as liaisons and transporting weapons. The different groups also helped considerably in the Allied escape routes.

Spanish Republicans were prominently involved in early acts of resistance, while the first German officer to be assassinated in France was shot by French ex-brigader Pierre Georges in the Paris metro on 21 August 1941. The resistance in Paris itself was commanded by French brigader Henri Rol-Tanguy, whom we left wounded during the first day of the Ebro battle in July 1938 (see Chapter 9). Veterans of the International Brigades played important roles in the resistance movements of the Netherlands and Norway. All four of the generals of Yugoslavian leader Josip Tito in the partisan war against the Nazis were veterans from the war in Spain. Indeed, if the Spanish Civil War was a training ground for Göring's Nazis, it was also one for the resistance movements across Western Europe. In France itself, Spanish Republicans played a key role in the liberation of much of Southern France, while in all, an estimated 50,000 Spanish Republicans fought either in the Free French forces or in the resistance against Vichy and the Nazis. A small number of these men also had an interesting part in the liberation of the French capital.

Paris

The high-speed TGV train from Barcelona took me comfortably towards Paris. The mountain of Canigó, historic symbol of the Catalan people, was clear to the left, strips of snow still between the clouds, dominating as ever. To the right, somewhere beyond the fields, there was the reminder of Argelès and the other camps. After Perpignan, we rushed along the coast to Narbonne. The views are stunning, with miles and miles of coastal lagoons, saltpans and dunes largely unblighted by the tourist sprawl that has ruined most of Spain's coast. Birds are everywhere; at one point, a flock of flamingos lifts away from the train. Then, we turn inland, moving smoothly through Central France, from the windows most of it looking flat, prosperous, green and a bit dull. Orwell described the scene in the penultimate paragraph of *Homage to Catalonia* as his train travelled this way in June 1937: "With every mile that you went northward France grew greener and softer. Away from the mountain and the vine, back to the meadow and the elm."

Six and a half hours later, the TGV arrives at the Gare de Lyon. Many of the brigaders who fought in Spain departed from this station and, above all, across the Seine at Gare de Austerlitz. Paris was the mustering point for thousands of volunteers from around the world. When arriving in the city, they first had to pass by the International Brigades' "secret office" located at 8 Avenue Mathurin-Moreau and run by Tito himself. A plaque in French on the building today remembers the brigaders' role in fighting Franco (see Fig. 12.1). It ends with the line "This was the first act of international resistance against fascism."

I was greeted at the station with a big hug from my old friend, now Dr Andy Flinn, with whom I'd discovered that plaque in Manchester back in 1985. We were meeting up in the French capital to celebrate our fiftieths and do a bit of history. After a couple of delicious French beers, I dragged Andy to the Hôtel de Ville, Paris city hall. Of the thousands of Spanish Republicans languishing in the camps of Southern France in 1939 who agreed to join the Foreign Legion, many ended up fighting with the Free French in North Africa against the German Afrika Korps, while others joined after escaping or being liberated from Vichy's murderous work camps in Algeria and Morocco. Most then volunteered under the command of General Philippe Leclerc, whose 16,000-strong 2nd Armoured Division by 1944 included some 800 Spaniards, along with many other foreign anti-fascists. After recruitment, they were shipped from Rabat to Liverpool, before travelling by train to Yorkshire, where they were stationed in and around Hull. Some 1,200 Republicans meanwhile fought in the British army.[3]

On the night of 31 July 1944, Leclerc's troops, now part of the 3rd US Army under General Patton, landed in Normandy. The division included the 9th Armoured Company, nicknamed "La Nueve" (Spanish for "nine") as it was made up principally of Spaniards, although it was commanded by its French captain Raymond Dronne (a Valencian Republican, Amado Granell, acted as his lieutenant). And although this was an official French unit, they were allowed to stitch a little Spanish Republican flag on their uniforms (as incidentally were the Spaniards who fought in the British army in the No. 1 Spanish Company). For the conservative French commander, they must have seemed a motley crew, with their blend of hardened anarchist veterans of the Durruti Column, socialists, communists and more moderate Republicans. These men fought a series of bloody battles as they pushed into the Normandy countryside in their American armoured vehicles painted with names sonorous of the struggle in Spain such as *Guadalajara*, *Brunete*, *Teruel*, *Ebro*, *Madrid*, *Belchite* and *Guernica*. Another vehicle was named *Don Quijote*— the name *Buenaventura Durruti*, the anarchist leader who had died during the defence of Madrid, was rejected by the French as being overtly political. By mid-August, Leclerc's soldiers found themselves just a few dozen kilometres from Paris.

The French were desperate to get to their capital before the Americans, and so, when news arrived on 20 August of the start of the uprising in Paris against the Germans, General de Gaulle requested permission from Allied Supreme Command to spearhead an advance. Among his best troops were the Spanish, now hardened from eight years of fighting fascists. However, without waiting for orders, "La Nueve" set off, 130 men in some twenty vehicles, on its dash for the capital on 23 August, meeting some German opposition. By 8 p.m. on 24 August, with Paris now in full revolt and the bells of Notre-Dame ringing out, they reached the city outskirts and at 9.22 a group under Amado Granell in a half truck named *Ebro* arrived at the square in front of the City Hall, where he was received by Georges Bidault, the head of the Conseil National de la Résistance. A photograph of the two of them appeared the next day on the cover of the communist-sympathising *Libération*, but the article falsely claimed Granell was an American. "La Nueve" were the first Allied troops to reach Paris, and, while claims that they liberated the city are hyperbole, they certainly played their part, as did upwards of 4,000 Spanish exiles in the city—along with thousands of French men and women and other foreign anti-fascists.

From Hôtel de Ville, we headed to Hôtel Le Meurice. This rather plush place was German headquarters in 1944. When Granell and his men reached the building, they were met with fierce resistance from elite German defenders. Several Spaniards managed to break through the defences and reach Paris's Military Governor Dietrich von Choltitz and his staff, whom they disarmed at gunpoint. They then allowed the general, who had defied Hitler's order to blow up the city, to surrender to a fellow officer, Lieutenant colonel Jean Fanneau de la Horie, a Frenchman, rather than a lowly Spanish Republican. In thanks, he gave another Spaniard, Antonio Gutiérrez, his wristwatch for having "honoured the rules of war", not that the Wehrmacht officer had likely respected any rules during his time in Poland and the USSR.

Three days later, this indomitable band of Spaniards marched in the victory parade along the Champs-Elysées. Four half-tracks of "La Nueve", with their resonant names from the Spanish struggle, were given the symbolic role of escorting de Gaulle's car, apparently to the general's bemusement, at one point driving past a large Republican banner unfurled by exiled Spaniards. The occasion was documented in a photograph depicting one of their trucks bearing the name *Guernica* as it drives past the Arc de Triomphe. How sweet it must have felt for those men after years of fighting, scarred by two wars, defeated in Spain and humiliated in France in 1939 to have contributed to fascism's defeat in Paris. But although more than fifty of the company's members received the Croix de Guerre for bravery, none were cited in de Gaulle's victory speech. "Paris is outraged. Paris is destroyed. Paris is martyred," he famously declared. "But Paris is liberated! Liberated by itself, liberated by its people with the help of the armies of France."

After a few days' rest, "La Nueve" took part in the liberation of Strasbourg and then turned their half-tracks to the battle for Germany, where they were involved in taking the Kehlsteinhaus, often called the "Eagle's Nest" in English, the infamous Hitlerian retreat in the Berchtesgaden Alps. But of the 144 men comprising "La Nueve" who had landed in Normandy, only a small number survived the war. And despite the hopes and expectations of the Spanish volunteers and part of the Spanish population, there was no Allied invasion of Spain. Then they were forgotten. Franco's Spain was never going to remember them nor any of the thousands of other compatriots who had fought against his allies, the Nazis. France, for its part, needed to stress the role of the French in the resistance to erase the memory of collaboration.

It was not until August 2012 that the French government allowed the last of the Spanish Republicans to parade with their flag during the sixty-eighth anniversary of the victory. It was a debt to history. This has been followed by homages from French and Spanish politicians and even from King Felipe VI in 2015. In recent years, the pendulum of how "La Nueve" are remembered has swung the other way, understandably perhaps, with books and newspaper articles exaggerating their importance in Paris's liberation.[4]

Next to the Hôtel de Ville, Andy and I came across a little garden named the Jardin des Combattants de la Nueve, named, as the plaque said in French, after "the anti-fascist Spanish Republicans who continued their fight in the 2nd Division. Heroes of the Liberation of Paris" (see Fig. 12.2). Wilted flowers, red, yellow and purple, in the colours of the Spanish Republic, had been placed to one side. If they'd been Americans, they'd have made a movie about them, but it was something at least.

Context: Franco and the Second World War

After 1945, the dictatorship promoted a mythical account of Franco's role during the Second World War. The Caudillo's great achievement, it was argued, was that he had resisted pressure from Hitler to enter the war on the German side. The reality was very different. The two men met only once, in Hendaye, just inside France, in October 1940. Encouraged by the defeat of France in June 1940, Franco made a series of territorial demands—Gibraltar and above all French North Africa—as a price for entering the conflict. Hitler was not impressed. He was aware that Spain was in no condition to contribute to the Nazi war effort, both as a result of the devastation of the Civil War and due to its vulnerability to British naval power. Until late 1942, however, Franco hoped to enter the war just before an Allied defeat but in time to claim a share of the spoils, an attitude that understandably earned the contempt of the Nazi leadership.

Though later myth claimed that Franco had little sympathy for the fascist powers, his pro-axis views were crystal clear to his ministers and can be seen in the support given to the German war effort. This included mineral supplies—most notably in the form of the considerable deposits of wolframite in Northern Spain, essential in the manufacture of tank armour—the refuelling and refitting of German submarines in Spanish ports, the establishment of German observation posts along the Spanish coast and the stationing of German aircraft—with Spanish markings—at bases in Spain. The height of the Caudillo's enthusiasm came after the Nazi invasion of the USSR in June 1941 and led to the despatch of the 47,000-strong Blue Division to fight on the eastern front. Faced with British protests, he argued there were two separate wars—one between the democracies and the Axis, in which Spain was "non-belligerent", and the other, a war against communism in which Spain was assisting Germany. Many, though not all, were hard-line Falangist volunteers. They joined the 250th Division of the Wehrmacht, fighting particularly during the siege of Leningrad. Around 8,000 Spaniards were killed and 10,000 wounded. As the chances of Nazi victory slipped away, the division was brought home in October 1943 to a rapturous official reception, although between 1,500 and 3,000 diehard Falangists chose to stay on, many dying in the final battle for Berlin, defending the Fuhrer's bunker to the end.

Despite its military and economic weakness, Spanish neutrality was crucial to the British. Its location at the western end of the Mediterranean and control of the Canaries meant that Spanish belligerency would threaten British shipping routes. Spain's economic vulnerability, however, enabled the Allies to apply pressure, though they were also keen to avoid the collapse of the regime, which might, they feared, lead to German intervention. The country was desperately short of wheat and oil. The Allies enforced a blockade but allowed limited imports. The British also spent some $13 million bribing top Spanish generals to encourage them to resist pro-Axis supporters within the regime.

By mid-1943, the Allied landings in North Africa (November 1942), the German defeat at Stalingrad (February 1943) and the overthrow of Mussolini (July 1943) made the eventual outcome of the war clear to Franco. He began to distance himself from the Axis. As well as withdrawing the Blue Division, he changed the country's status from "non-belligerency" to "neutrality" and dismissed his pro-Nazi foreign minister (and brother-in-law) Ramón Serrano Suñer. For those who had lost the war in Spain, however, there would be scant respite.

13

THE FRANCO REGIME

Francoist violence behind the lines

While Republican violence was largely committed in the context of the state's breakdown and the anger unleashed by the coup itself—and was condemned by the Republican government and curtailed by early 1937—on Franco's side, it was very different. We will never know with any certainty how many were murdered, although the number is today authoritatively given as between 150,000 and 200,000. The minimum estimate goes up every year as investigations uncover more evidence at a local level. Akin to the violence in the Republican zone, Francoist violence went through its "hot" phase at the start of the war, much of it committed by proxy groups—the Falange, the Carlists, local landowners—but much directly by the military. But unlike the Republican state, it was state-sponsored terror from day one in Franco's Spain. General Mola, the initial director of the coup, put it perfectly in Pamplona on 18 July 1936: "We must sow terror, we must impose the impression of dominion while eliminating without scruples everyone who does not think as we do." This was accompanied by mass rape and mass torture as means of spreading terror, tactics that, individual crimes aside, were not employed in the Republican zone. They went into village after village, seeking those who had voted for the left, electoral officials, trade unionists, teachers in the new schools, women who had dared to stand out.

The war was over for those who won. It wasn't over for those who had lost, and formally a state of war continued until 1948 and in practice for many years after. The regime now cleaved the population between "victors" and "vanquished". The sheer brutality of this was usually not clear to those looking at the country from outside. While those with close connections enjoyed the benefits of unbridled power, clientelism and corruption, those who lost the war faced execution, torture and imprisonment. Their families, meanwhile, were marked out as "scum", "barbarians" and "the anti-Spain" for many years to come. Those murdered behind the lines by both sides during the war were likewise divided: men and women killed by the left were now "martyrs" whose bodies were exhumed, reburied and remembered year after year in religious ceremonies, often honoured with statues and plaques; while those killed by the right lay where they had been shot in unmarked roadside ditches, ravines and common graves. After the war, at least 50,000 people were executed. A similar figure died of abuse in prisons and some 280 concentration camps. Somewhere between 700,000 and 1 million Republican forced labourers (the Spanish literature often uses the term *esclavo*—"slave") passed through these camps between 1936 and the late 1940s.[1] They were sent out to build the reservoirs that give us our drinking water today, the canals that irrigate the crops we eat and the roads on which we drive. An unknown but high figure died shortly after being released to avoid the inconvenience when their death seemed imminent. In all, as many as a million Republican prisoners passed through the regime's system of camps and prisons.

On both sides, millions of lives were ruined during and after the war. The pain of a mother whose son has been murdered, whether by a Falangist gang, a Francoist execution squad or a leftist militia is always the same, whatever the politics. All of this happened because a group of generals and their supporters refused to accept liberal democratic reforms.

Post-war Belchite, the new town and ancient histories

After my tour around Belchite with Juan Carlos, I walked across to the new town. Wandering around, it seemed a sleepy if not unpleasant place (population 1,527 in 2023) with the feeling of small-town conservatism, typical, in my mind at least, of similar places around the world. As I sat down at a bar terrace for a drink, a happy family celebrating a communion came out of the 1940s concrete church. Franco had ordered a new town to be built just 500 metres from the ruins (see Fig. 13.1). Its clean, neat little streets laid out in straight and carefully curving lines were designed to contrast with the so-called Marxist-created chaos of the ruined Belchite—although most of the damage by this stage had been done by his army and the Condor Legion. The work of building the new Belchite would be done by Republican prisoners who were housed in a concentration camp for the next five years on the outskirts of the town. They had destroyed it, Franco claimed, and now they would rebuild it. It was officially opened by Franco himself in 1954, although the last residents didn't abandon their old homes until 1964.

New Belchite has an unusual shape when seen from above. It appears that when planners laid out the new town, they mapped it closely on the street plan of an ancient Celtiberian settlement—Numancia,[2] a name probably familiar to many Spanish readers at least. Numantia, to give its classical English name, is famous for resisting the Roman expansion across the peninsula for twenty years starting in 153 BCE. This culminated in the thirteen-month siege of the town, after which the defenders chose to die free rather than live as slaves. In the nineteenth century, the story came to represent an essential piece in the construction of the national myth of Spain, similar to those supporting other nation-states across Europe—think of Boudica as a symbol of English nationhood. As they did with the Peninsular War against Napoleonic France, both Republicans and Francoists used the story in their propaganda to highlight heroic acts of defence (Madrid, Alcázar de Toledo) made by their side. A reminder of this today is the village of Azaña in Castile-La Mancha, which by complete coincidence was also the surname of the liberal Spanish Republican president Manuel Azaña, so hated by Franco and friends. Although the village's name had existed since at least the twelfth century and was therefore entirely unrelated to progressive Spanish Republicanism, it was unacceptable to the regime, which renamed it Numancia de la Sacra, in remembrance of the ancient siege and the regiment that took it in 1936. At the time of writing, most of its inhabitants steadfastly refuse to return their village to its former name of Azaña. Numancia was cited repeatedly in Francoist propaganda to extol the heroic resisters of Belchite and elsewhere. Franco made the point himself on several occasions. And the layout of its streets also drew attention to the defence of ancient Numantia.[3]

This use of an ancient past to fortify a version of the present did not stop at Belchite. It was a characteristic of the Franco regime, as it was in fascist-inspired regimes everywhere. Selected ancient histories would help provide historical parallels to the battles fought between 1936 and 1939 and form a historical basis for the new state. This included the veneration of the so-called Reconquista, itself a simplistic and problematic term for many historians today, describing an 800-year process in which Christian kingdoms, sometimes with the aid of Muslim ones, defeated other Muslim kingdoms often for territorial gains for ruling monarchs as much as being driven by religious motives. Whatever the case, for Franco's ideologues, the war against the Republic could be happily represented as a resumption of this Reconquista, which saw Franco, portrayed in propaganda as a living embodiment of El Cid, fighting a crusade to restore the old Spain and defend the Church (with the aid, without apparent contradiction, of some 80,000 Moroccan volunteers). The new enemies would be godless liberals, socialists, communists, anarchists, masons and, of course, as ever, the Jews.

A key site in this Francoist mythology was the remarkable archaeological remains of Empúries, 120 kilometres north of Barcelona, where Rome had first landed in the Iberian Peninsula in 218 BCE during their fight against Hannibal's Carthage. After emerging victorious, it then took the empire 200 years to conquer Iberia, in part due to its mountainous terrain and in part due to the dogged resistance of myriad local tribes and city-states, such as Numancia. All ancient history, but for Francoist historians Empúries was where "Spain" started to exist. The Romans were an essential root of Spain—despite their vicious war against Numancia. The Greeks had brought their civilisation, which was all well and good, but it was to the glory of the Roman Empire that the regime really wanted to connect. Its conquest of Hispana had created a united state undivided by warring tribes, inculcating a desire for order and discipline among its ruling elite, which, they fantasised, laid the foundations of the later imperial Spain, leading directly to their own fascistic state, which, the propaganda said, was "Una, Grande y Libre". Mussolini of course had similar ideas about his regime's origins.

Sometime after Belchite, I drove up from Barcelona to visit Empúries. The place was quiet on a warm spring Wednesday morning, save for a few tourists like myself. I wandered around admiring the ruins, although as always with these Greek and Roman places, you're not going to forget that much of the building work was done by slaves. What did come as a shock— although perhaps it shouldn't have—was to learn that slavery returned to Empúries in the 1940s in the form of Republican prisoners forced to work on the site digging up the old Greek and Roman walls. And the amphitheatre. And the Roman villa. And the new Roman town. All were unearthed by some 200 men toiling under atrocious conditions from sunrise to sunset under the watchful eye of sadistic guards. Physical punishment occurred every day, including beatings or being forced to carry heavy sacks of broken rocks all day long. The prisoners slept on the hard ground in shacks by the old walls and were fed a meagre diet of turnips, rice and scraps, which they augmented with lizards and snails to get a bit of protein. Local people helped them, in many cases passing them food, because their relatives were imprisoned elsewhere.

The prisoners at Empúries included anarchist veterans, survivors of the Ebro battle and even an ex-Barça football player, Josep Bayo. He had played in the 1–2 defeat by Real Madrid in the last pre-war cup final—then called the Copa del Presidente de la República—on 21 June 1936, a month before the generals rose and changed Spain forever. In 2022, a plaque commemorating the men forced to toil here was installed by Memorial Democràtic, the Catalan government's admirable historical memory institution. Why did it take so long? Empúries may be the pride and joy of archaeology in Catalonia, but it is an uncomfortable fact that much of the work done here in unearthing and modernising the site was carried out under the Franco regime, partly through forced labour.

La Pequeña Rusia

Before saying goodbye to Belchite, Juan Carlos said I should also visit "La Rusia". At first, I didn't understand—why would the old Soviet Union hold that answer? He repeated matter-of-factly "'La Rusia.' It's what everyone calls it. It's just over the hill."

We pull off the main road down a dirt track to a large stony field. In the middle stands a group of barrack huts laid out in three E blocks (see Fig. 13.2). All are abandoned today save for a few employed for storing farm equipment. Peering through broken windows into the gloom, it was clear some had been used in the past to house chickens. An information panel erected in front of one of the blocks gives some background. The complex was used to house the local women, children and elderly who had lost the war and were therefore not trusted to mix with regime-friendly families. Herein lies the nickname to this day "La Rusia" (all the defeated, whatever their ideology—or lack of it—were treated as "Reds"). Each small home was reasonable enough for a family: a kitchen, a living room and two bedrooms, although the thin, shoddily built walls would have offered scant protection from the freezing winters and scorching summers, unlike their stone houses in the old town. There was no running water; it had to be collected from the nearby river. A Guardia Civil station stood behind to keep things under heel. Presiding over the whole settlement is a small church, and between this and the homes, there is a large, flat open space, where the population could be gathered to listen to mass, to be lectured by the priest, to be harangued by the Falange.

The settlement is separated from their old town by a low hill. The intention was to house families in this disciplinary space and to keep these infected Reds, the anti-Spain, separate from the clean, trusted Christian population. Little Russia feels like a concentration camp, but this was not a formal prison. No fence was needed. There was simply nowhere to escape across the harsh plains of the Ebro Depression, and legal travel was impossible without a permit and money. Repression under Franco was diverse, ranging from extreme forms of violence to the more subtle ways seen at La Pequeña Rusia. Together, they form part of a veritable penal universe, formed by prisons, camps, forced labour gangs, reformatories for children and the wholesale exclusion of the defeated from public life. A small number of these sites have been memorialised around Spain such as here at La Rusia. The vast majority are almost entirely forgotten, outside of whispered memories and specialist writings.

Hunger years

Hunger was the order of the day in places like Little Russia. It is a pervading memory of the 1940s across Spain. People I've talked to over the years—so many have gone now—have often chosen, understandably, not to say much about the war years. What they did choose to talk about, particularly the women and those who were children, was the hunger. My mind casts back to the concrete silos I'd seen in Aragon. Hundreds were built across Spain, mostly during the early years of the Franco regime as part of its failed attempt to encourage but also control cereal production. Today, they stand abandoned in their hundreds as a reminder of the abject failure of the state's autarkic policies, aimed at making Spain self-sufficient. I like to see them as ugly memorials to "los Años del Hambre", "the Hunger Years" of the 1940s, when an estimated 200,000 people died in Spain of starvation. You can guess which side those who succumbed were on. It was also accompanied by widespread malnutrition, leading to spikes in deaths from infectious diseases such as typhus.

This awful post-war suffering had several causes. The war certainly played its part in food shortages. By 1939, livestock levels were, for instance, at pre-1914 levels, and the fighting was followed by a series of droughts and bad harvests. But the famine itself was the direct result of government policy. First, Spain sent huge food shipments to Germany to pay for the Condor Legion. Second, hunger was employed as a punishment and as an instrument of political repression through the refusal of ration cards and work to former Republicans and their families (and, at a local level, even the right to buy in shops). Although impossible to quantify, this was certainly a factor in many deaths. Third, there was the grotesque level of corruption by minor and leading Francoist officials, who syphoned off huge amounts of grain and other produce for sale on the burgeoning black market. But, above all, the policy of autarky itself was designed to reduce or eliminate food imports and to control food purchases on the domestic market. The consequence was huge profits for some and shortages and hunger for the rest. In the longer term, this led to the weakening of the Spanish economy, and by the mid-1950s, with the economy on the verge of collapse, the regime was forced to abandon autarky and open the economy to the international market.

All of this misery, accompanied by vicious repression enacted in village after village across the state by those who'd won the war, pushed many to find anonymity and just enough food in the shanty settlements growing around Spain's big cities. There was a huge one on Montjuïc just up the road from our flat, home to 30,000 people in 1950. My daughter's school is built on part of this settlement. A common sight in the 1940s was seeing families rummaging in rubbish tips for scraps. Perhaps they should turn one of the grain silos into a museum evidencing not only the hunger years but also the dictator's ideas about economics. Hunger is another form of violence.

Courts, expropriations and forced labour

As the new state established itself, first in areas under its control during the war and, from 1939, across the country, uncontrolled murders gave way to military courts. This was codified under the 1939 Law of Political Responsibilities, a cornerstone in the wider Francoist policy of punishing Republican supporters. It was aimed at giving the veneer of legality to what was a judicial system utterly rigged against the defeated. The law was retrospective, as its scope dated back to October 1934, criminalising activities—including membership and/or support of political parties, government service at a local or national level, and membership of the Republican armed forces—that had been legal at the time. This meant that anybody seen as a supporter of the Popular Front, or who had opposed in any way the July 1936 military rebellion, could be penalised in the form of fines, loss of public jobs, restriction of professional activities or confiscations of property. An estimated half a million people were prosecuted across Spain until 1945, representing 2 per cent of the country's then population of 23 million. Since prosecutions depended on evidence from figures such as village priests, Francoist mayors, local Falange leaders, landowners and employers, many people were implicated in the process.

A system of legal denunciation was implemented on 26 April 1940 to allow people to come forward and denounce neighbours, workmates and even friends, most of whom very probably had nothing to do with the alleged crimes. This was part of the "Causa General" (General Prosecution) set up to investigate any supposed crimes committed by those on the losing side. It helped instil an Inquisition-like state of fear, which would demonstrate to "good Spaniards" the horrors of "Red Terror". Crimes committed on Franco's side were never in any way investigated, in effect legally dividing the population between victors and vanquished. There was also another purpose. Encouraging people to denounce fellow citizens made a significant percentage of the population complicit, helping create a large class of beneficiaries who were now bound to the Franco regime. Their descendants number in the millions.

Many of those tried were punished with the expropriation of their property, enriching those who had won the war. This has been until quite recently something of a taboo. It ranged from large businesses, art and financial deposits down to humble farm plots and small bars. You can see evidence of this by strolling around any city or town in Spain. Although less so as the years go by, you'll come across bars, restaurants and shops that announce they were founded in 1939 or in the early 1940s, despite the dire state of the Spanish economy at the time. For these businesses to open, others had to close. At a national level, whole companies were taken, part of a corporate revolution, involving a profound shake up of the capitalist class. With few exceptions, almost all the companies listed on the Ibex 35, the Spanish stock exchange, such as Naturgy and Iberdrola, can trace their capital from winning the Civil War.[4]

Josep Fortuny

The fate of Josep Fortuny and his family is illustrative of the Francoist repression. Josep was the last Republican (ERC) mayor of Mollet del Vallès, 30 kilometres north of Barcelona. There's a black and white photo of him smiling and holding his little dog in his arms. He looks like a really nice guy: he was also a popular figure in the village because he was the *pastisser*, the cake maker. He, along with his wife, elected to go back to Spain with their two children after just a few weeks at Argelès camp. They believed that as he had done everything he could to stop the revolutionary violence in his town in 1936—including saving the village priest—he had nothing to fear. As soon as they crossed the border, the family were immediately separated. Josep was arrested, tortured and imprisoned at Barcelona's infamous La Modelo prison. Despite numerous testimonies in his favour, he was sentenced to death and shot in Barcelona on 15 June 1939. As with the 1,707 other men and women executed in Barcelona between 1939 and 1951, his body was dumped in the Fossar de la Pedrera, the mass grave of the victims of the Franco regime in Montjüic cemetery, Barcelona.

I have met his son, Pere, on a number of occasions through a monthly tour of the Fossar, which I used to do for Cementiris de Barcelona. Pere, almost eighty at the time, told me his father's story as we stood at the entrance to the medieval quarry, surrounded on three sides by sandstone cliffs. Fighting back the tears, he explained that the first time he came here aged six, it wasn't the beautifully landscaped space we see today but rather a "hell full of rats and snakes". In the middle was a 15 metre-deep pit, since filled in, at the bottom of which lay freshly dug mounds of soil. Underneath lay his father and other victims. As the bereaved family approached, one Guardia Civil roughly searched his mother, while the other shoved a machine gun into his six-year-old chest. "Com si portéssim una bomba a un cementiri", he exclaimed. Words I'll never forget. *As if we'd take a bomb into a cemetery.*

It didn't end there for the family. On their return to Mollet, the new Francoist mayor Simeó Rabasa first confiscated all of the once-prosperous family's property, their house and bakery. They lost everything. And to rub salt in their wounds, Rabasa ordered the shops in Mollet not to sell anything to Josep's family. Once prosperous, now they couldn't even eat and had to move, destitute, to a family member's flat in Barcelona and slowly, hunger stalking, with a degree of anonymity, remake their lives. Pere later told me who had denounced his father. On 14 June 1939, the same village priest whom he had saved in the summer of 1936 paid a visit to his mother and children, informing them smilingly as he held out his hand for young Pere to kiss: "This afternoon I'm going to sort something out with your father that you're going to remember for the rest of your life." He then proceeded to the prison. The next morning, Josep was shot in the Camp de la Bota (today's Forum), the killing ground of the Franco regime in Barcelona. "This stab in the back," he told me, thumping his heart with his fist, "I can never forgive."

In 1985, after years of campaigning by the victims' families, spearheaded by Pere and others, the Fossar de la Pedrera was redesigned and dignified as a memorial to the victims of the Franco regime by the Catalan government. It today functions as a space of memory for those who lost the war and is the most remarkable such site I have come across in Spain.

Women

In addition to the mass rape and other forms of abuse against Republican women, thousands were murdered or executed by the Franco regime and its proxies during the war, including 8 per cent of the 12,300 shot in Extremadura.[5] After the official end of the war, women on the losing side underwent a double defeat. The first for their ideas, being centre-left or revolutionary, and the second for their gender. Tens of thousands were imprisoned by the regime, and some were executed, most famously the "13 Rosas", the name given to the leftist women who were tortured and then shot in Madrid in August 1939. There are a number of memorials to them across Spain, including in Barcelona's Rose Garden in Parc de Cervantes.

Women accused of being leftists were forced to drink castor oil, causing severe diarrhoea, to humiliate them and had their heads shaven before being paraded around the town or village. Despite being a systematic practice, this has been a taboo and probably something the Spanish right itself feels ashamed of remembering. There is very little visual evidence of it. Just a handful of photos survive. In addition to the punishment itself, it was a way locals could identify the other side—women with shaved heads were a common sight in the 1940s. Large numbers of women were also forced into prostitution as their menfolk were either dead, in exile, maimed from the war or in camps or prisons. After the war, the Franco regime closed down almost all opportunities for women to work outside the home, leaving them few options to earn money to feed their families. There's also the case of Spain's stolen children. Nobody knows the real figure, but tens of thousands were forcibly taken by the Franco regime from 1936 onwards and either given to "good" Catholic families or sent to horrible orphanages run by the Church.

Women were kicked back into the Middle Ages and became even more subservient to their husbands. For example, a husband could legally give up his own children for adoption without his wife's consent, a 1938 law not repealed until 1970. In 1944, the Franco regime brought back "uxoricidio por honor", punishing only with banishment the murder or severe injury by a husband of his wife if he caught her *en flagrante* with another man (who could also be killed under the same terms). There was no sanction if he simply beat them up. He could do the same to his daughter aged under twenty-four under the same law, which was not repealed until 1961. Unless married, women under twenty-five were required to live at home. They did not begin to regain the rights and freedoms they had under the Republic until after Franco's death in 1975.

Cultural repression

The Republic's collapse in 1939 represented a total defeat for those who had professed support for progress, whether through a democratic republic or revolution. All forms of political activity outside the regime's single-party structure were now illegal. Across Spain, anything vaguely modern, liberal, progressive or revolutionary was banned (political parties, trade unions, press, films, books and so on). It was not just the formal achievements of the Republic since 1931 and the revolutionary changes since 1936 that were now outlawed. The entire progressive cultural edifice that had slowly emerged since the late nineteenth century was crushed as the new state waged a reactionary, fundamentalist Catholic and ultra-nationalist culture war. In town after town as Franco's army entered, auto-da-fe-like ceremonies were held involving the military authorities and the Church, in which huge piles of books were burned, as onlookers watched, arms outstretched in fascist salutes. Anything vaguely "Jewish–Masonic–Marxist–Separatist" was confined to the flames, as were novels by Tolstoy and Darwin's *On the Origin of Species* (1859). All aspects of life were now to comply with the vision of a unified fascist Spain, and this absolutely included the control of all areas of knowledge and academia. That the Francoist ideologues had by the 1950s largely abandoned this all-encompassing project does not mean that the original idea had not been a totalitarian one.

In Catalonia, older people have often bitterly reminded me of the suppression of their language. Their sense of grievance at being beaten up in the street or hit at school for speaking Catalan is patent. It wasn't ever illegal to speak Catalan, Basque or Galician in private spheres or in the street, but it could be dangerous to do so, particularly in the early years. Signs reminded the population to "Speak the national language" or "Speak Christian." The Catalan publishing industry was eradicated overnight. Teaching was now solely in Castilian. Babies' names could only be registered in "the language of the empire", and the first names of adults were altered in their national identity documents, all "Jordis" becoming "Jorges". From 1946, it became possible to re-publish classics, and this evolved in the 1960s into a certain tolerance towards publications in Catalan, Basque and Galician, albeit under the iron censorship that dominated all publishing.

In 1939, the Franco regime cleaved the people of Spain into two camps. The victors would be honoured as martyrs, while the losers were imprisoned, subjugated, censored and repressed—if they weren't killed. This can most dramatically be seen in the memorial Franco had built outside Madrid, all set in stone.

The Valley of the Fallen

Fifteen years of studying and working on the Civil War, but I'd never been to the Valle de los Caídos (Valley of the Fallen). I'd talked about how this fascistic monument to Franco's glory and a lament for the dead of his side was built and what it represented hundreds of times on tours and heard numerous people's impressions of their visits, but my knowledge was from a distance. Perhaps the stories of two people who had visited the site stuck in my mind the most. An American guy, son of a brigader, who when the guards weren't looking, deftly pulled out a specimen bottle of his urine he'd saved up over several days and poured it over the dictator's grave, before being escorted out by the guards. More recently, my friend Alma Mašić from Sarajevo, a veteran aid worker from the Bosnian Civil War, talked about her visit there with a European history group. What had most struck her, "aside from the grotesqueness of the place", were the tour groups bussed in from Madrid. She listened in to the spiel of the guides:

> Everything was framed in art history and architecture. Look at this lovely example of baroque painting, look at this beautiful medieval

tapestry, look at this sculpture of an angel. It was completely decontextualised from the history, so much so that it was absolutely contextualised—as fascist history. It was all so gross. And fucking fresh flowers every day on his grave.

To Madrid

I had been putting off going for years. I guess if it had been closer to Barcelona, I'd have visited earlier, but the idea of spending a couple of days and money on travelling to see the place really didn't appeal. But, as Mònica pointed out, it looked like they might finally remove the "cabrón", the colloquial Spanish equivalent of *bastard*. Still, I felt rather uneasy. It was now early October 2019, and the removal of Franco's body was seemingly imminent: the Spanish right, constitutional and ultra, clearly weren't happy. Just a week before, a screening in Valencia of the then latest film by Alejandro Amenábar, *Mientras dure la guerra* (While at war, 2019), was interrupted by a far-right group shouting Franco-era slogans such as "¡Viva España!", "¡Viva Cristo Rey!" and "¡Una, grande y libre!" The film tells the story of the famous confrontation at Salamanca University in 1936 between the conservative philosopher Miguel de Unamuno and the one-armed, one-eyed Francoist general José Millán-Astray, disfigured from war wounds he received in Morocco (he liked to call himself "The glorious amputee"). Meanwhile, Isabel Díaz Ayuso, the outspoken populist right-wing president of the Madrid region, attacked the plan to move Franco's body, asking what could come next: "Will they take the cross from the valley?" "Will they burn the local churches like they did in 1936?" All of this made it blatantly clear that the scars of the war were still raw in Spain. And six months earlier, in April, Vox had broken all expectations by winning 10.26 per cent of the vote in the national elections and have since become a seemingly permanent feature of the Spanish electoral landscape. The party is openly apologist towards the Franco regime.

The AVE speeds through the Sistema Central, the rugged mountain range that cuts across northeast Spain. Postcards flash past my eyes. Ruined settlements, African migrants working the vineyards (the grape harvest is late here on these cold slopes), bleak villages, pig farms again. So many pig farms in Spain, more swine than humans. Mountains tower above, casting deep shadows. Alder and poplar rise green along narrow rivers. At 300 kilometres an hour, it's all over too soon. Now the plains of the Meseta Central, the hunting estates of Guadalajara, soils red, soils black, a flock of sheep graze in a field of stubble by a wood. A mastiff looks towards the dark trees. There are a few wolves this far east. A gash opens in the relief, its river cuts deep through the rock, running lush through the drier land. The languages of Spain are rich in words for gorge and ravine: *desfiladero, barranco, garganta, congost, arribes, foz, gola...*

The next day, the early morning coach bound for the Guadarrama Mountains took me from Madrid city centre, still warm in mid-October. Straightaway to the right was a reminder of my destination: the Arco de la Victoria, built to commemorate the victory of Franco's forces, as shown in Fig. 13.3. There it stands in the Spanish capital, 49 metres high, undiluted, meaning exactly the same as it did the day it was completed in 1956, a stark memorial to a fascist uprising. Then, past the Palacio de Moncloa, official residence of the Spanish prime minister and the Casa del Campo park, where much of the fighting for the city had taken place in the autumn of 1936. We speed on through Madrid's prosperous northwestern suburbs, where those with the money have escaped to the ever-expanding residential estates and the cooler air. The Guadarrama range was soon visible, its bare, ancient granite peaks cloaked in cloud. And suddenly there ahead to the left, still miles and miles away but unmistakeable against the pine-clad mountainside was the cross, reputedly the largest in the world. Forty-five minutes later, the bus dropped me near the entrance, where I paid my 9 euros for the privilege.

The valley

I was dismayed to find there was no shuttle from the entrance up to the monument, but just as I set off an elderly Spaniard in a suit kindly offered me a lift, beaming as he announced to the guards that I was a "pilgrim". The BMW looked expensive. Unsurprisingly, Sr Ricardo (name changed) was an old Francoist, but I thought it might be interesting to hear what he had to say and took on the guise of an ignorant tourist—and in truth, it also saved me what would have been a 6 kilometre-steep, hot slog up the road. Ricardo clearly had pedigree, explaining he was born in Berlin in the late 1930s, where his father had taught Spanish. Everybody in his family had given all their gold and jewellery to help Franco's cause at the start of the war, as it was the Republican government in Madrid that controlled Spain's huge gold reserves, amassed, he correctly pointed out, from selling to both sides in the First World War. Ricardo had been coming to the mausoleum once a month to receive mass "ever since the socialists locked down the site ten years ago" (in 2009, it was closed to the public due to structural issues, but it was reopened again in 2012 after the victory of the conservative PP in national elections the year before). Every time he mentioned the socialists, who, of course, "wanted to dynamite the cross and start a new Civil War", he almost spat into his walnut dashboard as we drove somewhat unsteadily, his mottled hands slightly shaking at the wheel, through beautiful pinewoods, the memorial-mausoleum occasionally revealing itself, ever larger, as the road swung up. We were approaching the memorial, but Ricardo, surprised that I'd never been here before, insisted on giving me the full tour and drove around the back to the Benedictine abbey and hotel. He expounded every "S" sound, exaggerating the strong lisp characteristic of northern Castile, accompanied by a globule of spit: "The *S*panish founder of the monument"—he meant Franco—"created this *c*entre, *S*r Nick, as a *s*cientific [*sic*] in*s*titute to find an an*s*wer to why *S*paniards fought each other in a *C*ivil War. Philo*s*opher*s*, hi*s*torians, economi*s*ts, scientists, doctors all came here to discu*ss* this key que*s*tion." I was finding it harder to maintain the dumb smile. I was starting to feel a bit nauseous.

Thankfully, the cold mountain air rushed in as we opened the car doors. The setting Franco personally chose for the memorial, after considerable effort, is admittedly spectacular, beautiful even, a huge pharaonic esplanade, affording a panoramic view of the high peaks of the Sierra de Guadarrama, now cleared of cloud. A granite mount of boulders lies at one end, embedded into the face of which is the entrance to the basilica and mausoleum itself (see Fig. 13.4). Before we entered, however, Ricardo insisted I admire the cross—"150 metres high," he kept telling me, again and again, "each arm the length of not one but two saloon cars". I had planned to climb up the hundreds of steps to the base, but he informed me again that "the socialists had wanted to blow it up—as they had tried to do twice—and so it was closed down". In fact, there have been two failed attacks on the cross, but, as he surely knew, the first was carried out by the far left group GRAPO (Grupos de Resistencia Antifascista Primero de Octubre) in 1999, and the second attempt was at the hands of the Basque separatists ETA (Euskadi Ta Askatasuna) in 2005, not the PSOE government, which counted among their declared enemies.

Glaring down at you from the base of the cross are the four apostles. They are huge, muscled beasts, looking more like monsters from a violent fantasy video game than men of peace. Ricardo led me across the esplanade populated with small groups of American college kids and Franco nostalgics (i.e., fascists),

Fig. 10.3: Mina Canta. The Republic's remaining gold reserves and part of Spain's national art treasures were stored in secret in this old talcum mine, a handful of kilometres from the French border.

Lluís Companys.

Fig. 10.4: Part of an information plaque produced by the Catalan government's Memorial Democràtic, showing Lluís Companys's face scratched out in hate. The photo is by my friend Alan Nance who accompanied me that day in 2016.

Fig. 11.1: Memorial in the Republican cemetery at Argèles-sur-Mer. Among the Spanish and Catalan surnames are dozens of others from elsewhere in Europe, including Hirsch, Strauss, Blum, Hoffman, Lozowski. They very probably were wounded International Brigaders who succumbed on the beach.

Fig. 11.2: Château Royal de Collioure, location of an infamous punishment prison for International Brigaders and Spanish Republicans. A plaque remembers them.

Fig. 11.3: Tomb of Antonio Machado, Collioure Cemetery. A place of pilgrimage today to pay homage to the poet but also to the victims of Francoism and to those who fled into exile in 1939.

Fig. 11.4: Former International Brigaders at Gurs Internment Camp, France, 1939. Slovak brigader Janos Geza Pošner, Liz Kopp's father, is pictured, shirt off, on the right.

Fig. 11.5: A memorial installation on the Coll dels Belitres mountain pass, erected by Memorial Democràtic in 2009. It shows Manuel Moros's photos of Republican refugees flooding past here in January–February 1939.

Fig. 12.1: Plaque in Paris at the site of the enlistment office for the International Brigades, where thousands of "French and foreigners" joined before coming to Spain. "It was the first act of international resistance against fascism", the plaque reads. It is located in the Place du Colonel-Fabien, named after the International Brigader and resistance hero, in front of today's headquarters of the Parti Communiste Français.

Fig. 12.2: Plaque in the little garden next to Paris City Hall remembering the Spanish Republicans of La Nueve who fought in the liberation of Paris. Note the flowers in the colours of the Republican flag.

Fig. 13.1: Belchite Town Hall, built in a similar style to the monastery-palace complex of El Escorial. Much of the work on the new town was done by some 1,000 Republican forced labourers.

Fig. 13.2: The "Little Russia" camp near Belchite. Built to house local families deemed suspect by the Franco regime, along with, in some cases, the families of prisoners forced to build the new town. It was closed in 1945. An information panel at the site provides context.

Fig. 13.3: The Arco de la Victoria, Madrid. Built on the orders of General Franco and finished in 1956, it celebrates the Francoist victory in 1939. It has been described as the last fascist arch left in Europe.

Fig. 13.4: The Valley of the Fallen. Franco's body was still there when I took this photo. It's just about the creepiest place I've ever visited.

Fig. 13.5: Mints, sold in the gift shop of the Valley of the Fallen. They also used to sell lollipops.

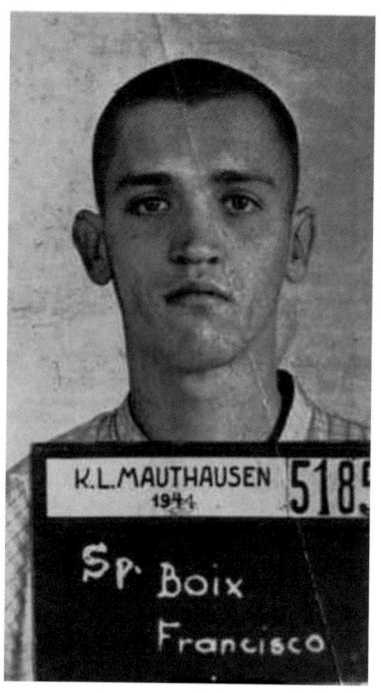

Fig. 14.1: SS mugshot of Francesc Boix taken shortly after his arrival at Mauthausen on 27 January 1941. Ricard Marco suspects this is a photocomposite Boix created after his liberation.

Fig. 14.2: Prisoners at Mauthausen being marched up the so-called "Stairs of Death" with granite blocks weighing as much as 50 kg on their backs. The SS guards would often kick back down prisoners when they reached the top; as they fell, they would take others with them. The Spaniards had a mantra for survival as they climbed each step, which took them back to Franco's war: "Una victoria más"... One more victory.

Fig. 14.3: Staged photo by US Army Corporal Donald R. Ornitz, recreating a day later the actual liberation of Mauthausen by the American Army on 5 May 1945. Francesc Boix can be seen just to the left of the flag with his camera.

Fig. 14.4: Mural remembering the victims of Mauthausen at Carrer de la Bòbila, 34, Barcelona. It was created by local school XXV Olimpíada.

Fig. 14.5: Francesc Boix during his trip to Kabylie, Algeria in May 1946. He always wore a winning smile for the camera outside of Mauthausen. This is the last image I show on my tour.

Orly 15-10-46
Paris

Fig. 14.6: Francesc Boix returning from his second appearance as a witness at Dachau. Taken at Paris Orly Airport in 1946, Boix gave this photo to American fellow communist Howard Pierson. It arrived in my hands via Kathleen Hammond through a remarkable twist of fate.

considerably more today than usual, I learned, due to the unfolding events, taking selfies. I'd wanted to enter the basilica alone, but Ricardo was proving hard to ditch and insisted on accompanying me, spluttering into my face when I asked him what he thought of the prospect of Franco being taken away. He bantered with the guards as my bag went through the metal detector. Our steps echoed on the marble floor as we walked along the voluminous tunnel decorated with medieval tapestries. Then we came to the entrance to the basilica itself, smaller perhaps than I'd expected but still huge and protected, as Ricardo pointed out, by two angels, not that you could have missed them. With their immense swords, they were clearly on the avenging spectrum of what is understood as an angel. The mass had started, and the far end of the church, where Franco was buried, was cordoned off. I became aware of music, sweet boys' voices. I thought it was a recording. "No," beamed Ricardo. "These are real boys who live and are schooled here. They sing a mass once a day." Imagine that. Sending your children to be educated at such a place. Suddenly, involuntarily in my mind, a second soundtrack appeared of bombs and screaming women and children, while on the third track Sr Ricardo wittered on about the meaning of some heraldic symbol or a painting, and how, he repeated, it was above all a place of reconciliation for all Spaniards. He'd come for his mass, and I said goodbye, my smile now almost a grimace, his eyes now cold, having by now sussed me out. I'd come back later when the rest of the basilica opened to us tourists, and anyway I needed to get out for some fresh air.

Conception and building

After dedicating considerable time and energy to visiting potential locations, Franco announced the project to build the memorial on 1 April 1940, the first anniversary of his victory over the

Republic. The Valley of the Fallen was initially conceived to render homage to those who lost their lives fighting for Franco, not, as Ricardo and many others claimed, to those on both sides. There was no room for reconciliation. This was the culmination of a wider characteristic of the Franco regime; it was in part a cult of the dead: the dead, of course, on the winning side. The country would be covered with funerary monuments—like San Simón, which I'd visited in Aragon—and well-tended cemeteries, while ceremonies held on key dates, year in, year out, would remind the population of Franco's dead in every town and village of any size.

Thousands of bodies of those who were killed in the war or had been murdered or executed by the Republican side were removed for interment here and stuffed into the crypts, usually, though not always, with the permission of their families. The bodies of many Muslim Moroccans who had fought for Franco were also dug up and transported to this Christian resting place, an idea their families would presumably have opposed, had they been informed. Republican dead were to remain forgotten in the mass graves. The design was influenced by the Egyptian tombs, by the architects of Nazi Germany, above all Albert Speer, and finally by El Escorial, the nearby palace-monastery of Philip II (I'd discussed its influence at Gernika), although this new memorial would be purposely placed at a higher altitude than the latter. And like these earlier works, the intention was for the memorial to "defy time and forgetfulness"—if you've ever visited, I doubt you'll forget it. As many have pointed out, it is clearly the work of a megalomaniac.

The project was supposed to be finished in a year, but it was immediately beset with huge problems and ended up taking almost twenty. The cost to the Spanish state at a time when half the country was starving was immense. Although some of those employed at the construction site were hired employees, most of the work, particularly in the first ten years, was done by forced labourers who were mercilessly exploited by the private companies who were contracted to carry out the work. It was a marriage of state interests and big business fed by corruption, a pattern repeated across the economy. Technically, these labourers were given the option of working on the site in return for a reduction to their prison sentences, which had been handed out by courts martial merely for having leftist ideas or simply for being Republican soldiers. The practice was based on the idea that their "sins" could be "redeemed through labour". Abuse was commonplace and malnutrition rife as the officials in charge syphoned off the meagre rations to sell on the local black market for personal profit. Fourteen men are known to have been killed in accidents on site, although many others died unrecorded in Madrid hospitals and hospices after being evacuated, as serious accidents were an almost daily occurrence. This is without counting the large numbers who had limbs amputated and those whose lives were later cut short through the silicosis they developed during the work.

The decision to bring Republican bodies to the mausoleum was only made in 1957—perversely, weirdly, sickly—as part of a broader effort to show a more human face to the rest of the world. The regime had reached agreements with the United States and the Vatican in the early 1950s and needed to improve its international image and prove that it prayed for the dead on both sides. So, it set out to scour the mass graves and cemeteries of Republicans executed or those who had been killed in battles such as the Ebro and brought them for re-burial here. In some cases, but more usually not, the family members knew but couldn't say anything. There was also a striking difference between the possibility of identifying the bodies of those who died on Franco's side compared with the Republican ones. The former were registered with their name, place of birth, family details and even the personal objects the bodies carried, while the Republican remains were brought unregistered and dumped en masse. In total, 33,847 bodies are interred in the crypts, of whom 12,000 have never been identified. The last transfer of remains took place as late as 1983, eight years after Franco's death, carried out by local councils who were presumably still keen to honour his work.

The two graves

There were far more people when I returned to the monument an hour later, but this time the guards eyed me warily and wouldn't let me in without showing my ticket—just me, I noticed. I think Don Ricardo had said something. I asked them how could I not have a ticket if you have to pay 6 kilometres away at the bottom of the hill. One said, even though he clearly remembered me, that I could be a "fugitivo del monte" who had got here hiking from outside. Another place, another time, it might even have been funny. But it was a term used by the regime to denote anti-Francoist guerrillas, or people simply hiding out in the hills after escaping from Franco's prison system. In the Valley of the Fallen, a place of penitentiary punishment, those words felt a little bit chilling. After some fumbling, I found my ticket, and they had to let me back in. The service was over, so visitors could go all the way to the altar.

I came first to the marble gravestone, embedded flush into the floor of the basilica, of José Antonio Primo de Rivera (1903–36), the eldest son of General Miguel Primo de Rivera, the dictator who ruled Spain from 1923 to 1930. José Antonio was an upper-class lawyer and the founder of the Falange Española, the unreservedly fascist party within the Francoist coalition of reactionary groups whose purposely violent actions did so much to create a sense of ungovernability in the lead-up to the July coup. The charge of illegal possession of firearms led to his arrest in March 1936. With the war in full swing, he was found guilty of conspiracy and military rebellion by a Republican court and executed in Alicante on 20 November 1936 (incidentally the same day of the year as Franco died). Many suggest José Antonio's death was welcome to Franco since it removed a potential rival while at the same time creating a useful martyr for the Falangist and wider Francoist cause. He became widely idolised, with a cult of personality developing around his figure, his name written on the façade of thousands of churches across the country, where they can sometimes still be seen.[6] In 1939, José Antonio's body was relayed in a coffin in a torchlit procession on the backs of Falangist admirers for 467 kilometres from Alicante to El Escorial. Wreaths were sent to the funeral by Hitler and Mussolini. In 1959, he was reburied, again brought by torchlit procession, here in the Valley of the Fallen.

But most people that day had come to see the other grave, up a couple of steps and closer to the altar, above the Falangist leader, the hierarchy unmistakable. You could hardly see this one for the red and yellow wreaths and bouquets. Just a few of the letters "FRANCISCO FRANCO" were visible. One fellow pulled off the cellophane wrapper—6.49 euros it said. They must have cleared the flowers away every day to stop them from overflowing. More wreaths, one huge, the size of a man, were arriving as I left. A woman was taking what looked like a grotesque selfie as she angled on one leg to get her face and the grave into the frame. I guess some visitors were just curious, or even a few, like myself, with, let's say, a hidden agenda, but most were evidently there to pay homage and say goodbye to the dictator's resting space for forty-four years. Franco wasn't going to be dumped at sea by the Spanish Navy as the eminent British historian Paul Preston recommended. His new spot was to be next to his wife Carmen Polo in a Madrid cemetery, so his followers would be able to stare reverentially at the new slab soon enough. Franco himself probably didn't intend to be buried in the Valley of the Fallen anyway and left indications that he should be interred next to Polo. It seems that on his death the diehard followers around him had his body sent here, even though he hadn't died during the war—making him the only person interred here, to my knowledge, not to have done so.

I wondered what portraits these well-wishers had hanging in their living rooms. And I bet, as I write in 2025, quite a few of these artworks have been dusted off since with the recent normalisation of far-right politics in Spain. Many Spaniards owe Franco a lot—huge fortunes but also modest ones were made by many of those who won the war: through the handouts, corruption and the mass expropriation of the losers. Many of their descendants are either unaware or prefer not to become aware, but some are eternally grateful. The crowds of visitors included families with young children, one with a baby in a pram. Some of the men looked genuinely frightening, but most were weirdly normal. There were quite a few dressed in Barbour jackets, a typical attire of your wealthy *Madrileño*. Two little boys were dressed in sailor suits. You wouldn't have batted an eyelid if you passed some of the others on a Barcelona street. And on either side, as they reverentially whisper their tributes, hidden behind heavy doors, all of those bodies.

Out of the bunker

On the way out, the gift shop was doing a roaring trade in tote bags, ash trays, mugs, soap, fridge magnets, the usual... all bearing the outline of the mausoleum and cross. I leafed through the glossy book of photos of the site. It made no mention of the prison labour that had been used. My fellow guide Catherine Howley had visited the site a few weeks before while working with the BBC on a news report and acquired a box of mints from the shop embossed with the Valley's image (see Fig. 13.5). I sometimes use the mints on the tour. I see them as the banalisation of murder encapsulated in a little tin of sweets. Before leaving, I picked up a hefty piece of pale granite from close to the basilica entrance and slipped it into my bag. It looked like it had been worked, perhaps hacked out of the space that became the mausoleum. It made me think about the cubic metres of toil and pain, the wasted years and broken families, that went into hollowing out the space. I've used it sometimes on a tour. People hold it, feel its weight; for some, it manages to take them to the place and the horror.

There was no path threading down what is a beautiful valley, so I had to walk back down the road, and although the mountain views, woods of pine and oak and birdsong were lovely, the journey was marred by the constant comings and goings of cars, some very expensive. I couldn't help thinking that the noise inside some of the vehicles mouthing off about *rojos*, separatists, foreigners, women, homosexuals, Catalans would be infinitely worse. I moved away from the road and scrambled down, through pine needles, acorns, moss and twigs crunching underfoot, the truffling work of wild boar everywhere, to a fast stream where I threw cool water over my face and sat and ate some nuts, watching crested tits flit among the pines and tried to will the sound of the water to cleanse the dark left by Ricardo and the dictator's grave.

At the bottom of the road by the entrance, several news crews were reporting that the abbot of the memorial and church was refusing to give the state permission to enter to remove Franco's remains. Santiago Cantera, an ex-Falange candidate in national elections, and at the time of writing *still* the Benedictine prior of the abbey attached to the Valley of the Fallen, claimed there had been no forced labour and that prisoners were treated as if they were in a health spa.

Moving the bodies

Two days after my visit, the Valley of the Fallen was closed; two weeks later, on 24 October 2019, the coffin containing the dictator's remains was exhumed from the basilica in compliance with the 2011 Historical Memory Law. The coffin was borne out by members of the dictator's family, with the old slogans "¡Viva España!", "¡Viva Franco!" ringing out loud and clear. A helicopter paid for by the Spanish state transported it to Mingorrubio municipal cemetery, where his remains were re-interred alongside those of Polo, as he would probably have wanted. The whole thing was broadcast live on Spanish state TV. Fittingly, Ramón Tejero, the priest given the task of saying mass at the ceremony, was the son of the Guardia Civil lieutenant colonel Antonio Tejero, who led the failed 1981 coup.[7]

In 2023, José Antonio's remains were also removed to a different cemetery in Madrid. Since then, change has been slow. Meetings exalting Franco are now banned at the Valley of the Fallen, there have been some changes to the webpage and the information panels and the site's official title have returned to the valley's old name of Cuelgamuros. More importantly, there have also slowly been some exhumations of bodies so they can be returned to their families, despite attempts to block this by right-wing lawyers. Some have argued that this showcase of Spanish fascism should simply be blown up, but I believe they are wrong—first and foremost because it is a mass grave, but also because it is part of the tragic history of modern Spain. However, we still seem a long way from creating a space where visitors might feel as they do visiting, say, a Nazi work camp. Any significant work in this direction runs the serious risk of being derailed once a right-wing government wins a national election. You can even get married in the basilica. Even though his bones have been physically moved, the dictator's presence still stalks Cuelgamuros in the same way it haunts many other places in Spain. Not because of anything spectral, of course, but because part of the legacy he left behind is still in many people's minds... and is growing.

14

MAUTHAUSEN

The photographer of Mauthausen

I'd left Francesc Boix, the young Catalan photographer from my street, possibly being marched across a beach in Southern France. In September 1939, he was conscripted into a labour battalion to work on defences in the Vosges, part of the Maginot Line—one of some 12,000 Spanish Republicans employed in the attempt to complete this pharaonic defensive structure designed to withstand a German attack. Although conscripted, dressed in old French army uniforms and poorly paid, the Spanish were no longer prisoners and now had a degree of freedom. They were often popular with the local women because of the aura associated with being anti-fascist fighters, and men would stand them drinks in bars, knowing they had little money.

Nazi Germany invaded France in May 1940, sweeping around the Maginot Line and rendering it utterly useless. Boix was captured on the night of the 20–21 June and was moved, along with other Republicans, to a series of prisoner-of-war camps in Northern France and Germany. The Nazis saw the Spaniards as political enemies to be treated as such. Their fate was sealed after a visit to Germany by the Spanish foreign minister and Nazi-admirer Ramón Serrano Suñer, Franco's brother-in-law. While the smoking gun of a document is yet to be found, historians are clear that the Franco regime disowned the Republicans, allowing the Germans to declare them stateless citizens and hence to be worked to death. Had Franco agreed to take them back, it would have hardly made a difference. Those Republicans who were deported to Spain faced torture, concentration camps and firing squads. The SS were merely lending a hand in this work.

On 27 January 1941, after two days crammed with other Spanish Republicans in a railway wagon, Boix arrived at the SS camp complex of Mauthausen in Austria (see Fig. 14.1). He was twenty-one years old. The camp, which included some fifty sub-camps, had been established in 1938 for the most "Incorrigible Political Enemies of the Reich", where the order of the day was extermination through labour in quarries, munitions factories and assembly plants. It is considered among the worst of all Nazi work camps, where more than 90,000 humans were either worked to death or otherwise murdered under the direction of camp commandant Franz Ziereis. Thousands were Spanish Republicans, many of whom died in the sub-camp of Gusen.

I have never been to Mauthausen. In this sense, this final chapter of the book, the one that is the most important for me to tell, is based on a falsehood. I've told the story of the Spanish at the camp so many times. I've read thousands of pages on the barbarities committed and stories of survival. I've often imagined walking through its barracks and quarry in my head. I even organised several virtual tours to the camp during the COVID-19 pandemic—I used Google Street View to help the participants imagine we were there. As much as the place has drawn me, it also repels me. Maybe I'll go next year. Maybe I'll never visit.

Boix and his fellow prisoners were forced to strip before being passed like cattle through showers. They were then given a striped blue and white uniform bearing the blue triangle used to identify foreign forced labourers, with an "S" superimposed on top to denote "Spanier"—or "Rotspaniaer"—Red Spaniard (although this is sometimes taken as *staatenlose*—stateless). Each prisoner was then assigned a number to replace their name. Boix's was 5,185. Quick-witted and having already managed to pick up some German, he was assigned as a translator, and by the end of the year he managed to get a relatively good position —privileged within the context of hell—working as a slave technician in the SS photo lab (the *Erkennungsdienst*), developing the thousands of photos the Nazis obsessively took to document the camp and its inmates. The photos served partly to feed the bureaucratic obsession of the Nazis but were also often simply handed out as souvenirs. Most were police-type portraits taken of each prisoner on their arrival, but the images also depicted executions and other barbarous acts committed by the camp's guards, inmates lying murdered on the ground and, crucially, visits by leading Nazis.

Many of the Spanish prisoners were sent to work in the granite quarry. The most salient feature of the quarry, if not the whole camp, is the stone steps known as the *Todesstiege*, the "Stairs of Death", often used simply as a punishment. Prisoners were forced to lug granite blocks weighing up to 50 kilos up 186 steep, irregular steps, one prisoner behind the other. Many, weak from hunger, would lose their footing and fall, taking others with them like dominoes. The steps were particularly treacherous when wet or iced over. The SS guards would also force already exhausted prisoners to race up the stairs carrying their loads. Other times, the guards just kicked them down when they got to the top. Many of the Spaniards who died at Mauthausen were murdered here. Those who survived each ascent uttered a mantra of survival to themselves: "¡Una victoria más!" One more victory.

287

One notorious photograph shows prisoners waiting to climb the steps while others are already ascending with blocks on their backs (see Fig. 14.2). It is impossible to know whether Boix developed the photograph—he certainly didn't take it: most were by the SS photographer Paul Ricken.

Boix, despite privations, was in a considerably better situation working in the photo lab than those in the quarry. After the German defeat at Stalingrad in February 1943, the SS started to destroy records of their appalling system. Boix and several others were ordered to burn all of the photos and negatives. Under the direction of the clandestine communist network in the camp, they set out to steal several thousand negatives and photos to be used as future evidence against their tormentors. They handed them to a group of young Spaniards aged between thirteen and sixteen—the only ones allowed outside to work in a private quarry run by the company Poschacher (you can still buy granite from this sizable family company today). En route, the young resisters passed the negatives and photos to a rather brave Austrian woman, a social democrat called Anna Pointner, who hid them behind a stone in her garden wall. These images represent by far the largest photographic record of the barbarity of the Nazi camps because the SS destroyed almost all the records. In fact, there are apparently more photographs from Mauthausen than all the other camps put together—thanks to these terribly brave Spanish lads and an Austrian woman.

Exact numbers are not known, but somewhere between 9,000 and 10,000 Spanish Republicans were deported to Nazi camps. More than 7,000 were murdered. At least 7,251 ended up at the Mauthausen complex, of whom at least 4,379 were murdered.[1] Another 2,000 or so died in other camps. The survivors evidently could not return to Franco's Spain and were given residency in France. Republican women were also deported to SS camps, above all several hundred who were sent to Ravensbrück near

Berlin. The Ravensbrück survivor Neus Català campaigned tirelessly to recover the memory of these women, arguing that, if the Spanish Republican men were the forgotten victims of the Nazi camps, the women were the "oblidades entre els oblidats"— the forgotten among the forgotten.[2]

Throughout the Nazi camp system, the levels of murder enacted against Jewish, Roma and Soviet prisoners were particularly horrific. What is noticeable at Mauthausen is that the Spanish had higher survival rates, physically and psychologically, than all other groups of inmates, quite simply because they understood why they were there. As they struggled with those granite blocks on their backs, they saw their hardship as a continuation of the struggle that began in 1936. They were brought together by the shared memories of the war against Franco. Anti-fascism defined them. This was manifested in greater solidarity towards each other, often through the communist underground, although non-party members did not always benefit from this solidarity. At night, in their cramped, stinking, lice-ridden barracks, they'd sing ever so quietly songs of love but also words from the battles of Madrid, Aragon and the Ebro—"¡Ay, Carmela!" and the others. The Catalans also sang their anthem "Els Segadors". In the dark heart of the 1940s, the music they made helped them to lift their hearts and dream of their homes on the other side of the European continent.

The death toll at Mauthausen could have been much worse. In May 1945, as the Allies drew closer, the SS—driven by the need to cover up all evidence and by their murderous madness—set about killing the remaining prisoners and ordering incriminating documents to be burned; they ran out of time and fled on 3 May as news arrived of the approaching US army. The camp was left in the hands of a few older guards. On 5 May, Spanish Republican prisoners including Boix rose up and overpowered the guards in their section of the complex. The next day, the Americans were welcomed at the gates by armed Spanish Republicans. It was the last Nazi camp to be liberated. Shortly after a photo shoot was staged recreating the event (see Fig. 14.3). The scene taken by a US army photographer is a remarkable one. We see a Sherman tank swamped by ex-prisoners in striped uniforms holding their fists in the air. A long banner confected for the occasion from the SS cotton bedsheets is unfurled across the gates, proclaiming "Los españoles antifascistas saludan a las fuerzas libertadoras" ("The anti-fascist Spaniards salute the liberating forces"). Boix can be seen to the left of a flag flying above the banner holding the Leica camera he had taken from the Nazi photographer. He had already set out to work, photographing the camp's liberation, a unique perspective in terms of other camps: piles of murdered prisoners; liberated inmates sitting around dazed; a gas chamber; the Americans' real, unstaged arrival. He also photographed the interrogation of Ziereis, mortally wounded after being shot by the Americans while trying to escape from the area.

A few days later, Boix visited Pointner to pick up the negatives and photos and took them to Paris. Initially, the French Communist Party felt uneasy about publishing them. Stalin's declared policy of seeing Soviet soldiers captured by the Nazis as traitors who should expect nothing but death sat uncomfortably with the treatment of liberated communists from Western Europe. Sense prevailed, and the Communist Party-aligned magazine *Regards* dedicated an issue on 1 July 1945 with shocking photos of the camp. Meanwhile, Boix, like the other Spanish Republican survivors, was given residency in France. Liberated they may have been, but by 1945 many were at the limits of their resistance, and half were dead within a year. The survivors bore the nightmare for the rest of their lives.

Witness

On 28 and 29 January 1946, Boix appeared for the French prosecution as a witness at the Nuremberg Trials, the only Spaniard called to the stand. His declaration, which you can watch on YouTube, supported by photos taken by the SS, was short and harrowing. He described slave labour, torture and how the SS guards received bonuses for shooting Jews. He commented on one photo he had developed:

> This staged the scene of an Austrian who had escaped. He was a carpenter in the garage and he managed to make a box, a box in which he could hide and so get out of the camp. But after a while he was recaptured. They put him on the wheelbarrow in which corpses were carried to the crematorium. There were some placards saying in German, "Alle Vogel sind schon da," meaning "All the birds are back again." He was sentenced and then paraded in front of 10,000 deportees to the music of a gypsy band playing a song "J'attendrai". When he was hanged, his body swung to and fro in the wind while they played the very well-known song, "Bill Black Polka".

Boix testified to the presence at the camp of high-ranking Nazis: Himmler, Speer, and Ernst Kaltenbrunner—the latter of whom had denied any knowledge of the camps and was convicted and hanged because of Boix's testimony, the highest-ranking member of the SS to be condemned. Later in the year, Boix was also a witness for the US prosecution at a second trial in Dachau against sixty-one other Nazis who had worked at Mauthausen, completing his work testifying against the horror.

In 2022, a *Stolperstein* was embedded in the pavement beneath the plaque in my street in Poble-sec, one of now well over 100,000 so-called "stumbling stones": little brass-fronted concrete cubes installed around the world in places associated with the lives of victims of Nazism. It was a moving event enlivened by a group of very young musicians playing Republican songs from the war. What I really liked was that the whole show was run not by historians or politicians, but by students from the local secondary school, XXV Olimpíada. Shortly afterwards, the students painted an interesting memorial that brings together elements from the story framed with rolls of negatives: prisoners laden with blocks ascending the steps, his camp number (5185), the blue triangle with the "S", Boix pointing at Nuremberg. It can be seen at Carrer de la Bòbila, 34 (and is reproduced here in Fig. 14.4).

Soon after his liberation, Boix started to work as a photo reporter for the French communist-aligned press (*L'Humanité, Ce Soir* and *Regards*). He covered party meetings and demonstrations against Franco of exiled Republicans but also football matches, the Tour de France and art exhibitions, including a shot of Picasso showing his work to the Spanish communist leader Dolores Ibárruri. In June 1946, *Regards* published a travel reportage of his trip to Kabylia, Algeria. The front cover shows a young girl in traditional dress smiling at his camera. It's barely a year since his liberation from that hell, and Boix seems to find in her face hope for a post-war world. Ricard Marco, who had helped unearth Boix's photographs from the war, explained to me that in 1948 Boix's name began to disappear from the press. He was ill. Later in the year, he had two operations on his ailing kidneys. On 4 June 1951 (not 7 June, as online sources have it), he died in Paris from kidney failure. He was thirty years old, as his obituary in *L'Humanité* noted, dying so young due to "the abuse he suffered in the concentration camps of Daladier and Hitler".

Francesc had joined the youth section of the PSUC, the Catalan communist party, probably in 1936, aged sixteen. Its leadership certainly leant towards Stalinism, despite the more plural nature of the party in Catalonia. After Mauthausen, he became a member of the French Communist Party, whose position was more unreservedly Stalinist. My impression is that Boix himself, probably like many of the young Catalan communists around him, was certainly a brave anti-fascist fighter, but he wasn't a Stalinist ideologue. Rather, he was drawn to the gregariousness and togetherness of the party and to the excitement of the fight and the cause. I like to imagine he saw himself fighting for social justice in Catalonia and for the Spanish Republic rather than for the interests of the USSR. We don't know how he would have developed politically had he survived longer. Would he have left the party, as so many did after the Soviet invasions of Hungary in 1956 or Czechoslovakia in 1968? Or would he have stayed like many other Spanish did, stressing their anti-Francoism rather than the Soviet ties of the Spanish party, which in any case was moving towards Eurocommunism in the late 1970s? Or would he have died an embittered old Stalinist? Whatever the case, I suspect that the action and even fun was always more important to him than the ideology. How would he have developed as a photographer? Ricard pointed out to me that "[h]e always had a camera around his neck, but his work was all too brief. Just a couple of years in Catalonia, barely a man and with scant experience, followed by photographing the liberation of the camp and working for a few years in France. He was certainly getting better, picking up contemporary techniques, but," he concluded, "he died too young to fulfil his promise."

Echoes

In 2018, I was involved with Ricard in a talk about Boix at my local library in Poble-sec. As we were almost finished, an old guy sitting at the back stood up and pulled a huge wad of old photographs out of his rucksack. They were all either taken by Boix or of Boix. As August Andreu passed around the well-thumbed photos to our open-mouthed amazement, he explained that his father Hector had been a fellow communist and a close friend of Paco, as Boix was known to those around him. The Andreu family had lived opposite Boix's house in Poble-sec, even closer to ours, and the young Paco spent long hours in their Barcelona home. By 1945, the Andreus were in exile in Montpellier. "He came to stay with us in the summer of 1946," August explained. "I was just four years old." He showed us a photo of himself as a young boy on top of Francesc's shoulders on a beach near Montpellier. I asked August if he happened to remember anything about Boix, being so young at the time. "Of course I do," he shot back. "We used to go to the beach all the time and whenever my father wasn't looking, he'd buy me another ice cream," he giggled. "He was that kind of guy, but I never saw him after 1947," he sighed. "I suppose he wasn't well by then. I've never forgotten him, such a warm-hearted man." The photographs have since formed an exhibition showing another aspect to his life. I now take part in a free tour in Catalan every month or so on Boix's life in Poble-sec with August, now in a wheelchair, and Ricard Marco and other local historians. It's a good way to remember and thank Francesc for how he's changed my life.

The story of Boix keeps coming back to me in strange ways.

In June 2015, a woman called Andrea from New York came on the tour. She explained to the group that her parents had been communists and had helped collect scrap metal on the streets of Brooklyn in the late 1930s to raise money for the Republican cause. Andrea came up to me at the end visibly moved. To my great surprise, she told me she too had a copy of the last photo I always show on the tour: Boix grinning on top of a donkey during his trip to Algeria in 1946 (see Fig. 14.5). It's a great image, although you have to pity the animal underneath him. Andrea explained that when her mother had died, she had come across an old scrapbook of her parents' times as members of the American Communist Party. Some of the pages referred to a visit they made to Europe in 1948. She had no idea who the people depicted in the photos were, but, she insisted, Boix on the donkey was in the scrapbook. It's a very distinct photo, but I have to say I secretly thought she might have been mistaken.

A few days later, after recovering from jetlag, Andrea sent me some photos of the scrapbook, including the very same image of Boix. On the other side of the page is a cut-out from an American newspaper of Boix's testimony at Nuremberg. The name of the article is "Star Witness Incriminates Nazis: While Mauthausen Prisoner, Spanish Republican Steals 2,000 Negatives". It describes Boix as "a curly-haired, smooth-faced lad" who "treasures his memories of the day prisoners revolted and liberated themselves while the Americans were drawing nearer". She also included an image of the back of the photo. On the rear, it says it was taken in Kabylie, Algeria, in May 1946. There is a dedication in French to her parents from a "young Spanish communist", signed "François". He happily called himself Francesc, Francisco, François. I checked it with a series of known Boix signatures. It's his. He had the habit of giving away photos, a relatively expensive item back then, as a memento to people he liked.

This chance circumstance certainly left me in wonder as to how a daughter managed to reconnect in Barcelona with her parents' visit to Europe in the 1940s, but there was also another story waiting for me.

Sometime later, another American woman came on my tour. Kathleen Hammond, a Spanish-language teacher, was taken with the story of Boix. When she returned to Boulder, Colorado, she decided to introduce it as a reading topic in her university classes. At the end of the course, one of Kathleen's students wanted to give her a present in thanks and managed to track down a copy of *Francisco Boix, el fotógrafo de Mauthausen* (2015), the only biography of Boix, by Spanish historian Benito Bermejo. It's not particularly easy to find in Spain. In the US, there was one single copy, second hand, on offer. When Kathleen unwrapped the book and opened it, she was stunned to find two original photos taped inside. The first shows Boix smiling at the camera. On the other side is a handwritten note signed by Boix to a man called Howard Pierson. The second shows Boix in front of a Boeing B-29 super fortress and is dated: "15-10-1946, Orly [Paris]" (see Fig. 14.6). On the other side, Boix had written in Spanish: "To my American friend Howard Pierson, with my deepest affection for the community of the cause which unites us. Francisco Boix Paris 29-10-46."

There were keys to the mystery. A little sticker inside indicated that the book belonged to Pierson. And he is referenced in Bermejo's book. As a young journalist, he had been doing military service in Germany as a journalist for the *Stars and Stripes*, the US army newspaper, which had published the article Andrea had sent me. I can't prove it, but my strong guess is that it was written by Pierson. Bermejo, Boix's biographer, had managed to track down Pierson and includes in his book the interesting first encounter between the two men. One day, the American, also a communist, was walking past a room on the military base where he was stationed when he heard somebody playing a familiar tune from the Spanish Civil War on the piano. I fancy it was "¡Ay, Carmela!", the song I'd listened to in the Ebro, and my guess is he knew it from the Pete Seeger recordings published in New York in the 1940s. The two young men hit it off and despite the distance kept in contact by letter for some time. Boix either gave the photos to Pierson at the Dachau trial or sent them to the US. Many years later, Bermejo sent Pierson a signed copy. Presumably, he taped the treasured photos of his friend inside. Pierson died in 2014. Kathleen tried to contact the family to return the photos, but they showed no interest. She kept them for some years. In 2021, terrible grass fires swept through residential areas of Boulder, destroying almost 1,000 buildings, close to her own home. With rising temperatures, Kathleen became increasingly worried about the disaster returning and started to distribute heirlooms around the family. The importance of the Boix photos also weighed upon her, and in 2022 she brought them to Barcelona and gave them to me to form part of my walking museum. I, too, felt the weight of their presence in our cramped flat with rambunctious children. After discussing it with Kathleen, I donated them to Poble-sec library, where they are now on permanent display in memory of the centre's namesake.

Boix's anti-fascist politics aside, he was also someone who was full of life. You can see this very much in August's testimony but also through the dozens of photos of him outside of Austria—whether in Spain at the front or having a laugh with his mates in France, he always has a lovely, winning smile. He was also handsome—he looked a bit like Elvis. I tell people on my tour he was a "Jack the lad", as we say in British English, which might be a regular Joe in the US. Younger folk would probably call him a "bro". He liked to drink, to dance, to flirt, to mess about. He was a bit of a charmer. It was often the charmers who had the *joie de vivre* or the resilience to survive the hell. This appalling history was thrust upon him. He did the right thing at the right time, which I think is probably what a hero is. I like to think he's a universal hero of my street. He was thirty years old when he died, a young man from Poble-sec to whom history had given the role of documenting Nazi barbarity.

EPILOGUE

MEMORY POLITICS

The Franco dictatorship continued for thirty-seven dark years. It went through its extremely murderous phase between 1936 and the late 1940s, during which time it had a clear totalitarian project. This project, in the main, failed, and what emerged from the 1950s was an oligarchic authoritarian dictatorship in which different groups vied for power under Franco's supervision. Economic reforms in the late 1950s imposed by the International Monetary Fund, the arrival of mass tourism and the remittances sent by the millions of Spaniards who went to work in Northern Europe in the 1960s brought a remarkable economic turnaround, leading to material improvements, and by the late 1960s many workers in the cities were aspiring to have cars. Among the middle classes, there was also a certain cultural opening, provided this was not politically oriented. Meanwhile, any overt dissent or independent trade union activity was violently suppressed.

Franco died in his hospital bed in 1975; he was succeeded as head of state by King Juan Carlos. His death was followed by what is usually called "the transition": key events in this were multi-party democratic elections in June 1977, the drafting of the Spanish Constitution of 1978 and the failed military coup of 23 February 1981. A cornerstone of the transition was the so-called "Pacto del Olvido" (Pact of Forgetting), an informal understanding under which the Francoist crimes of the war and the dictatorship would be forgotten by the left in return for a parliamentary democracy under the figurehead of a king, and the promise of social peace, development and a degree of redistribution. The Amnesty Law of October 1977 ensured that no one would be brought to account. There was no Truth and Reconciliation Commission. This silence was probably tacitly supported by a high percentage of society in the 1980s and '90s.

The relative silence over those murdered was never going to last. There are more than 120,000 bodies in some 2,600 unmarked mass graves in Spain, representing what cultural anthropologist Francisco Ferrándiz has called "an underground landscape of terror", in a country that has been a member of the European Union since 1986. In Spain, however, although the survivors and their children were wary or even afraid of talking about the past, their fears were not shared by their grandchildren, some of whom started to ask why grandparents were buried in places like the village dump. To this, we should add the extraordinary work of many dogged local researchers and historians.

This has helped to engender a wide-ranging movement aimed at breaking the silence, which has changed the panorama in twenty-first-century Spain. First a civic movement developed that puts pressure on local authorities to open up the graves. It's an expensive process that has often been met with resistance. The opening of mass graves has been accompanied by a cultural and history movement, manifested in art, movies, TV documentaries and novels. A seemingly never-ending supply of new works of history is published every month in Spanish and Catalan on every imaginable angle of the war and the dictatorship. The Civil War probably comes up somewhere every day in the press in Spain.

At a municipal level, a large number of memorials, plaques and small interpretation centres, some of which I have discussed in this book, have been created in recent years, initially in Catalonia and then later in the rest of the state—there are well over 150 in Barcelona, if you have a mind to look for them. The culmination of this movement was the Democratic Memory Law of 2022, which annulled all the sentences for military rebellion imposed by the Franco regime.

One example of all this work may suffice. Marina Ginestà of the Hotel Colón photo, who had returned from Caracas in 1950, died in Paris on 6 January 2014, a couple of weeks short of her ninety-fifth birthday. In recent years, thanks to the photograph, Ginestà has become a well-remembered figure in Catalonia. The image has featured on a number of magazine and book covers and on television news reports. Barcelona city council even reproduced the image in the form of plants growing on a wall garden in the Plaça de les Dones del 36 (Square of the Women of 1936), which you can see in the district of Gràcia. In 2016, to commemorate the eightieth anniversary of the outbreak of the war, the council put up 520 posters across the city with Ginestà's image and a quote from the Catalan poet Màrius Torres: "Jo vull la pau, però no vull l'oblit!"—"I want peace but not forgetting." I like to think this sums up the attitude of many Catalans and indeed that of progressive Spain.

This attempt to break the silence has been countered by two things. First, as generational ties to the past are snapping, younger people are increasingly uninterested in what happened in the 1930s. It's a long time ago, and why should they care about what happened to their great-grandparents? I don't even know the names of mine. This is a natural process in every modern society, in which it becomes the responsibility of historians and educators to fill the gap as family memories fade. There is, however, another problem: the counter-narrative of the Spanish right, who have become angered and emboldened by the success in bringing the history of the war and regime to light. The old line, which is still very much there, is that both sides did bad things, so let's not talk about it—even though one side did nothing but talk about it for thirty-seven years. This attitude is still prevalent and was trivialised to the extreme in November 2022 when PP leader Alberto Núñez Feijóo described the Spanish Civil War as merely "a punch-up between our grandfathers and great-grandfathers" rather than an annihilating war unleashed by murderous generals killing hundreds of thousands and ruining millions of lives.

Spanish democracy today is seated uncomfortably upon these crimes, and the refusal of most of the right and its supporters to adequately condemn the 1936 coup and the murder it wrought is an uneasy presence in the heart of parts of the state and society. To compound things, we now also have a much more radical line openly expressed by the far-right party Vox, which is influencing the supposedly liberal-conservative PP, bringing out latent neo-Francoist attitudes within the party that were previously partially hidden. This line not only avoids condemning the 1936 coup but rather appears to fully support it. An example. In 2024, during a televised debate in the Balearic parliament to repeal the previous historical memory law, the speaker, a member of Vox, expelled two parliamentarians for displaying a photo of Mallorcan communist and feminist Aurora Picornell, who was tortured and murdered on the island in 1937. As he demanded they leave, he grabbed her photo and ripped it up. This seems a fine metaphor for the type of reconciliation offered by the far right.

What's happening now in Spain is an increasingly belligerent and nasty memory and history war, which is getting worse and worse, straying into territory I would not have believed possible when I started this book. Evidently, this cultural war isn't taking place on its own. There's one going on across the planet, as we move into dangerous, uncharted waters. I've been saying words to that effect in recent years near the end of my tour. Maybe I used them for rhetoric, but in 2025 they're feeling very real.

APPENDIX 1

AN ALPHABET SOUP

On the left

The left was split between, first, those in favour, nominally at least, of the liberal democratic Republic, that is, those broadly supporting the constitutional system and the progressive reforms introduced since 1931 (either because they believed in this or, in the case of the PCE, because of geopolitical strategy); and, second, those in favour of some form of socialist, anti-capitalist revolution. There were major differences within both of these groups and, often, disagreements within the parties and unions themselves. It is worth stressing that these divisions were important for their militants, but for many others, support waxed and waned as the fortunes of war changed. Many in, say, the Catalan working class probably had a foot in both the revolutionary and Republican camps, depending on which way the wind blew—as people often do. In the first weeks and months, it blew very much towards revolution; as the war dragged on, this moved back to more support for the Republic. The following is a description of their political backgrounds, but their military positions evolved as the conflict continued. With the war quickly going badly, all of the groups—including a majority of the anarchist movement and the revolutionary POUM—came to accept the need for a centralised military command and government, whatever the nuances in strategies.

The (nominally) constitutional left

ERC (Esquerra Republicana de Catalunya—Republican left of Catalonia)

The ERC was founded in 1931 by a merger of several parties. In its early years, the party was a loose federation of mainly middle-class Catalan republicans with a principally social-democratic ideology, though divided between those who followed Macià in demanding independence and supporters of Companys who advocated Catalan membership of a federal Spanish state. The party was the leading electoral force in Catalonia between 1931 and 1936 and formed the bulk of the Catalan government for most of the war.

Izquierda Republicana (Republican left)

Centre-left Spanish republican party that formed the minority government from the 1936 elections to the outbreak of the war: its leader, Manuel Azaña, was president of the Republic during the conflict.

PCE (Partido Comunista de España—Spanish communist party) and PSUC (Partit Socialista Unificat de Catalunya—Unified socialist party of Catalonia)

The PCE was a minor partner in the 1936 Popular Front electoral alliance, but during the first five months of the war, the party grew from 30,000 members to 100,000. It was replaced in Catalonia by the PSUC, a pro-Soviet communist-affiliated party formed by a merger of the Catalan sections of the Spanish socialist and communist parties along with smaller groups on

23 July 1936. It also had a strong Catalanist identity but was ultimately subservient to its Spanish partner.

Some readers may be surprised to see the inclusion of the communists in the non-revolutionary left. The party's stance in Spain was dictated by the demands of Stalin. The Soviet Union was in a difficult geopolitical position by 1936, between the threats from imperial Japan and Nazi Germany, and so Stalin was desperate for an alliance with the Western democracies. Supporting revolution in Spain would prevent this. Moreover, as the Civil War spread, the PCE and PSUC concluded that only a centralised military command based on the broad democratic front of the Republic could defeat Franco—as did all leftist parties and unions.

PSOE (Partido Socialista Obrero Español—Spanish socialist workers' party)

The PSOE is the main social democratic party in Spain and, at the time of writing, the senior coalition partner in the country's government under Pedro Sánchez. It was founded in 1879, making it the oldest party in the country, and was by some way the largest of the left in the 1930s. However, it decided not to join the Republican government due to divisions between a more social democratic wing under Indalecio Prieto and a more revolutionary, though broadly pragmatic one under Francisco Largo Caballero. Caballero would be prime minister from September 1936 until the crisis arising from the 1937 Barcelona May Days, when he was replaced by an ally of Prieto, Juan Negrín, who led the Republic until its defeat in April 1939. The PSOE had scant support in Catalonia, where Catalan republicanism and anarchism dominated among the working class, the peasantry and progressive middle class.

UGT (Unión General de Trabajadores—General union of workers)

Socialist trade union founded in Barcelona in 1888. Prior to and during the war, the UGT had a greater presence among white-collar workers in Barcelona than the CNT. In Catalonia, the union attracted many POUM militants, as well as communists and ERC members. In other parts of Spain such as the Basque Country and Madrid, the union attracted large numbers of manual workers and was much larger than the CNT. Like the socialist party (PSOE), it was divided into more social democratic and more revolutionary factions.

The revolutionary left

CNT (Confederación Nacional del Trabajo—National confederation of labour)

The CNT was formed in Barcelona in 1910 as a confederation of anarcho-syndicalist labour unions. Being anarchist, it wanted a society without a state and a form of communism based partly on individual liberty but above all on local community control. Being syndicalist, it advocated for a society based around working-class control of the workplace. Held together by class consciousness, the CNT dominated proletarian society and politics in Barcelona until 1939. The union was at the head of the workers' revolution that engulfed Barcelona in the summer of 1936. As the war developed, it became deeply divided between more revolutionary factions and those, probably the majority, who, while still being anarchist, were in favour of working with the Republic.

FAI (Federación Anarquista Ibérica—Iberian anarchist federation)

Founded in Valencia in 1927, the FAI was a loose and ill-defined organisation of anarchist militants that aimed to safeguard the

CNT's anarchist principles, on occasions by violent means, though its members also included pacifists. The two are often abbreviated as CNT–FAI because of their close relationship.

FIJL (Federación Ibérica de Juventudes—Iberian federation of libertarian youth)

Often abbreviated to Juventudes Libertarias, the FIJL was an anarchist youth movement founded in Madrid in the early 1930s. It enjoyed huge support among young working-class men and women in Barcelona.

Mujeres Libres (Free women)

The anarchist women's organisation—independent from the CNT—with some 30,000 members across Spain by 1937.

POUM (Partido Obrero de Unificación Marxista—Workers' party of Marxist unification)

The POUM was an anti-Stalinist Marxist–Leninist party, sometimes referred to as Trotskyist. This is despite the party breaking with Trotsky after he referred to its strategy as "erroneous and criminal" for supporting the Popular Front, rather than trying to infiltrate the PSOE. While they enjoyed considerable support in Catalonia, elsewhere in Spain they were tiny.

On the right

While the right were certainly divided and had somewhat different visions for Spain, they had far more in common. They believed in private profit and property, hierarchy, the Catholic Church, military discipline and the primacy of men over women, the employer over the worker, the landowner over the peasant. In April 1937, the Franco regime forcibly merged the Falange Española and the Carlists and outlawed all other groups to form a new ruling party, the Falange Española Tradicionalista y de las Juntas de Ofensiva Nacional Sindicalista (Traditionalist Spanish Phalanx of the Councils of the National Syndicalist Offensive), a mouthful often shortened to FET, the only legal party in Spain until 1977.

Carlists

Carlism was an extreme traditionalist movement arising from the First Carlist War (1833–9) that sought the establishment of a separate line of the Bourbon family on the Spanish throne, supporting an ultra-reactionary regime. The Carlists had some support in the south of Catalonia and among wealthier classes in Barcelona and were still powerful elsewhere, particularly in Navarra. Their militia, the Requetes, had begun military training during the Second Republic.

CEDA (Confederación Española de Derechas Autónomas— Confederation of Autonomous Right-Wing Groups)

CEDA was a right-wing Catholic party strongly influenced by the Nazis and Italian fascists. Its leader, José María Gil-Robles, declared his intention to "give Spain a true unity, a new spirit, a totalitarian polity" and stated that "[d]emocracy is not an end but a means to the conquest of the new state. When the time comes, either parliament submits or we will eliminate it." The party held rallies inspired by those of Nuremberg and in April 1934 threatened to lead a "March on Madrid" to seize power, as Italian fascists had done in the 1922 "March on Rome". CEDA had little support in Catalonia.

Falange Española

Founded in 1933 by José Antonio Primo de Rivera, son of the dictator General Miguel Primo de Rivera, the Falange was heavily influenced by Italian fascism, advocating a strong national syndicalist state, but, unlike Mussolini's party, it was characterised by its strong Catholicism. At the start of 1936, it enjoyed scant support across Spain, polling just 0.7 per cent in the February general election, though its support grew massively in the months preceding the July military coup, during which time it employed extreme violence to destabilise the Republic and so justify its overthrow. Members of the Falange were responsible for many of the atrocities committed by the right behind the lines during the war.

The Basque centrists and the Catalan right

Lliga Catalana

This conservative party representing the Catalan bourgeoisie was not involved in the 1936 military plot to overthrow the Spanish Republic. Its founder, the Catalanist politician Francesc Cambó—also not involved in the coup—became a major financier of the Francoist war effort. In 1939, most of the Catalan right pragmatically elected to forget its Catalanist traditions in order to protect its economic interests. They continued to do this throughout the Franco dictatorship, despite being unhappy about the regime's fervent anti-Catalanism.

PNV (Spanish: Partido Nacionalista Vasco; Basque; Euzko Alderdi Jeltzalea—Basque nationalist party)

Formed in 1895, the PNV was, and is today, a conservative Catholic party. The party supported the Republic during the war and led the autonomous Basque government from October 1936—when it was established by the Republican government—to the fall of the Basque Country in June 1937.

APPENDIX 2

FURTHER READING

If you're new to the topic, I'd recommend looking at one or two of the excellent introductions available. Personally, I'd probably go for Helen Graham's *The Spanish Civil War: A Very Short Introduction* (Oxford: Oxford University Press, 2005) or Julián Casanova's *A Short History of the Spanish Civil War* (London: I.B. Tauris, 2013). Anthony Beever's *Battle for Spain* (New York: Penguin, 2006) is probably the best introduction from a military perspective.

For those who want to go further

Paul Preston's *The Spanish Holocaust* (London: HarperCollins, 2011) is a harrowing read from the world's leading expert on the war. It charts the barbarity on both sides and pulls no punches while highlighting the difference between bottom-up violence on the Republican side and the state-sanctioned terror unleashed by the rebels. This is possibly Preston's crowning achievement, although all of his work is worth reading, including his monumental biography of Franco.

Ronald Fraser's *Blood of Spain* (London: Allen Lane, 1979), despite being published in 1979, still offers a remarkable oral history of the war based on interviews carried out with survivors in the early 1970s.

Adam Hochschild's *Spain in Our Hearts: Americans in the Spanish Civil War* (Boston, MA: Houghton Mifflin Harcourt, 2017) is a superb telling of the role of American fighters and journalists in Spain as well as, for example, Texaco's support for Franco.

British readers can't go wrong with Richard Baxell's *Unlikely Warriors: The British in the Spanish Civil War and the Struggle against Fascism* (London: Aurum Press, 2012).

Giles Tremlett's superb *The International Brigades* (London: Bloomsbury, 2020) provides the best overview of this unique fighting force.

A fresh read from a different perspective is *Archaeology of the Spanish Civil War* (London: Routledge, 2016) by Alfredo González-Ruibal.

Sebastiaan Faber's writings on the cultural aspects of the war are fascinating: see, for example, *Memory Battles of the Spanish Civil War: History, Fiction, Photography* (Nashville: Vanderbilt University Press, 2018) and *Exhuming Franco: Spain's Second Transition* (Nashville: Vanderbilt University Press, 2023).

Much of the superb writing about the war in Spanish and Catalan is sadly not available in translation.

Tours

I'd like to recommend the following tours around the war in Spain:

For the Ebro battle and Aragon: Alan Warren of Pdlhistoria.

For the Ebro battle (in Catalan and Spanish): Terra Enllà.

For Madrid and surrounding battle site: both Dr Almudena Cros of Across Madrid Tours and David Mathieson of Spanish Sites.

NOTES

INTRODUCTION

1. John Blake and David Hart (dirs), *The Spanish Civil War* (Granada Television, 1983).

2. Dolores Ibárruri is renowned for adopting the slogan "¡No Pasarán!" ("They shall not pass!"), which epitomised Madrid's heroic resistance to Franco's forces. The term was originally coined by Catalan writer Apel·les Mestres in a poem he wrote in 1914 as a protest against the German invasion of Belgium. With the Spanish capital in mind, a banner carrying the slogan was unfurled during the Battle of Cable Street on 4 October 1936, when protesters prevented the police from allowing Oswald Mosley's British League of Fascists to enter the mainly Jewish East End of London. It has since come to be widely used by the political left. For example, on 3 March 2022, TV Rain, one of Russia's last independent media outlets, was forced to stop broadcasting indefinitely because of its coverage of the invasion of Ukraine. At the end of the last broadcast, the staff gathered in front of the camera, raised their fists and proclaimed in Russian "No to war" and then two final words in Spanish, "No Pasarán." A second example: on the night of 7 July 2024, the slogan was chanted by thousands of jubilant Parisians, celebrating the defeat of the far-right National Rally in the legislative elections.

3. Aris Hagis was born in Limassol, Cyprus, in 1910 and emigrated to the United States in 1930. He came to Spain in March 1937 with

the American volunteers of the Abraham Lincoln Battalion and saw action at Brunete, Teruel, and Aragon before returning to the US, where he died in 1974.

1. ORIGINS OF THE SPANISH CIVIL WAR

1. See Sebastian Balfour, *Deadly Embrace: Morocco and the Road to the Spanish Civil War* (Oxford: Oxford University Press, 2002).

2. "Jewish Immigration from Eastern Europe to France", Yad Vashem, n.d., https://www.yadvashem.org/holocaust/france/jewish-immigration-from-eastern-europe-to-france.html

2. BARCELONA: JULY 1936

1. Across Spain, while the figures are a matter of debate, some 70 per cent of the officer class supported the coup, whereas the various police forces were more evenly divided.

2. https://www.lavanguardia.com/internacional/20220917/8527886/ochenta-ocho-balazos-plaza-catalunya.html

3. Mikhail Koltsov, *Diario de la guerra de España* (Paris: Ediciones Ruedo ibérico, 1963).

4. John Langdon-Davies, *Behind the Spanish Barricades* (New York: National Travel Club, 1936).

5. Interviewed in 1981 by Martha Ackelsberg in *Free Women of Spain: Anarchism and the Struggle for the Emancipation of Women* (Bloomington: Indiana University Press, 1991), p. 72.

6. Mateo Santos, *Reportaje del movimiento revolucionario en Barcelona* (n.p., 1936), https://www.vscw.ca/index.php/es/node/482

3. HOMAGE TO ARAGON

1. Luis Buñuel, *My Last Sigh* (New York: Vintage Books, 1983).

2. Quoted in Antony Beevor, *The Battle for Spain*, rev. edn (New York: Penguin, 2006).

3. In comparison, perhaps 1,200 were killed during the French Revolution; in the latter case, 20,000 clergy were also forced from

the priesthood and a further 25,000 went into exile. See William Doyle, *The Oxford History of the French Revolution* (Oxford: Oxford University Press, 1990).

4.　Julián Casanova, *A Short History of the Spanish Civil War* (London: I.B. Tauris, 2013).

5.　Francisco Espinosa and José Luis Ledesma, "La violencia y sus mitos", in Ángel Viñas (ed.), *En el combate por la historia. La República, la guerra civil, el franquismo* (Barcelona: Pasado y Presente, 2012), pp. 495–6.

6.　See Paul Preston's magisterial *The Spanish Holocaust* (London: HarperCollins, 2011) for more details.

4.　ORWELL IN ARAGON

1.　Harry Pollitt, "Mr Orwell Will Have to Try Again", *Daily Worker*, 17 March 1937.

2.　George Orwell, "As I Please", *Tribune*, 1944.

3.　*Barranco*: ravine. Often dry much of the year, they are characteristic of the Spanish landscape. So many were murdered in such places during the war.

4.　Andy Durgan's comprehensive study *Volunteers for the Revolution: The International Militia of the POUM in the Spanish Civil War* (Leiden: Brill, 2025) has gone a long way in shedding light on their particularities and underlines the similarities with the European members of the International Brigades.

5.　Joaquim Oller Viladrosa, "La Guerra Del Piojo", https://jeanfiguier. wordpress.com/2016/10/20/la-guerra-del-piojo/

6.　Kindly translated by Alan Nance.

7.　Jay Allen, "Slaughter of 4,000 at Badajoz, 'City of Horrors,' Is Told by Tribune Man", *Chicago Tribune*, 30 August 1936.

6.　GERNIKA AND THE MAY DAYS

1.　Ukrainian President Volodymyr Zelenskyy evoked the destruction of the Basque town, if not Picasso's painting, when he addressed the Spanish parliament in April 2022 with the words. "We are in April 2022, but it seems like we are in April 1937 when the whole world learned [of the destruction] of one of your cities: Gernika", much to the discomfort of the PP and the ire of the Spanish far-right Vox party. An indication of the latter's position is reflected in the declaration of the journalist María Jamardo a couple of days later on the primetime Telecinco programme *Ya son las ocho*: "Neither were those who bombed Gernika so bad, nor were those who were bombed so good." Let's reflect on that for a moment: "Neither were Nazi pilots so bad, nor defenceless Basque women and children so good."

2. "Camaradas: han de ser enterrados el encono y la competencia que conducen al odio y el desastre. Los trabajadores somos hermanos; no enemigos. ... el fascismo es el enemigo de todos."

3. Albeit in prisons controlled by the Republican state and therefore safer than in Stalinist-controlled centres. Some twenty POUM leaders were still languishing in Barcelona jails in January 1939 as Franco's forces approached. All were released or escaped and managed to cross the French frontier into a very uncertain exile.

7. BELCHITE AND THE FALL OF ARAGON

1. Their story is reflected in the documentary *Over the Sky of Azerbaijan* (Volya Productions, 2013), which charts the experiences of some 500 Republican pilots trained in the USSR during the Spanish Civil War and the involvement of those who survived the terrible attrition in Spain, fighting in the Soviet air force against Nazi Germany at Stalingrad and the rest.

2. Bill Bailey, *The Kid from Hoboken: An Autobiography* (San Francisco: Circus Lithographic Prepress, 1993).

3. A smaller battle near Alfambra between 5 and 8 February saw the last great cavalry charge in Western Europe, in which Francoist mounted troops routed Republican defenders.

4. Joe Joyce, "What O'Duffy Did When He Came Home", *Irish Times*, 12 June 2009, https://www.irishtimes.com/opinion/what-o-duffy-did-when-he-came-home-1.782808

5. Stéphane Michonneau, *Fue ayer: Belchite; Un pueblo frente a la cuestión del pasado* (Zaragoza: Prensas de la Universidad de Zaragoza, 2017).

6. Many of the victims were women and children who were forced into

the church, which the Germans then set on fire. Those who tried to escape were machine-gunned. A total of 247 women and 205 children were murdered in this way. Paradoxically, the local priest had previously refused the Spanish families' admittance to the church as he saw them as the "Children of Satan".

7. David Ferrer Revull, *Recuerda: Españoles en la masacre de Oradour-sur-Glane* (Barcelona: Autoedición, 2019). A plaque in Oradour-sur-Glane remembers their deaths.

8 The ground-breaking Thames TV series *The World at War* (1973) is introduced by the story of Oradour, just as the Granada series starts in Belchite.

9. Antón Castro, "Las raíces aragonesas de Serrat", *Heraldo*, 21 June 2018, https://www.heraldo.es/noticias/ocio-cultura/2018/06/21/las-raices-aragonesas-serrat-1250601-1361024.html

10. Manuel Vicent, "Para Serrat", *El País*, 21 March 2010, https://elpais.com/diario/2010/03/21/ultima/1269126001_850215.html

11. Those who died in the sinking of the *Ciudad de Barcelona* are remembered in Malgrat de Mar by a sandstone sculpture created by English artist Rob MacDonald. The work, known as Solidarity Park, was created with community participation incorporating an international education project and has expanded to an annual festival connecting the events of the war in Spain to activism today against racism and other forms of bigotry.

12. Mark Derby, *Kiwi Compañeros: New Zealand and the Spanish Civil War* (Christchurch, NZ: Canterbury University Press, 2009).

13. Remmel was among the 500 surviving German brigaders to end up in the GDR. Many fought throughout the Second World War in resistance movements, while others spent hellish years in Nazi camps. Historians have gone as far as to say that the war in Spain was the foundation myth of the GDR. In its early years, former brigaders formed the core of the state's new army and police and provided numerous leaders in almost every area of the country's cultural, industrial and repressive administration. This was supported by a considerable cultural output in the form of medals, postage stamps, books, films and vinyl records, many of which featured the voice of the German tenor Ernst Busch.

14. His escape is described in Ian MacDougall (ed.), *Voices from the Spanish Civil War: Personal Recollections of Scottish Volunteers in Republican Spain, 1936–39* (Edinburgh: Polygon, 1986), though his name is not mentioned. It has the feel of a far-fetched cinema plot, but the far-fetched can happen in times of war. The American, an East Coast seaman, was then picked up by a Francoist ambulance, whose crew were secret Republican sympathisers. "They murdered the wounded fascist inside the ambulance, gave the American his place and uniform, and took him to hospital, where knowing no Spanish, he feigned loss of voice." Sometime later, he managed to escape from Franco's Spain and told the story to Scottish brigader John Dunlop.

8. THE BATTLE OF THE EBRO

1. My global figures for the Ebro are from the historian Andreu Caralt, who is currently writing a comprehensive history of the battle.
2. One of these commandos was Rubén Ruiz, the seventeen-year-old son of "La Pasionaria". He was later killed fighting in the Red Army in 1942 during the retreat into Stalingrad, becoming one of a small number of foreigners to be awarded the Order of Lenin, the Soviet Union's highest order.
3. See *Alvah Bessie's Spanish Civil War Notebooks* (Lexington: University Press of Kentucky, 2002). It's a highly recommended and fresh read.
4. Jack Jones, *Union Man* (London: Collins, 1986).
5. The story of the unit's role in running the cave is told in Angela Jackson, *Beyond the Battlefield: Testimony, Memory and Remembrance of a Cave Hospital in the Spanish Civil War* (n.p.: Warren & Pell, 2005).
6. For many years, it was believed that Wainman's collection was lost. However, in 2013 his son, known by the pseudonym "Serge Alternês", managed to recover his father's photos and published a selection in the book *Live Souls: Citizens and Volunteers of Civil War Spain* (Vancouver, BC: Ronsdale Press, 2015).
7. In total, around 9,000 litres of blood were collected in Barcelona during the war.

8. Ladino, the old language of Sephardic Jews, a version of Castilian Spanish, left Spain during waves of repression ending in the final expulsion of 1492. Like Yiddish, it was almost annihilated as a spoken tongue in the Holocaust. Estimates vary, but there are perhaps 50,000–100,000 remaining speakers of Ladino worldwide.

9. ECHOES OF THE EBRO

1. Heath visited Barcelona in July 1938 as a defender of the Republic despite being president of the Conservative students at Oxford and described seeking cover in a bomb shelter during an Italian air raid on the city.

2. He asked me for the story to remain anonymous and so the names are invented.

3. Echoes of the Spanish Civil War are too numerous to count. In April 2023, Amalie Høgsbro Jørgensen, a woman from Copenhagen who had been on my tour, sent me a video of a rather lovely piece of singing in Norwegian by Danish women's choir DR Pigekoret with music by Otto Mortensen. It becomes so much more powerful when you know the history behind it. "Kringsatt av fiender" ("Surrounded by enemies"), also known by the poem's original title "Til ungdommen" ("To the youth"), was written by the Norwegian poet, communist and journalist Nordahl Grieg. It was inspired by his time working as a journalist reporting on the war in Spain and was written as a message of hope in darkening times to young Norwegians. In 1940, he reported on the Norwegian resistance to the Nazi invasion before escaping to the UK. Grieg was killed as a correspondent covering a British bombing raid over Berlin in December 1943.

    After the 2011 terrorist attack in Norway, when the far-right nco Nazi Anders Breivik murdered seventy-seven people, mainly on the island of Utøya, the song became the music that united people across Scandinavia. Amalie explained its significance to me: "Singing the song together in a big crowd can have an incredibly strong effect on people. Most of the time people sing it simply because it's uplifting. It works well for singing in a group in social get-togethers, at school gatherings etc. But on a few occasions, it has become the symbol of something bigger. The unity of people. This was the case after the massacre on Utøya in 2011. A video of the memorial church service held in Oslo cathedral shows the queen of Norway visibly in tears as the choir sang Grieg's words." Words first felt in Spain, echoing down.

Utøya belongs to the Youth League of the Norwegian Labour Party, which uses the island as a summer camp. Two days before the murders, on 20 July, a rather modest plaque, screwed to a birch tree (which seems rather Scandinavian to me), was unveiled remembering four party members who had died fighting fascism in Spain: Gunnar Skjeseth, Martin Schei, Torbjørn Engebretsen, and Odd Olsen. Underneath their names are several lines from Grieg's poem:

> Neat stacks of cannon shells,
> Row upon row
> Death to the life you love,
> All that you know
>
> War is contempt for life,
> Peace is creation
> Death's march is halted
> By determination.

4. Ernest Hemingway, "Dispatch on the Bombing of Tortosa", 15 April 1938, in William White (ed.), *By-Line Ernest Hemingway: Selected Articles and Dispatches of Four Decades* (n.p.: Arrow, 2002).

10. THE FALL OF CATALONIA

1. Perhaps the macaques were captured while grazing the cedar forests of the Atlas Mountains by Spanish zoologists in the wake of the final Spanish victory in 1926. It brought home to me later that the history of modern zoos is intrinsically linked with colonial expansion and war. European imperialism did not just systematically conquer and exploit native populations but also collected or captured huge numbers of plants and animals that were exported back to Europe

for profit but also for scientific study and display in natural history and zoological collections. The macaques of Barcelona Zoo were, I'm sure, a source of delight for local children, but they also represented Spanish colonisation through war, which had brutalised its officer class with important consequences in 1936 and afterwards.

2. Bernat Montsià, "Les bèsties del parc" (1931), quoted in Olga Merino, "Réquiem por Júlia", *El Periódico*, 17 July 2016.

3. Henry Buckley's *The Life and Death of the Spanish Republic* (London: Hamish Hamilton, 1940).

4. Increasingly, La Jonquera has become associated with sex tourism. Men, these days often very young, head here to a series of brothels, some of Europe's largest, which are effectively legal on this side of the border. Many come from France, where prostitution is illegal. As Jordi Cabezas, mayor of La Jonquera, put it in an interview: "The region has become France's brothel." The women, always young, come mainly from Eastern Europe but also from South America, Africa and China. Many are trafficked. They are modern-day slaves.

5. Translated by Peter Bush and quoted in Pete Ayrton (ed.), *¡No Pasarán! Writings from the Spanish Civil War* (New York: Pegasus Books, 2016). First published in Spain in 1995 as part of the collection *Enero sin nombre: Los relatos completos del Laberinto mágico* (Barcelona: Alba Editorial S.L.).

6. A curious example of the deep cold between the two states surfaced in a football match during the 1960 European Nations' Cup. After defeating communist Poland, Spain was tied against the USSR. Franco forced the Spanish team to boycott the match for fear of losing to his ideological enemy, which gave the Soviets a free pass to the semi-final. They went on to defeat Yugoslavia 2–1 in the final in Paris. It was a propaganda victory for the USSR and a propaganda disaster for Franco's Spain. But the regime learned its lesson. Four years later, Spain playing at home beat the USSR 2–1 in the final at Santiago Bernabéu to the delight of the regime's press.

7. Federica Montseny, *El éxodo: Pasión y muerte de españoles en el exilio* (Barcelona: Galba Edicions, 1977).

8. Antoni Rovira i Virgili, *Els darrers dies de la Catalunya republicana* (Buenos Aires: Agrupació d'Ajut a la Cultura Catalana, 1976)

11. FRANCE

1. The official figure of recorded deaths at Argelès is 215, but this does not reflect large numbers who died after being moved to hospitals after suffering the appalling conditions of the camp, especially in Perpignan, and those who died outside of the camp. See "La mortalité du camp", Mémorial du Camp, n.d., www.memorial-argeles.eu/fr/1942/1942/la-mortalite-du-camp.html

2. The quote comes from Rosemary Bailey, *Love and War in the Pyrenees: A Story of Courage, Fear and Hope, 1939–1944* (London: Orion, 2008), p. 39. Blending history, biography, place writing and travel, Bailey tells the story of the people in her Pyrenean village who helped Spanish Republicans, and who were caught up in occupation, collaboration and resistance. It is a beautifully written book that deserves a wider readership.

3. The story of the fate of the Spanish Republicans at Argelès is narrated in the 2020 graphic novel *Josep*, which was turned into a touching, award-winning animated film of the same name. It focuses on the experiences of Catalan artist Josep Bartolí during his time in the camp and his unusual friendship with a camp gendarme. Bartolí documented the horror of the camp. Some of the originals are on display at the Exile Museum in La Jonquera. His angry sharp lines forming bleak hellish visions tell the story of the suffering of the inmates. Later, the film (and book) follows Bartolí's exile in Mexico, where he became a close friend and lover of Frida Kahlo. The book—and film—brought tears to my eyes. I strongly recommend it.

4. *L'Humanité*, 13 May 1939.

5. Grégory Tuban, *Camps d'étrangers: Le contrôle des réfugiés venus d'Espagne, 1939–1945* (Paris: Nouveau Monde éditions, 2018).

6. Eulalio Ferrer Rodríguez, *Entre alambradas: Diario de los campos de concentración* (México, DF: Pangea, 1987).

7. Translation by Alan Nance.

12. INTO THE EUROPEAN ABYSS

1. See Paul Preston, *The Last Days of the Spanish Republic* (London: William Collins, 2016).

2. "Who Built the Atlantic Wall?", Concrete Borders, n.d., https://www.fronterasdehormigon.com/en/who-built-the-atlantic-wall/

3. See Séan Scullion's comprehensive and highly recommended *Churchill's Spaniards: Continuing the Fight in the British Army 1939–46* (n.p.: Helion, 2024).

4. A thumping, journalistic read is Evelyn Mesquida's *The Spanish Republicans who Liberated Paris* (n.p.: Christie Books, 2015; English translation), as is Paco Roca's excellent graphic novel *Los surcos del azar* (Bilbao: Astiberri, 2013) (translated into English as *Twists of Fate*), while Diego Gaspar Celaya's academic study *Banda de cosacos: Historia y memoria de la Nueve y sus hombres* (Madrid: Marcial Pons Historia, 2022) offers a more nuanced understanding, downplaying while still praising the epic nature of their involvement.

13. THE FRANCO REGIME

1. Carlos Hernández de Miguel, *Los campos de concentración de Franco: Sometimiento, torturas y muerte tras las alambradas*, New York: Penguin Random House, 2019.

2. The resemblance, as Dacia Viejo-Rose points out in *Reconstructing Spain: Cultural Heritage and Memory after Civil War* (Brighton: Sussex Academic Press, 2014), "seems uncanny".

3. These days, you'll more likely hear the expression "resistencia numantina" to describe a particularly "heroic" football performance, perhaps by an underdog, playing against the odds.

4. This wholesale plunder is superbly charted in journalist Antonio Maestre's book *Franquismo, S.A.* (Madrid: Ediciones Akal, S.A., 2019). He makes the point that this mass "acquisition" of property at the end of the war is probably a major reason behind the hostility of many on the Spanish right towards demands for opening up mass graves and memorialisation, for fear of what else might be questioned.

5. María José Rodríguez, "El 8% de las personas asesinadas durante la represión franquista en Extremadura eran mujeres", elDiario.es, 25 August 2018, https://www.eldiario.es/extremadura/sociedad/personas-asesinas-represion franquista-extremadura_1_2756410.html

6. Even in the right light in faded letters on Barcelona's main cathedral, despite being cleaned off in 1997.

7.   On 23 February, Tejero, commanding 200 Guardias Civiles and soldiers, entered the Congress of Deputies, the lower house of the Spanish Parliament, which was in the process of electing a new prime minister, and held the deputies hostage, with the entire episode being filmed by Spanish state television (RTVE). Away from the parliament, the most serious developments were seen in Valencia, where fellow plotter General Jaime Milans del Bosch declared a state of emergency and ordered tanks on to the streets. However, seven hours later, at 1 a.m., King Juan Carlos, whose own role has never been fully clarified, gave a nationally televised address denouncing the attempted coup. The next morning, the insurgents surrendered. It was all over in a day. When I ask older friends how they remember that day, they often talk about the fear they felt, sometimes about how they planned to flee to France, but also, unless they were doing military service, how they watched the events unfold on their TV sets. In that sense, 23-F, as it is called in Spain, was the world's first televised coup and an early example of people experiencing history through a screen. You can watch the RTVE footage on YouTube of Tejero entering the chamber as a civil guard fires his machine gun into the ceiling. See, e.g., https://www.youtube.com/watch?v=3rmrfVqqEEM

14. MAUTHAUSEN

1.   Gómez Bravo Gutmaro and Diego Martínez López, *Rotspanier: españoles en el complejo concentracionario Mauthausen-Gusen* (n.p.: Grupo de Investigación de la Guerra Civil y el Franquismo, Ministerio de la Presidencia, 2022).

2.   Neus Català (1915–2019) was captured in 1943 while working for the French resistance and, after torture, deported to Ravensbrück in 1944. She moved to France after her liberation and continued the struggle against Francoist Spain and chaired the Association of Victims of Ravensbrück before returning to Catalonia in 1978. Català collaborated with writer Carme Martí to produce a moving novelised version of her life, *Un cel de plom* (A leaden sky [Badalona: Ara Llibres, 2011]; not translated in English), later adapted as a powerful theatrical production.

LIST OF ILLUSTRATIONS

All photos by the author unless otherwise indicated.

LIST OF ILLUSTRATIONS

INDEX

333

INDEX